Finally FULL
of
You

Unlocking You

Maria Salomão-Schmidt

Finally Full Of Yourself!: Unlocking Your Spiritual DNA
by Maria Salomão-Schmidt

Published by Happy Me Living

www.happymeadvantage.com

www.coachmemaria.com

www.happymeliving.com

Cover: Carlos Ferreira, Sketchtank

Illustrations: Karyn Knight Detering, Ideas Take Shape

Author photo: Natalie Sisson

Print ISBN: 978-0-9981912-1-8

Ebook ISBN: 359-2-85933-609-1

Beautiful Linda,

May this book

bring your heart

much joy!

Love,

Maria

This
book
is dedicated:
to Sophia,
to Olivia,
to Mialotta,
to Isabella,
to Douglas,
to Christopher,
and
to You,
who
seeks ways
to activate
and
live from
your
most
authentic
self.

Why do you stay in prison when the door is so wide open?

—Rumi

Contents

We are at a time in humanity when we have incredible technologies and we are being asked to marry these with an equivalent transformation of heart.

—Jack Kornfield

Introduction

(Psssst...Don't skip it. This one is worth reading!)

For most of my life I was a "good girl." I morphed, sacrificed and contorted myself for what I had been taught was the "right" way to live. I had a lot to be thankful for and I was thankful. Turns out you can be thankful and still uninspired. On paper, especially compared to most people on this planet, I "should" have been inspired. After all, I lived an extraordinary life. I had followed the formula of success and had the things we are all taught to dream about... I got a good education, started my own PR firm, traveled the world, had homes in Boston and San Francisco, got to meet and work with some of the world's most amazing people and companies. I had as much "freedom" as I wanted but I did not feel free. I took workshops, read piles of books, asked, learned, sought out the answers. I did not realize at the time I lived in a cage of my own making. I always felt like something was off but it was like that for most everyone around me so I accepted that.

I found myself constantly holding back on the things I was called to do, for the things I was supposed to do. One of those things was motherhood. Since I was the oldest of four kids with an almost 8 year span, I started taking on that role very early. Because I suffered as a child, I have a very soft spot for children, especially abandoned or lonely ones. That core wound, in part, drove me to find the answers in this book. Pain is part of the human existence, but suffering does not need to be. I always wanted a big family and did not care if the children came through my uterus or through just my heart (as I believe children who are step, adopted or fostered come into our lives). I was already looking at adoption and other creative ways to become a mother in my mid 30s, when I found the love of my life Douglas Herbert Schmidt.

Doug helped me with one of my life's deepest dreams, to bring beautiful babies into the world with someone I adore and who adores me. Doug made it even easier by already having a magnificent six year old son, Christopher, whom I fell in love with at first sight. That "little boy" is now over six feet tall but he still melts my heart. After two years we decided to start having children. Doug and I met later in life so we began making up for lost time (wink, wink, nudge, nudge). We had two amazing little girls, first Mialotta, then Sophia within fourteen months of each other. Even with all of life's bumps, our three children were the light of lives. It is sometimes when you think everything is starting to fall into place that what begins falling is you... not because of how worthy you are, but because it's the only way to learn how to fly!

"How do you become when your life blows up?" My "perfect" life blew up the day I held my dead baby girl in my arms. Although I did not realize it at the time, the sudden and heartbreaking death of our beloved youngest daughter Sophia cracked me wide open. Everything else I had ever "suffered" became irrelevant. After her death, I could no longer stomach the niceties, polite rules and curtain talk that create the inauthentic conversations in our lives. It gave me a form of courage and boundaries that I would not have otherwise.

What many who have had loved ones pass know, is that just because the person dies, the love, and even the relationship, does not stop. I found that for me to connect to Sophia, I had to let go of the heaviness of how I had been living my life, always trying to be a "good girl." Although there's a part of me who weeps at my writing this next phrase... there's a gift to her having died. Thanks to the amazing intervention of Gary Zukav (author of *Seat Of The Soul*) and Oprah Winfrey (more about this story later in the book) I realized on a core level that since I cannot bring her body back in this lifetime, I have chosen to look for the gifts. Sophia's death has led me to all the amazing information you'll find in this book. In a sense Sophia has become my spiritual teacher, showing me the world of energy that has been mostly invisible to me, so I can show it to you. It has taken me almost a decade to write. It's my life's work. I have put my whole heart into it.

The ride has been "bumpy." I have written this book four times and burned it three times because it just was not at the level it exists. You are holding number four in your hands right now. It was downloaded, imagined, created and magnetized from the most authentic vibrations I know how to access. It was written as a gift, in honor of the life of and death of a little angel that I have the honor of calling my daughter. I have presented this work in a way that will make your life more about

Maria Salomão-Schmidt

the FLOW of it because that is where you will find your life's spiritual DNA. When each of us accesses and uses our spiritual DNA, we heal our lives from suffering. You know all those holiday cards you've received and written saying "peace on earth" in them? This is finally how we bring peace to the world.

Stop "Efforting" and Start Flowing

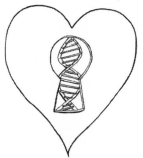

Life does not have to be this hard, confusing or painful. If you have been feeling stuck, depressed or frustrated, *Finally Full of Yourself!: Unlocking Your Spiritual DNA* is the book for you. In it, I offer you the strategies you need to "shift" your life, so that it reflects the life of your dreams. Your dreams come from your spiritual DNA. They are your own unique roadmap for this lifetime. Your dreams are constantly calling and guiding you. When you allow your dreams to guide you, you live authentically. The more we awaken to our own unique authenticity, the more we get to live in peace, harmony and Love—things often found to be off limits, except in fairy tales. This book is written to show you how you can attain this flow.

Think of it this way. Have you ever heard of a beached dolphin? She instinctively knows how to swim but she can't get in the water, where she flows naturally. Where many of us find ourselves today is similar to that. You have built-in instincts that can guide you, but you just don't know how to get into that flow. You think you can, but you keep getting beached. This book teaches you how to get back into the rhythm of whatever you want your life to look like. Being in that flow is where your happiness lives. It's where your heart is happy. This is where and when you feel whole. Unless you are living an inauthentic, cookie-cutter life, no two lives are the same. Imagine how wonderful it's going to feel to learn how to stop efforting and instead live your own unique life's path, the way you design it? So exciting! Let's not waste another moment! Get ready to say, "Hello!" to your authentic life. Let's begin!

A change would do you good.

—Sheryl Crow

FINALLY FULL OF YOURSELF

ENERGY DISCLOSURE

You are here on Earth to let your own unique greatness discover you. This book that you're holding in your magical hands right now is one of the most powerful tool boxes any human being can come across. Inside are all sorts of invaluable tools for the next phase of human evolution that you can use and share for the rest of your life. The tools are wrapped in humor and examples, so that you can more easily open the gifts each will give you. The type of learning I have specifically chosen for you involves shedding your "shoulding" and embracing your "playing." Feed your *inklings*! *Finally Full of Yourself* is your own personal guide to turning your blocks into flows. Blocks are feedback, not punishment. Many wonderful "secrets" are revealed through them.

Remembering To Check-In To Your Life

If you want to get on a flight, you check-in. You can buy the ticket, pack your bags and even get to the airport early, but if you don't *check-in*, you'll never get on that flight, and your trip will never happen. Checking in is key.

I ask you to check into your life. I know that it's been confusing, painful, depressing, lonely and messy—very messy at times; but that's about to shift. It's time you tapped into your gifts, the ones that only you have to give to the world. Yes, it's time!

There's a difference between doing what does not feel good and what's uncomfortable. "Feeling uncomfortable" is absolutely necessary. It's what expansion and growth look like. "Feeling good" means you are on track, activating your spiritual DNA; therefore not feeling good means you are out of alignment with your life's flow. Let me ask you, "Did you have to DO anything to activate your body's DNA?" Your physical body looks and works the way it does because of DNA and environmental conditions. There is nothing you *do* or *did* to get your DNA. It's just part of the "you get a life package" on Planet Earth. Your energy body works exactly the same way. It also has a built-in energetic, or spiritual DNA that directs you towards your life's purpose.

Maria Salomão-Schmidt

It's my life's work to help you find your life's purpose. Sharing the "how" with you is why I was born. By being authentically me (my own unique "flavor" in the world), I've been able to receive some of the amazing information. This information helps you connect to your natural flow, the parts of yourself you've been blocking. From now on, it's about accessing and living the life you've dreamed about, because dreams are actually how we humans get our life's mission. Dreams are direct communication from our spiritual DNA.

I am thrilled to be giving you many of the answers to the questions you've been so desperately seeking! These answers are not "from" me, they came "through" me. You get to choose which ones fit you. The intention is to bring you more *freedom* and *flow*. *Finally Full of Yourself* is chock full of what the divine Oprah Winfrey, whom I believe is Earth's godmother, calls *"ahas!"* As you well know, the human journey can get pretty messy here on Planet Earth, but if you're holding this book, at this specific moment in time, you're ready for this life-enhancing knowledge.

Have you noticed all the shifts going on? We're experiencing an *evolutionary growth spurt*. It's all happening right before our eyes. For the first time in human history we're bearing witness to something never seen before in such a short period of time. It's time to evolve! Everything flows, where it flows, because we're all connected to each other. The perceived disconnection from one another has caused much conflict, pain, violence and war. Nothing happens in a vacuum on Earth, everything is interwoven. It's time to start paying (even deeper) attention to all the amazing things that are and have been always happening right in front of you. They are things you might have been oblivious to, until now. This is where your "efforting" diminishes and the happiness rises for you in this lifetime! Welcome to the next stage of your own personal evolution!

Helpful Bonus Tools

We're on the brink of the biggest human shift so it's completely understandable that you might be feeling overwhelmed. In order to help you better grasp the concepts that will help you, throughout the book you'll see the following three symbols below. They're specifically designed to help you incorporate the lessons into your life so you increase your levels of happiness and decrease your blocks.

TASK - The smiling heart lets you know there's an exercise that goes with the specific chapter topic. The exercise helps you apply what you just read specifically to your own life.

BREATH - It's one of the fastest and most powerful ways to center yourself. Breath is one of the most basic tools you get in this lifetime. When you see this symbol it's a reminder to breathe. It's also one of the most under-utilized gifts we humans possess. More about breath in Chapter 3.

JOURNAL - Journaling is one of best tools for processing through things that normally block you. Targeted journaling helps even more because it helps show you where you need to focus. The more you journal, the more the energy in your life flows.

Maria Salomão-Schmidt

Everything is energy and that's all there is to it.
Match the frequency of the reality you want and you
cannot help but get that reality. It can be no other
way. This is not philosophy. This is physics.

—Albert Einstein

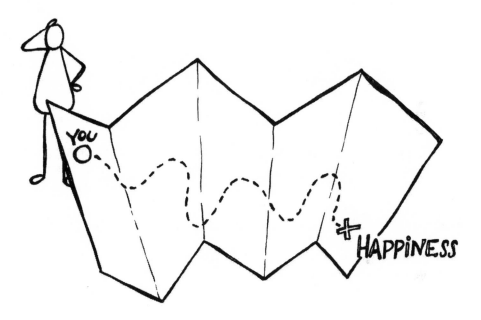

Chapter 1. Where Have We Been?

No matter where you grew up, chances are that most of us learned from a very early age how to take care of our bodies. You learned all of the things that it needs to survive. You know what to eat, even if you don't always eat what would be best for your body. You know you need to drink water. If you forget any of these things, your body gives you feedback. If you ignore the feedback, it gets bigger and bigger until you decide to shift or until the body simply stops working, and you die. To maintain a happy and healthy fully functioning human body, you need to take care of it. Even though we human beings are all very different from each other in many ways, we're all made up of two basic parts: matter or physical (*meat body*) and soul (*energy body*).

Most of us think of ourselves as having only a physical body, which we mainly focus on, and then a soul. As we are evolving, we're starting to realize that this way of thinking is a bit of a misrepresentation because as you just read, we actually have *two* bodies. The energy part of us, what some people call a *soul*, also is a *"body"* of sorts. The major difference is that it's comprised of energy. As we move further into this new dawn of human evolution that some call the Age of Aquarius, we're starting to pay more attention to both the energy and meat bodies. Why is this an important distinction? Well, with your *meat body*, there are certain things you need to learn and do to take care of it such as:

Feed it	Exercise it
Listen to it	Clean it
Maintain it	Rest it

In fact, much of our childhood is about learning how to take care of our "meat" bodies. We play sports and exercise to build muscles and coordination. We're taught that bedtimes are important so we can get enough sleep. We have rituals around meals. We're taught to have bath time, brush our teeth and cut our nails. There are millions of books written on how to use, move, grow, sculpt, maintain, nurture and take care of our *meat* body. What has been greatly disregarded is our second body, our energy body. It is from learning how to take care of our energy body that you can find most of the solutions you have been seeking, yet, most of us have never learned how to take care of our energetic bodies, or that we even had one, really. Many contemplate the energetic body when death is imminent, and fears of going to "heaven" or "hell" sets in. It is clear that we all have a good understanding of how to take care of our bodies, but who teaches us how to take care of our energy? *Finally Full of Yourself* is the book that shows you how.

The Age of Aquarius Defined

Earlier I mentioned the dawning of the Age of Aquarius. For those who need more clarity, that simply means that we're ending a cycle that happens every two thousand years. This shift is referred to as the *changing of the ages*. The last one coincided with the arrival of Christ.

Maria Salomão-Schmidt

We're in the process of leaving Age of Pisces, and entering into Age of Aquarius.

You may be wondering, "What does this have to do with me?" This affects everyone on our planet. We're going through a time on our planet of massive energetic shifts. You can see it in every aspect of life from technology to human rights, and weather to politics. Things that were once considered strange like veganism, meditation, alternative medicine, Reiki, being transgendered, telepathy and psychic ability are now becoming more commonplace as we continue to evolve. Just like everything on this planet, human beings are also shifting. We're becoming more and more aware, not only of the energy around us, but that *we are energy*. You're bearing witness to one of the most exciting times to be alive!

People have already begun looking within themselves for answers, instead of outward to money, possessions and other people, as many human beings have done in the past. More and more people are living more and more *enlightened* (meaning living from within the light, which is their energy). This enlightenment increases all of the following on our planet: flow, kindness, release and truth.

Taking Out The Soul... To Uncover Your Core!

Do you know the adage that, "when you ASSUME, you make an "ASS" out of "U" and "ME?" Well, there are some things you've heard so many times that you assume permanence with them. We make an assumption and never *notice* the word again. "Soul" is one of those words. We're in love with the word "soul." In order to get to the best learning position, however, it's important to stop saying "soul," at least for now. Why? Sometimes to move forward, you have to step back and lean into what is uncomfortable.

The ground-breaking research I am presenting in this book is pre-religion so it simply does not matter what your specific religious beliefs are. "Soul" often has a religious connotation linked to it. You might not know what that means right now, but keep reading. It'll make sense to you soon. Just know that the more simply you can look at things, or *notice*, the more you can shift your life. Stagnation comes from making the most basic assumptions. Those *assumptions* are the invisible glue that keeps you feeling helpless, confused, depressed and stuck.

From now on, to move your life forward, I will refer to the human body most of the time as the *meat body*. This simple shift will give you information that you did not even know you had. It will help you *notice*.

To notice is to connect to your life. So the goal is less *ASSUMING* and more *NOTICING*.

Whatever (Whoever) controls your FOCUS
controls your life.
—Maria Salomão-Schmidt

Why Our Bodies Have Become the (Perceived) Enemy

Most of us grow up thinking that we *are* our bodies, and that our bodies are us. The word "body" has been hijacked! Slowly over the years, the focus has shifted to paying more and more attention to what is "wrong" with your body and what needs to be "fixed." Billions of dollars every year are spent on re-focusing your attention on what your body *should* look like. This *programming* is so strong that it even affects how very young children see themselves.

During my talks; lectures; speaking engagements and retreats, I've learned that for most people the phrase "my body" activates very negative judgment. This affects our lives because it sets the vibration for how we feel about and treat ourselves. The more human beings dislike their bodies, the more likely they are to buy more products. Because this method of making money has worked, there are whole industries that have been built to reinforce these ideals. The more it's reinforced, the more it becomes normal. The more it's considered normal, the less people notice or question it. This is the most dangerous stage because this is where all checks and balances are dropped. Without any monitoring, it becomes like an undetected cancer, wreaking havoc and causing suffering throughout the human race.

We humans have many examples of this, where money comes before ANYTHING else. Historically, in order to make as much money as possible, several industries have directly dictated what's considered "beautiful," especially for women. By setting the beauty and body bar to the type of body that most of us don't have, most of us buy products and services to conform to the beauty standard. One of the industries is the razor industry. In mainstream US culture, shaving, especially for underarms and legs is considered basic grooming. You just do it.

When I was 22, I was working in Japan and for winter break decided to travel to Thailand for a month. While on the beach in Koh Samui with my friend Tracey Neret, I noticed that many German women, even though they were hip and beautiful did not shave their armpits or legs. Having just graduated from Boston College, where you would not have been caught dead not shaving, I was, as the British say, gobsmacked by all those hairy legs and armpits because I have never even questioned not shaving. In my mind not shaving was "gross." I had labeled it under "must do" and not thought about it again. Hanging around with and seeing so many women my age not shaving I was able to *notice* something I had *assumed*. I had been conditioned by whom or when I have no idea, that to not shave was ugly. Without even realizing it I had assumed this as a truth, and judged others when they did not follow suit. This experience left me wondering what else I was assuming in my life.

Shaving is not the only artificial need that has been created for us. There are many more. For example, when I was a flight attendant for Delta Airlines, I was surprised to find that flight attendants had a weight requirement. Interestingly, the pilots did not have any weight requirements at all. Before flight attendants got on a plane, we had to step on a scale to weigh in. We could literally be fired for weighing above what Delta considered an appropriate size. It was an incredibly degrading experience, even if you were within the weight. Flight attendants had an image to uphold and we had to be able to fit that model, or lose our jobs. I had several friends who did because they weighed 5 lbs. more than the airline thought they should.

In the fashion world, our attention is mainly focused on the *models* themselves. Without this key focal point, the industry would have a very hard time being able to define beauty. The word "model" is defined as "a system or thing used as an example to follow or imitate." So the word itself basically means, "Hey, you over there. Yeah, you! This is what you *should* look like." If that were not enough, then they added the word *super* in so that now it's "super model" like the ultimate model. I modeled for a short time and I can tell you that whenever I told people that I was a model, I felt them treat me differently—as though I was suddenly *more important*. Even with all the negative ramifications, there is definitely still a *wow effect*.

Because only a very few human beings look like models, they are seen as "special" and given lots of attention, that is why many little girls dream of being one. From the outside, it looks like these women have everything they want, including love, clothes, money and attention. These basic beliefs fuel this industry. De-constructing this industry further, we can ask what are the qualities chosen for models? In other words, what does one need to look like to model? Here are some startling facts from the Center for Disease Control and Prevention:

- The average model is 5´10˝ tall and weighs only 107 lbs. In comparison, the average American woman is 5´4˝ tall and weighs 166 lbs.

- Size 6 is considered a plus size in the modeling world.

- Most runway models meet the body mass index criteria for anorexia.

- Twenty years ago, the average fashion model weighed 8 percent less than the average woman. Today, she weighs 23 percent less.

- Plus-size models, a decade ago, averaged between size 12 and size 18. Today, the majority are between size 6 and size 14.

- Half of women wear a size 14 or larger, but most standard clothing outlets cater to sizes 14 or smaller.

- Half of girls aged 9–10 report they feel better about themselves when they are dieting.

- Forty-two percent of girls 4–10 wish they were thinner.

- Four out of five children reported worrying about being fat.

For the last three decades, I have tested this at my workshops. As soon as I say, "Let's talk about your body," it causes people, especially women, to squirm a bit. If I ask how they feel about their body, they usually almost immediately either cross their legs or arms. The word "body" is definitely a loaded word that we've been conditioned to judge. Even models themselves, who in our society are supposed to represent "perfection," are often incredibly critical of their own bodies. Let's take a moment to stop and notice. Does this way of living make any sense? Does any of this feel good to you as you read it? It does not, does it? It is pure madness!

From an energy point of view, repetition of something that is not working for the majority of those involved this, is a form of trapped energy. Think of it as a huge "energetic fur ball" that we humans can either choke on, or work through our system. The first step is *noticing*. Everything shifts with awareness. By reading this and being open and leaning into it, you're accomplishing the first step of shifting into your most authentic life. Remember that to notice is to connect to your life.

The second step is to go back to the core of things as much as possible, before judgment or opinion. Going back to the core of an issue is where we can best shift the pattern of disconnection. In the example of how we see our bodies, I ask you to join me in referring to a human body as a "meat body." I know it might sound a little strange at first, but this part is vital because it allows you to look at the subject with *fresh eyes*. Our bodies, at one of their most basic level are flesh and bone. There is no judgment, it just does whatever your DNA tells it to do, as long as the environment and nutrition are there. It's from this point of reference that the massive shift back towards a more authentic you unfolds. The more of us that begin to do this, the more balance we will bring back to our world.

So in this chapter you've started examining your two bodies *(energy and meat)* and how they affect how you see yourself and those around you. Understanding this is incredibly helpful to start seeing things work on this planet. In Chapter 3, we dive in even deeper. We're taking it bit-by-bit because this information is best if it's digested in bite-sized pieces.

 JOURNAL TIME... Here's an interesting exercise that may test you more than others. If you want to experience what feeling small and uncomfortable feels like, you can do it here. Activate your imagination and answer the following questions: How would you feel if you were at the beach and saw a woman in a bathing suit who did not shave her armpits or legs? How does that feel to you when you picture it? Lean into that thought. Notice what comes up without judging. Now picture a man on the beach in swim trunks who also did not shave his legs or armpits. How does that feel? Compare what came up in each scenario for you.

> *Women have fought so long and hard for*
> *our rights and equality, and now all*
> *our attention is put on being a size 0.*
>
> —Pink

*One thing I realized, in life, is that you can't just go
by how a person reacts to you.*
—Louis C.K.

Chapter 2. From Fire To Energy— The Next Biggest Human Shift

For me the biggest *aha!* came when I realized that most of the problems we have, we look at from a physical or "meat" point of view. It takes a long time to change or even shift matter. As I mentioned earlier, we're all made up of not one, but two bodies—a *meat body* and an *energetic* one. We're just beginning to learn how to play with the energy side of us, which is our core. Our bodies dramatically change over our lifetimes, but our *energy body* maintains itself throughout our lifetimes and beyond. If you want to change something in your life, it is harder to do it in the physical world; but with energy, things can shift instantly. If you've ever wondered why energy healing, such as Reiki, can be so instant and powerful, now you know. What was once thought of as *woo-woo* is now given as treatment in many hospitals, healing centers and businesses.

Since most of our attention is usually focused on our bodies, we don't always address the energy side. As a Reiki Master Teacher, when I am teaching students Reiki, I include a heaping dose of energy basics. This is so they have a context to how energy works, otherwise it's too foreign to them. It's almost akin to our great ancestors playing with fire and not knowing how it works. They knew they needed fire to stay warm and cook food, but they also knew it could hurt, destroy and even kill if misused. For our ancestors, the nomadic cave people, an important energy source was fire. Now, we are entering the dawn of another massive evolutionary human milestone. We're being called to learn how to use that part of us that we have been ignoring, much to our planet's detriment—our *energy body*.

Shifting From Suffering

Many of us are afraid of "change," because we've associated it with pain. We've been conditioned to fear what we don't know. There's a proverb, "Better the devil you know, than the devil you don't know." Its meaning, that if you have to choose between a familiar but unpleasant situation and an unfamiliar situation, choose the familiar one because the unknown situation may turn out to be worse, is energy-limiting. This type of belief keeps us small.

Most people have two completely different lives in their head. They have the one they are living—what we can call their "should" life, and the one they wish they could live—their "dream" life. After decades of coaching, I can tell you that although people say they don't know what their dream life would be they begin to describe it effortlessly when asked just a few questions. Once they start, the details they describe of what it would look, feel, sound, taste and smell like is so descriptive that it even shocks them. They don't know from where it comes from. There are two main reasons why this is so:

- One, is that as a society, we're so focused on what's not working, that we look for (notice) what we don't want.

- Two, the reason why this is so buried is that many of us fear change for that is what we have been taught.

Why do people stay in painful situations? Why does someone not leave her abusive partner? Why do we not leave our life-sucking jobs? Why do we accept an ordinary life? Why do we keep eating when we want to lose weight? Why do we live small versions of ourselves? We do all these painful things, even when we know they are not in alignment (don't feel good), because our attention is focused elsewhere, and we have been taught to fear change. Sounds disheartening, but I've got some good news for you!

I'm afraid of changin', cause I built my life
around you.
—Stevie Nicks

My goal is to help address issues that get in your way and keep you from making the changes you need. You'll get more clarity as you continue reading this book. The next issue is fear of change. So allow me to address this head-on so you can get back to living the life of your dreams... for that is how you access your spiritual DNA!

As we deconstructed the term "body," we are now going to do the same for the word "change." The mainstream belief is that if you are not happy "change something." Change is not what we are going for here, at least initially; it's too big of a leap. It's like going from first grade to high school, way too much, too soon. Instead, the word we want to embrace is "shift." To understand the difference you "get to" (instead of "have to") slow down and notice the subtleties.

To shift is more in alignment with the visual of a train effortlessly switching lines once someone has lowered the railroad switch lever. "Change" is the by-product of many smaller shifts, in any given circumstance, back into the alignment that is naturally and effortlessly yours. Much of the way you have been taught to live your life is very painful and takes a whole lot of *efforting* energy! This is why you and many others sometimes feel tired of living. Once you get the sense of how your energy works, you'll get the feeling of how easy, freeing and fun being you is! One of my coaching clients said it best: "It feels like peace."

One little person, giving all of her time to peace,
makes news. Many people, giving some of their time,
can make history.

—Peace Pilgrim (Mildred Lisette Norman)

Why I Do This

All of my life's bumps, unrest and lessons kept leading me to paths I would not have normally taken. Eventually, I enrolled in the Rhys Thomas Institute of Energy Medicine's three-year energy program, which taught me all about chakras, energy, Emotional Freedom Technique (EFT), past lives and psychological profiles. I also learned how to do table healings and chakra balancing work. While there, I also started taking Reiki from one of my very favorite people, the beautiful Joy Dorsey of Barrington, Rhode Island. Joy is a magnificent Reiki teacher.

Maria Salomão-Schmidt

I really took to Reiki and eventually become a Reiki Master Teacher. I love, love, love teaching people Reiki because it provides a gateway to learning about energy. Reiki is a wonderful gateway to learning about your energy body. What a wonderful gift to be able to see people shift into their peace and power right before your eyes. It's humans *de-cluttering* their false energy patterns and embracing their connection with their spiritual DNA!

 JOURNAL TIME... Take moment to notice... Start being more present in your life. How has your life shifted recently? In the last month? In the last year? In the last five years? In the last 10 years? How does it feel? What created these shifts?

> *We can bomb the world to pieces,*
> *but we can't bomb it into peace.*
> —Michael Franti

Things I Want To Remember/Research/Review:

Grumpy: "Ask her who she is,
and what she's a-doin' here!"
Doc: "Ah, yes. Now what are you,
and who are you doin' here?"
—Snow White and the Seven Dwarfs

Chapter 3. Unlocking and Opening Your Human Toolbox

IMPORTANT: All of the things you're learning about in this book are nothing anyone else can give you. They're all things with which you were born. You've just never known how to use them, or that you even had them. If you had, you never would have needed to buy so much stuff or try to morph into someone else's opinion of who you *should* be to feel loved, seen and whole. So think of our journey together as an easy way to start unwrapping all those amazing gifts you never even knew you even had! It's a shift from "doing" because you're not enough, into "being" your unique flavor on this planet!

Your 7 Helpers

The shifting began the moment you were called to pick up *Finally Full of Yourself*. The life lessons never stop because there's always a constant flow of movement, even if you're lying down. Plus, you're in many lessons in each moment. The difference now, with this book, is that you don't have to *effort* alone. This time you get to have your questions answered so that you can start living in your own "zone," your own authentic vibe. You get to consciously create the life you want from a place of natural flow, and not from a place of struggle.

Ever notice how your radio works? There are radio waves all around you, but without focusing on the channel you want you have to tolerate whatever you land on. Our gifts are always all around us too, but sometimes we're going so fast and focused on other things that we don't see them. We don't know if we're doing it "right" or going about things the "right way." Having a lack of direction or sense of purpose can make life feel even more frustrating.

Since we're at the beginning of the book, I'm giving you a quick 7-point checklist to help you live your best life. Just like Snow White had her seven live-in helpers to assist her, I have designed this simple, fun, memorable way for you to remember the built-in helpers that you already possess. They are some of your most valuable resources and will keep you focused on growing your energy so that you are full of yourself.

This chapter was inspired by the Seven Dwarfs. As you read about the helpers, you may discover that the lines blur in this section between both your two bodies, as one flows into the other. When the *meat body* is healthy, it promotes your *energy body*'s natural flow. This is when your life feels good and things seem to effortlessly show up. When your *energy body* is aligned, your *meat body* also becomes healthier. It's during this time that you feel full of yourself.

1st Helper - GROUNDING

If your body had a label on it, it would say "Made on Earth." If you think about it, it's pretty amazing that EVERY part of your meat body was made from the elements found on earth. According to Wikipedia, "Almost 99% of the mass of the human body is made up of six elements: oxygen, carbon, hydrogen, nitrogen, calcium and phosphorus. Only about 0.85% is composed of another five elements: potassium, sulfur, sodium, chlorine and magnesium. All are necessary to life."

Everything works and flows in a certain rhythm, both physically and energetically. Indigenous people understand this concept. The chakras are the energy "hubs" of our energetic body. The first chakra, of the seven main chakras is the closest one to Mother Earth. It is the energy that connects us to her. I call our beloved planet mother or Mama Earth because our bodies are literally a product of this planet. To connect to the Earth is to be grounded. Our society, however, is often encouraging us to be busy. The "busier" we are with our lives, the more ungrounded we get. We tend to be more in our head, thinking versus feeling. It is also when we allow others control over our life because we are not present in it.

To Fly, Ground Thyself Exercise... To help get you grounded enough to create a good intention for your day, your event or your life, I'm sharing the advice I often share with my clients. One of the easiest and quickest ways to ground is to go barefoot. The closer to nature or earth you can be, the better. The soles of your feet are incredibly sacred. Think about it. They are your most constant connection point to the Earth. Every morning when you get up, your soles are usually the first connection point to earth. If you're present to it, it actually can be a very powerful way of getting up. Most of us race through getting connected and grounded in the morning, and thus completely miss this sacred way to start your day full of yourself. The most happy people have morning rituals. If you don't have morning rituals, I highly suggest you create some. Morning rituals can be anything that helps align you to your flow. It's about setting your "channel" for the day ahead including meditating, running, yoga, yodeling, journaling, walking the dogs, writing morning pages, etc.

"Grounding" is such an important Helper because, if you get too ungrounded, then little things (like losing your keys or tripping on a rug) turn into huge things (having a car accident or falling down hard). Grounding is your life calling you back to the present moment, back to your body, back to the right now. By the way, sleeping is also a form of "Grounding"—in that to fall asleep, you must surrender to the present moment.

I invite you to notice and use the 1st Helper (Grounding) as a time to activate the 6th Helper (Intention) and set your intention for the day. Remember not just in the morning, but any time you're feeling overwhelmed, put both FEET on the ground. Wiggle your toesies. Smile. This may seem simple, and it is. This is how "helpers" were designed. It confirms for us that we don't need to learn anything else to be happy, because it's already in us. We are already whole.

2nd Helper - HYDRATE

Water. Water. Water. We're mostly made of water. Water represents "flow" in our life. Without enough water we have dryness, which is a type of stagnation. Organs and other body parts don't function well without water.

You might start noticing that when you ignore any of the Helpers, you can tell because you tend to find yourself craving sugary and/or caffeinated drinks. For me, it's black tea. I can drink enough to make the Mad Hatter gasp. Whenever I get too much in my head, I find I start craving sugary black tea more. When I succumb to the cravings, I notice that my skin, teeth, energy levels all give me feedback as to how it's affecting me. My skin gets dryer, my teeth become less white and my energy level is more sporadic. Recently, our family took an epic 33 day road trip from Vancouver, Canada to Tijuana, Mexico; then back up to the Grand Canyon, Sedona, AZ , Santa Fe, NM and Albuquerque, NM. We had an absolute blast! Because the climate there is much hotter and drier than I'm used to and because I drank a lot less water and more black tea than I normally do, I got a killer headache that really set me back. It was a doozy. When we don't have enough water, it becomes a slippery slope unless we notice it and go back to the water. Drinking water on a consistent basis makes a huge difference to your body's health and your life's flow.

3rd Helper - MOVEMENT

Sitting is the "new smoking." This is something I heard a scientist say and it really stuck with me. For the human body to work properly, it needs to move. Our ancestors moved all day long. Think about it. They were almost always walking, standing or squatting, but not sitting, like we do today. With the invention of television, videos, video games, computers and cars, that come with modern day life, we've become a sedentary culture. In order for human beings to be healthy and connected to their internal guidance system, they need to have plenty of movement. Moving our bodies activates something power-ful in us. It's not optional. It is absolutely vital.

Sorry couch and desk potatoes! One of the best things to do for your body is move it.

I Like To Move It Move It

I Like To Move It Move It

I Like To Move It Move It

Ya Like To... (MOVE IT!)

—From the movie *Madagascar*

("I Like to Move It" is a song by American
electronic dance duo Reel 2 Real)

Movement can be fun too. Just think of *The Ellen Show* with the exuberantly magical Ellen DeGeneres. My dream is to one day dance with her because she uses dance to reverberate love into the world! Ellen brings people together and gets them into their peak state of being, accessing happiness and authenticity in those moments. This in turn helps her audience do the same. I know it feels good to her but I don't know if she realized how much she is helping the planet shift towards peace and love because of her authenticity. Take a moment and watch her show, especially the dance segment. Notice the joy she stirs up and sends into the world. It's almost humanly impossible to watch without smiling!

There are all sorts of creative and fun ways to bring more movement into your own life. In our house we, like Ellen, love dancing. So on some nights we have a dance party after we're done with the dinner dishes. We turn up the music and dance like fools all over our kitchen. Everyone has a blast and my Fitbit loves it!

I could not finish this section without mentioning one of the most amazing forms of movement, besides dance, I know. That is yoga, which means "union with your source." Yoga substitutes being hard/stiff/rigid/hunched (like people in nursing homes) with being soft/flexible/supple/aligned (like happy, healthy babies). It does this not only with your body, but also with your mind. Lack of movement simulates aging. The more flexible your body, the younger you will feel. If you have tried yoga and it did not suit you, keep exploring. There are so very many kinds of yoga and teachers, even within the same type of yoga.

I had a very bad car accident in my twenties in NY on my way to work that hurt my back in such a way that doctors told me that I would have limited mobility for the rest of my life. I did not accept that and looked for ways to heal. Yoga helped me heal. Today I'm able

Maria Salomão-Schmidt

to freely move, as long as I keep doing the yoga. The body knows. I highly recommend yoga to everyone, because unlike most any other movement, it's also about the inner journey.

I first experienced yoga when I was dragged by my housemate to an ashram in San Francisco. I cannot believe how nervous I was about going. Growing up Catholic, this was way out of my comfort zone at the time. As it turned out, I absolutely loved it and have been doing it ever since. I explain it to people this way, "it clears out your pipes." Wherever you are holding stress or pain, yoga helps you shift it. For me, yoga is absolutely one of my very favorite things about this lifetime!

4th Helper - BREATHE

This sounds pretty basic, but most people have never been taught to breathe properly. Breath mirrors how you live your life. You can check where you are in any given moment by stopping and noticing your breath.

Use your breath. It's the most sacred and profound connection we have between this world and the next/prior realm. The less breath you have, the less life you have. The more breath you have... (say it with me) the more life you have! By more life, I mean you feel the wholeness that you are, instead of the hole-ness that most of society lives. Breath brings energy to your entire body. It is critical. You can live without food or water for a lot longer than oxygen.

By the way, just because you are breathing does not mean you are getting the proper amount of breath. Get into the habit of checking in with your breath on a regular basis because it's always giving you vital feedback. For example, if you start thinking about something very intently your breath will become shallow. So right at the time when your brain needs more oxygen, you're giving it less. When you start paying attention to things like this, you can effortlessly adjust for the best results. These small shifts help you become full of yourself, your highest form of authenticity.

Within the 4th Helper, Breath, is also meditation. Meditation is not what most people think it is. Many equate it with being hard to do and something outside of themselves, but meditation is the way humans connect with the core of their being, their energy body. It's absolutely sacred work that each of us has access to any time we desire. Play with your sacredness of breath in as many moments of every day as you can because it's one of the keys of unlocking your authenticity.

 Look for this symbol throughout the book as a gentle reminder to take several deep breaths.

5th Helper - GRATITUDE

 Trust is a key element of authenticity. Being grateful builds your trust muscle. It also increases your ability to connect with others and shows how to see and focus on more beauty in the world. Those who find the gifts in both the simplest and hardest of life experiences are the ones who are rewarded with the most amazing gifts. Being able to slow down and notice your life's gifts is what makes the ride worthwhile. This is where peace and wisdom come from. Gratitude leads to the gifts. It's that simple. When you lock on to what is not working, you get more fear, disconnect and conflict. To go back into your own unique flow, look for gratitude by asking, "What is the gift?" Wherever you go, always pack "your attitude of gratitude." Start bringing the question, "What am I grateful for?" to all your conversations, not just that one on the third Thursday of every November.

 The Walk of Gratitude... This is a happiness-restoring exercise that my husband Doug and I do in the mornings when we walk our dogs... Next time you go for a walk, choose a part of your walk, for example from this tree to that tree, and during that time ask over and over, either out loud or silently, "What am I grateful for?" The more you do it, the more you'll notice the amazing results in your life. In a way, it's like a walking meditation that aligns your vibration to the level of your heart.

You've got to be a thermostat rather than a thermometer. A thermostat shapes the climate of opinion; a thermometer just reflects it.

—Cornel West

Maria Salomão-Schmidt

6th Helper - SETTING YOUR INTENTION

Most people are getting knocked around by life because they don't know where they want to go, what they want to do, or who they are. No matter how much they *try*, life eludes them. They serve many masters outside of themselves, but ignore the most important one, their own inner guidance (internal GPS). Your internal GPS is always there, whether you notice it or not, and whether you believe it or not. It's much harder to find someone who has a strong intention who feels sad about life. This is because when human beings have a focal point accompanied by a strong belief or desire, the energy stays at a higher focused vibration. There aren't many things that can keep that person from their dreams or life purpose when they have a strong intention. If you've ever watched the Olympics you've seen this over and over again. Intention gives you clarity. Without clarity there's confusion. Intention also gives you direction. Before you begin anything, your day, a project, a trip, it's important to set your intention. May this book serve as a gentle reminder to have INTENTION in how you live your life. This Helper is the most completely ignored of the Seven.

7th Helper - RELEASE

This is the least "pretty" of the Helpers, and sometimes the hardest for us humans to do. This is where we hold on to our "shoulds" because we're afraid of not being liked, or of doing the right thing. We spend lots of "efforting" energy to hold on to the things that don't belong to us because we've been taught and accept the "life is hard" school of thought.

The record-breaking movie *Frozen*'s main song is "Let It Go." To embrace the song's theme has to do with letting go on all levels: Relationships, Things, Situations, Labels, Thoughts, Actions... all of it. Purge yourself of the "have-tos, what-ifs and shoulds." Slow down and give yourself the space to notice that icky feeling that tells you that something doesn't "fit." You're getting these feelings for a reason.

Notice them. Listen to them. Believe them. In doing so, you call your energy back. More about calling your energy back in Chapter 8.

Each day more and more of us are starting to understand that we can take our lives up a few notches and emerge into living in the EXTRAORDINARY. If you break EXTRAORDINARY down, you get that it's living with "more than just the ordinary." You still live the ordinary part of your life, but you also get that extra layer, the "extra" one. It's about living at that next level—the one you have dreamed about your entire life but could not figure out how to get there. With so much information and access to almost any kind of item or resource in the world, it's a mystery that so many people live unhappy lives. That frustration keeps people small and inauthentic.

JOURNAL TIME... From all the Helpers that you read about, what's your favorite? Which Helpers are the one(s) you want to increase in your life? What would shift for you if you were to remember to use your Helpers more often?

Anchor Exercise... Pick an anchor that will bring Helpers front-of-mind for you. Anchors are visual reminders and activities that bring your focus to where you want it go. What anchors do you need to help you focus on your favorite Helpers? For example, for Helper 3 (Movement), if you want to bring more movement into your life one thing you can do is put a photo of Ellen up as a reminder to dance. As long as it makes you smile you know it's working.

In every moment start exactly where you are.

Start right now!

—Maria Salomão-Schmidt

Neo: "...I don't like the idea that I'm not
in control of my life."
Morpheus: "I know exactly what you mean. Let me
tell you why you're here. You're here because
you know something. What you know, you can't
explain. But you feel it. You felt it your entire life.
That there's something wrong with the world.
You don't know what it is, but it's there. Like a
splinter in your mind—driving you mad. It is this
feeling that has brought you to me. Do you know
what I'm talking about?"
—From the movie The Matrix

Chapter 4. You Might Feel Alone... But You Never Are

Let's Inspire Each Other

It's about connecting to something that's both a part of you, and also bigger than you. By taking this journey, you are learning things and getting answers that you never would have understood before because it was not the right time. We as humans have gotten to a place where we have both evolved and devolved to show up in this moment in time. This book was written with as open of a heart as I can in each moment. By doing so, I have opened up the possibility that you'll do the same. When one is inspired, it's contagious. It's simply the way we are built. We're connected to each other, even when we can't see it. We are ONE.

It's my vision that by noticing what you focus on, you can begin making choices of how you want to see the world. When we operate from our own unique core, we live with a more open heart, which will in turn inspire others to do the same. When that continues to spread, then we ignite our viral vehicle for establishing deep peace and true prosperity on earth, simply by default.

Straightforwardly put, my intention in writing this book is to free you from the boring, painful, disconnected, "Night of the Living Dead"-like existence that many of us are trained to live out. Many of us have been giving up our decision-making abilities to someone else either because we haven't really noticed, or have lost the energy to do what we wanted to do. When you read this book, you'll be able to have those two critical elements back!

You've started to collect the tools and call back the energy to be your authentic self. This is true freedom! The energy on our planet has shifted in such a way that living in the dark, like this, is no longer serving us. We're creating massive amounts of pain, death, suffering and pollution from this type of disconnected living. Earth can no longer support us living without our internal GPS activated. I invite you to explore and see how being "authentically you" is the key, not only to being truly connected and happy, but also to live out your life's purpose.

If you plan on being anything less than you are
capable of being, you will probably be unhappy all
the days of your life.
—Abraham Maslow

How This Book Is Different

I have been reading self-help, business, psychology and how-to books for many decades. One of the things I dislike is that even though I get a few cool *ahas!* or quotes, nothing much changes after reading them. The intention of this book is to give you tools that'll instantly shift your focus. Shifting from being stuck to flowing back into alignment will lead you to your life's purpose. It'll uncover the reason of why you took the trouble of even getting a body and being born! There's much to explore so let's go even deeper! In a way, you get to watch yourself "evolve" right before your very own senses! How cool and terrifying is that?

Maria Salomão-Schmidt

Stuff Coming Up

Whenever you move forward in your life, there's the possibility that your *saboteur* will come for a visit. Your saboteur is there to make sure whatever you're working on does not manifest. Although many don't see it that way, its purpose is to protect you from going too far from what is "normal" or "acceptable" so you don't get into difficult situations. The saboteur likes routine. It does not like newness. It means well. You'll know it has arrived when you feel procrastination and resistance to something you really want to do. The *saboteur* will also call in backups like the *trys*, *shoulds* and *have tos*. When you notice these popping up, do exactly that—*just notice*. Give it no energy, just like with a puppy that you don't want to rile up! Don't play with it, if you don't want it to play with you! That goes for both puppies and your *saboteur*! When you're feeling stuck like this, use your breath and focus on that for a bit. This will help ground you. Once you have grounded yourself, now focus your attention on what you *want*. Just like in meditation, don't ever look back at what you *don't want*. Put your focus on where you want it to be.

Is It Hard?

"Hard" is how you've been living, blocking yourself. What I am teaching you is not hard, but it is most definitely "wicked" messy, as we say in Massachusetts. Don't forget this now, and then get all surprised and upset later. You have been warned! ;)

Even though we live during the most abundant time in human history where we have more freedom, stuff, opportunity and access to almost anything we can imagine, many of us are still incredibly unhappy. The perception that *life is hard* is the reason why stress-related *dis-eases* are wreaking havoc in our bodies. We've all heard it's not what happens to us but what we do with it that matters. How many books have you bought? How many classes have you attended? Many times do you get excited by what you learned and then each day it fades away a bit more until there is nothing left? Much of the information out there requires you to DO MORE, LEARN MORE, TRY HARDER. It can be totally exhausting!

The information in this book is actually based on the fact that you already *know* everything you need to know. Where you have gotten "stuck" is on what you're focusing on. Whatever you focus on sets the course for your life. You'll see that I have already, and will continue to, say some version of that last sentence over and over and over again in this book because it really is the key to you finding your life's path. It happens in each moment. Curious though, it's also the easiest lesson to forget because it's so darn simple.

What we're going to do is DECONSTRUCT familiar concepts and words that you've *assumed* are "true" because they haven't changed much in the last hundred years; but with this huge evolutionary growth spurt we are on, DECONSTRUCTING is a wonderful way to declutter and re-purpose those communication tools that are hurting instead of helping you be heard and understood. Just like cleaning a closet, it's an incredibly messy process, but is also incredibly rewarding and refreshing. This is what we're doing with your life, going through the messy stuff so that we can uncover your exceptional life. I'll delve deeper into this later on.

For now, take a deep breath, drop and roll your shoulders and know you are at the *right* place at the *right* time. Focus on the *right now*—this very precious moment in time. So, let's savor these words and lessons together as we make the world a better place by each discovering who we really are.

JOURNAL TIME... Who inspires you? Who do you inspire? If either of these questions are hard for you to answer, lean into the icky. Find out where you are feeling "off" by simply noticing what is coming up. Notice when you make it about you instead of realizing that it is just feedback.

It is now that my life is mine.

—Amy Gill

Maria Salomão-Schmidt

Life on earth can never be fully understood. Life and
all it holds is too big for humans to understand.
There is the possibility for more joy than they ever
comprehend and there is the same possibility of pain
and suffering. Humans have embraced pain and
sorrow much more fully than they have embraced joy.
This is why the world suffers.

—Jan Krause Greene (I Call Myself Earth Girl)

Chapter 5. Poverty, Poison & Pissedocity

This next section can be very painful. For many, even just the thought of it is enough to shut them down. Unfortunately, that's one of the reasons suffering continues on Earth. I invite you to summon up the courage to face what feels "icky" because the only way to get rid of something is to go *through* it. Bring your *7 Helpers* with you as you take on this journey and lean on them, for they'll help you get to the other exceptional side of living from your heart's purpose.

If you are going through hell, keep going.

—Winston Churchill

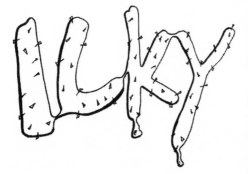

As of the writing of this book, our beloved Mother Earth is in the worst shape it's ever been, and the trajectory is moving in the direction of much more needless loss and pain. Two of the biggest causes of suffering, wars and poverty continue to expand and grow at alarming rates. Misery, sadness, destruction, chaos, stress, hopelessness, heartache and pain also expand in their wake.

No matter how many technical and medical advances we make, we seem to make money our first priority and for that reason, our planet is showing significant signs of being in major crisis. Here are just a few examples, in no particular order, of what I mean...

- Planet Earth can't digest plastic, yet, we keep making more that cannot be recycled.

- Much of our food is full of chemicals and pesticides and being genetically altered. When we ask to identify which foods are GMOs, large corporations sue. They even sued the State of Vermont when its citizens passed a bill asking for GMOs to be identified.

- We are running out of clean, safe, drinkable water.

- Our animals are dying at unprecedented numbers. In the last 40 years, 50% of the world's animals who are living in their natural habitat have died! Think about that for a moment!

- Our children are more overweight than any children in history, yet corporations continue to put their processed, unhealthy food in our schools because they give schools money.

- People of color and women are still being discriminated against at alarming rates.

- Women with the same experience and education still get paid less money for the same work as men.

- The prison population continues to grow at alarming rates. Although America is only 4.6% of the world's population, we have a horrifying 25% of the prison population!

- Most think the sex & domestic slave trade happens "somewhere else" but it's happening in middle class American neighborhoods right under people's noses. Many have been kidnapped from other American cities, had their faces reconstructed by the kidnappers so as not to be recognized and been drugged to perform sexual acts. Their families will never see nor hear from them again. They have no idea what happened to their child. This shocking act against humanity continues because most of us don't even know it's happening so the unspeakable suffering keeps growing, like a poisonous weed strangling as it grows. This veil of ignorance and silence is a poison to our human race.

Maria Salomão-Schmidt

- Our oceans are so full of trash that in the Pacific there is even a huge "island" of plastic trash. Fishes' and birds' lives are being cut short because of the plastic they ingest, due to the breakdown of plastic into small pieces.

- Corporations use vast amounts of money and lobbyists to control government policies that affect everything in our world including our food, our environment and our lives. They even have managed to have the US Supreme Court give corporations the same status as a person. While a select few are getting extremely richer, the poverty rate is exploding.

- Media, now owned by a very few, re-directs our attention to meaningless news broadcasts so that we focus on those issues instead of what is really going on. Remember "whoever controls your focus controls you!"

Now What?

The points above are just a very small handful of what is going on! It can be so overwhelming that most people just shut down, which is incredibly unfortunate because it just makes the problem grow even faster. With very few checks and balances in place and most people tuning out, those whose main interest is making money above all else begin creating the world more and more in the image that helps line their pockets. Meanwhile, this kind of unnatural imbalance is destroying our world. If you stick a frog in hot water it jumps right out. If you stick a frog in warm water, it just slowly sits there as the water heats up until it is too late because it has gotten slowly used to it, even if it was killing her/him. Unfortunately, like frogs placed in warm water that comes to a slow boil, many of us haven't woken up to the reality that is staring us in the face. People often become dormant, living in a cruise-control-like state as they enter "analysis paralysis" that turns them from PEOPLE to SHEEPLE.

For those who begin to notice, they may also feel powerless. The fear is that:

1. It's too late.

2. I'm only one person. What can one person do?

3. It's too big and confusing for anything to change.

4. This is just how the world is. There is no choice.

5. I don't want to make trouble. Making waves is out of my comfort zone.

6. How will people think of me or treat me?

But if you are reading this, it's not too late! You have been led here, to this information, for a reason. Your time is now! Remember that whatever you were born to do, it's based on what you love to do. Your "instructions" and directions have always been within you, just as it is for each blessed blade of grass. It is always in your internal GPS. Look for it! It is there to serve you! It is not based on worth or ability, it is just yours because it's part of you.

For over two decades, I've been coaching people, who like you, feel like they want to make a difference but don't know where to start. The difference in the intuitive hits I get now compared to when I started coaching, is massive and consistent. Because of the "calling back my energy" work I've d one, it has allowed me continuously to uncover my reason for being. My life's powerful mission is BEING THE FIRE THAT IGNITES YOUR LIFE PURPOSE. In other words, my fire helps SPARK YOU to your life's powerful mission!

Maria Salomão-Schmidt

A fulfilling life requires embracing or bearing witness to, difficulty, rather than running away from it.

—Friedrich Nietzsche

YES! You Are Feeling A Growing Sense of Urgency

The really cool thing is that when I coach, I get intuition hits on my clients. Don't be too impressed, because intuition is just us connecting to our energy body. It's our innate ability. We all have it. The more you're open to the universal energy within, the stronger your intuition hits are. Now, it's important to note that they don't come in the form of a telegram or anything like that. Nothing fancy. Just something pops into your head and you allow it to share its message with you. If you immediately shoo it away, it's less likely to come back. You get my drift? *Energy works by using your imagination and focus.* Use those vital tools to begin communicating at this amazing level. This is why "play" is so important because it frees you in a way that connects you to the things your five senses can't pick up.

When I first started coaching, it was rare to get a strong "sense of urgency" intuition hit that the person in front of me activate their life's purpose. Now, however, I have this massive "sense of urgency" sensation with almost all of my coaching clients! I would say the energy has greatly shifted over the last few years and is so strong that I now not only see it, but sometimes I even hear the vibration pulsating.

After reading the list of statistics earlier in this chapter, we can all begin to see why the energy is getting even more intense. Hard as it may be, it will only get worse if we don't stop and check in. The most common complaint I hear is, "I don't know where to start?" You know the answer as well as I do... Start where you are. As you begin exploring the energy side of yourself, you start realizing how very much there is to learn and how very much we still don't know. Much of this is new to me too, but what I can tell you is that something has definitely shifted and it is getting louder—much louder. I know this with all my heart.

Our planet, Mother Earth, is calling to us because we are off-balance. Although it might turn some people off, I personally like using the term Mother Earth, as I mentioned earlier in the book, because it is a phrase that connotes the feelings of connection and gratitude. We were all birthed on earth using all the amazing resources from this planet so she is, in a sense, our body's "mother." So when people think about the earth in this manner, they are one step closer to noticing.

When this happens, you wake up to the fact that we're polluting where and what our children eat and drink. Even the weather is helping us wake up with all these highly erratic and powerful storms and climate change patterns. Our system of checks and balances is off and the call for course correction is growing. Those who place the importance of making a profit before all else are running our world into the ground, and in many circumstances, being "rewarded" for it. There is nothing wrong with making money, but it's how one goes about it; and if it's done in an unconscious way at the expense of others and our environment, then this is no longer a *win-win* situation in the end. Having money as your number one goal, above all else, can only lead to more destruction of our planet.

Ultimately, we have the power to change our course and to continue taking the appropriate steps to reverse and prevent further damage. We have everything we need to be successful in this endeavor. We just may have never fully understood that we had the power all along. *Finally Full of Yourself* is designed to help you activate your energetic DNA, the part of you that will give you *freedom and flow*!

The courage to finally write this book comes from a sacred, loving place. This book is my answer to that call I am feeling getting louder and louder. By reading *Finally Full of Yourself* you'll find how you can serve in the world too. Even more exciting is that if you're reading these words there are no accidents or coincidences. As my longtime mentor Dr. Wayne Dyer says, "Coincidences are simply two right angles 'coinciding.'" I know in my heart of hearts you were meant to read it, just as I was meant to write it!

If you remember nothing else I ask you to keep feeding and following the voice of your intuition. It's that energy that led you to this information and it will continue leading all the days of your life. You only get into *trouble/pain/suffering* when you block out your intuition. It leads you to the things that will wake you up to your life's purpose, because your mission, the reason for your being born, is what this world needs unleashed right now.

There's a simple reason why things are not working but it's only simple if you notice what's happening and why it's happening. There is a poverty, a hunger, a longing, of the spirit. You may be living out of old, out-dated habits of what worked for our ancestors, but realize that time has passed on in our evolution. It is time for a massive shift. Just as our bodies have evolved, our energy too has evolved. All over the planet we are seeing signs of people moving more into a different

Maria Salomão-Schmidt

way of living and being. So, enough yapping, now that you have a bit of background, let's get right to the heart of the matter... because it's from that place that this all gets sorted out.

JOURNAL TIME... Your spiritual DNA is always calling, leading and guiding you on our path, even though you might have not even considered that possibility. When have you felt it pulling your forward? Write about those rare moments that you tend to notice, but then brush off as, "not important."

JOURNAL TIME 2... This chapter has a lot of the dark stuff we don't like to address so having another journal option helps you clear your shit even better. From the list at the beginning of this chapter what stuck out the most for you? What do you wish you could help solve? What calls to you? Write about what comes up for you? How do you feel you can serve?

> *Even if you never do anything about this, you've benefited from an unjust system. You're already the winner in a game that was rigged to your advantage from the start.*
>
> —Jonathan Kozol

*Her life's calling was continuously reaching out to
her, giving her clues, subtle only because her
attention was elsewhere, if only she slowed down
long enough to take notice.*
—Maria Salomão-Schmidt

Chapter 6. Our Family's Secret Blueprints

Don't blink! We live in an unprecedented time in human history, for never have human beings faced this much change, happening this quickly. For two million years, we humans did things pretty much the same way from generation to generation. Change did happen, but it occurred oh-so-very slowly over a v-e-r-y long time.

Today, running around living our busy lives, we often don't think much about our ancestors except for a few photos, heirlooms, stories or mementos; but much of how we do things, especially the unconscious stuff, are things we picked up from our family. These are secret "family blueprints" of how to be in the world that have been unconsciously passed down over time, under the radar (even to us) because it's just how we do things. For the most part, the way we operate in our lives, our perceptions of our world, how we treat ourselves and others, where we live, who we pick as partners, how we raise our kids, and so much more comes from how we were indoctrinated by our parents. Our parents learned from their parents, and so on and so on. There are times when a parent's behavior is so contrary to the soul of the child, that the child makes a vow to do the exact opposite. This happens a lot, but you will find that other parts of how that child does things, will still match up to family blueprints of others in his/her family.

Life Through Flow Points

Why we do what we do is influenced by how our ancestors went about their survival. We're both energetically and cellularly connected to them, whether we are conscious of it or not. When we become more present in our lives we can finally notice what unconscious patterns have been repeated over and over through each generation. Some patterns are being repeated in the most subtle of ways.

Why is this important? This whole journey is about calling back your energy so that you can be full of yourself, fully you. Through our energy body we make connections. Where there's a flow we've created flow points, which allow the energy to continue moving and expanding. When we make certain connections to somethings, the energy creates a stuck point and there's a lack of movement. Calling our energy back is about turning those stuck points back into flow points.

More about calling your energy back in Chapter 8. For now, remember to notice if you're experiencing flow points or stuck points when you read the following questions.

- What is going on around you?
- What you do in certain circumstances?
- How you do it?
- Why you do it?
- Who you attract into your life?
- What you attract into your life?

Although we tend to think we are very unique, much of how we live our lives has to do with covering up or blocking our true uniqueness, or flavor, in the world—because uniqueness means being different. Historically speaking, "different" was not a good road to be on. Others saw it as dangerous, and many times people were demeaned, ostracized and even killed. There is a lot of fear wrapped up in being different and a lot of "reward" for following the well-traveled path dictated by society.

No matter what your story is, when you start digging in deep, you realize just how fascinating it can all be once you slow down and begin to dissect how you are using your precious life force; in other words, your magnificent life's energy—your core.

 Field Trip Exercise... When I was a child, I spent hours and hours at the library because I discovered that books could not only transport me to magical places, but also teach me useful life information. From a very early age I was hooked on books. One of my favorite ways to play in the world is with authors like Napoleon Hill, Florbela Espanca, Dr. Seuss, Shakti Gawain, Wayne Dyer, Florent Chavouet and Og Mandino. I HIGHLY recommend all of them! Which leads us to this exercise...

HOORAY! It's a field trip! The purpose of this one is to combat "busy" and the dreaded, "I'll do it one day" syndrome. This will give you a chance to slow down and do something simple, so you can start shifting how you race through life, missing many of the really precious parts. Now, many times when I'm reading a book, I don't do the exercises which defeats the whole point, really; but sometimes it's hard to when I am in reading/processing mode, to stop and do an exercise. When I'm in the flow, it's difficult to stop. So, for this exercise, you don't have to do the actual assignment right now. Just go get your calendar and book at least a 30-minute appointment with yourself within the next seven days for this wonderful adventure! The sooner you do, the sooner your life will continue to shift in the direction of your dreams. Stop now and get your calendar before you begin this next adventure...

The Goals: 1. Build Trust. 2. Work your Intuition muscle. 3. Activate your Imagination.

Description: Here's a fun, free exercise that helps you build your level of trust in the world. Most of us hold back because of a huge lack of trust. We're taught by society that the world is a scary place and that you can't trust people. HAPPINESS cannot happen without trust. Since most of us could use a lot more trust, through doing this easy exercise, you'll see some amazing results.

Your Mission: So, when was the last time you went to a library, just for you just to play and explore? Some of the most magical places on earth are libraries! Each book carries the energy of the author and when you read these books, you can more easily tap into that energy. It's easy to see why books are still so popular even with all the other things and technological devices diverting our attention. Most people read to get information or for entertainment, but, whether they know it or not, they're also connecting to the energy of that book.

SLOWLY use your finger to go through the authors' names below. *Notice* which names catch your fancy. Pick a few names you have not heard before and go find the book at the local library. Get out of your familiar environment. If they don't have the author there look him/her up online, but only if they don't have the book at the library. Have fun being an explorer. Play with what you find. Jot down notes and ideas that pop up. See where it leads you. Each person who does this exercise will get the perfect results for them... Give yourself this gift and see where it takes you. It's a wonderful way to connect to all that amazing wisdom that is always all around us... wisdom that is completely useless if we don't connect to it. Here's your chance to do something human beings have never been able to do until now, access the wisdom of some of the most amazing people who have ever lived! How incredibly amazing is that?

List of Names to Explore... I invite you to see what you find when you focus on this specific group. Drop your assumptions and open you up to new adventures.

Here's your list:

Jane Goodall, Fernando Pessoa, Napoleon Hill, Robin Casarjian, Derrick Bell, Sheryn MacMunn, Shakti Gawain, Mitsuyo Kakuta, Malala Yousafzai, Geoffrey Canada, Wayne Dyer, Sark, Naoki Higashida, Iyanla Vanzant, David Elkind, Jan Krause Greene, Debbie Ford, Elie Wiesel, Jack Kerouac, J. R. R. Tolkien, Antoine de Saint-Exupéry, Richard Bach, Trina Paulus, Carlos Castenada, Ethel Lilian Voynich, Stieg Larsson, Zora Neale Hurston, Albert Camus, Brené Brown, Haruki Murakami, Charlotte Brontë, Margaret Wheatley, Nora Garcia, Serena Dyer, Elizabeth Gilbert, Esther Hicks, Jonas Jonasson, Eckhart Tolle, Julia Butterfly Hill, Rayya Elias, Joline Godfrey, Dr. Christiane Northrup, M. Scott Peck, Clementine Bihiga, Annelise Orleck, Barbara Ransby, Kris Carr, Tama Kieves, Mary Shelley, Holly Bellebuono, Robert Parker, Eudora Welty, Alice Walker, Dr. Becky A. Bailey, Barbara Ann Brennan, Don Miguel Ruiz, Paulo Coelho, Marianne Williamson, Anodea Judith, Deepak Chopra, Jonathan Kozol, Julia Cameron, Anthony Robbins, Louise Hay, Florent Chavouet, Caroline Myss, Florbela Espanca, James Redfield, Les Brown, Gloria Steinem, Amy Tan, Robert Fulghum, Jonathan Kozel, Ernest Hemingway, Oriah Mountain Dreamer, Louisa May Alcott, Anne Frank, Loretta Laroche, Milan Kundera, Edith Wharton, Margaret Atwood, Jung Chang, Jill Bolte Taylor, Banana Yoshimoto, Nicholas Kristof/Sheryl WuDunn, Martin Luther King, Jr., Anne Lamott, Gary Zukav, Mark Nepo and Og Mandino...

WARNING: Notice when your brain wants to get the "right" answer. Start getting used to the world where there is no "right" answer. Some of you will negate this exercise as being too simple, but even Olympic athletes get great by repeating simple tasks over and over again. Take that in for a moment and digest it. Your path is sacred, messy, humbling and beautiful. Leave nothing on the table. If you live it with all you have, the most magical things begin unfolding in your life. Lots of people are out there with half-lived lives. Drop your membership to that "club!"

Pay no attention to the man behind the curtain.
—Wizard of Oz

Things I Want To Remember/Research/Review:

Maria Salomão-Schmidt

We need much less than we think we need.

—Maya Angelou

Chapter 7. The Happiness Glass Ceiling

When you live in a world where you have reduced gratitude, you lose out on the amazing gifts before you. It's equivalent to receiving a magnificent gift and never opening it. If you play videogames at all, it's like passing by that extra bonus flashing-something-or-other and choosing not to activate those points. This type of lack of engagement affects your life on an energetic level. It lowers your vibration, which is another definition for "how you feel." You can *physically* feel it when your vibration lowers. It feels "heavy" and you feel *depressed, hopeless* and *exhausted.*

As of the writing of this book, so many people live in these lower vibrations that this has actually has become "normal." Being sad is so prevalent that if someone shows excitement for simply being alive, people say they are crazy, or maybe even think they are on drugs. On the other hand if someone complains or sees things as half-empty, others may feel more connected to them because they are also on that lower vibration which feels so *familiar* to them.

Mind Movie Exercise... Activate your imagination for this exercise to see if it's in alignment with what you have experienced on this planet too. I'm going to use this as an excuse to really have fun, so let's even pick the characters to play out this example. You can pick any actors you wish. I'm including some of my favorite here.

Characters in our Mind Movie:

Main Character - Francesca: Isabella Rossellini

Co-workers - Stella: Rose Leslie, Marilyn: Shirley MacLaine, Joan: Chrissy Teigen, Susie: Melissa McCarthy, Victoria: Corrine Petteys

Take One

Scene begins... Francesca holds her head as she painfully walks toward the office's break room. On the other side of the door she finds five of her co-workers (Stella, Victoria, Marilyn, Joan and Susie) volleying gossip back and forth as they add more sugar to their morning beverages.

"What happened to you Francesca? You look like crap!" said Stella, just before biting into her lox and cream cheese toasted sesame bagel. Francesca shakes her head, while shrugging her shoulders, "I have no idea. I just woke up tired and fed up. Thank God it's Friday." All the women nod in agreement. Francesca sits down and they continue on this low vibration, this time trying to outdo each other to see who had the most shocking (bottom feeder) details about last night's celebrity tragedy. Fade to black (literally and figuratively)...

Take Two

Scene begins... Francesca almost skips as she dances toward the office's break room. On the other side of the door she finds five of her co-workers volleying gossip back and forth as they add more sugar to their morning beverages.

"What happened to you, Francesca? You look so happy! Did you win the lottery or something?" said Stella, giving the others a knowing look. Francesca shakes her head, as she giggles, "I have no idea. I just woke up feeling great! I'm happy it's Friday!" All the women look at each other and roll their eyes. Francesca thinks about sitting down, but it somehow does not feel right. She pours herself an Ayurvedic special hot tea and wishes her co-workers, "a great day!" Even before

Maria Salomão-Schmidt

Francesca leaves, the five women lean in and start talking about how strange Francesca was acting. "Maybe she's on drugs," they whisper. Fade to black.

DOROTHY *"Oh, now?"*

GLINDA *"Whenever you wish."*

DOROTHY *"Oh, dear—that's too wonderful*

to be true!"

—Scene from The Wizard of Oz

Because of how very low expectations are here on earth presently, it's like there is a *Happiness Glass Ceiling* out there. Every time someone gets "too happy," they hit it in the eyes of those around them who feel more comfortable being miserable than happy. Later in the book I will explain why that is specifically. For now, I will go back to the break room in our Mind Movie.

In these two scenarios, you have been given examples of how people behave when they are both in the same "operating system," and when they are operating in a different one. This is a wonderful example that many of us have experienced—and, if we are honest, have participated on both sides. We live in a world where we want to belong, so sometimes we join the "herd" because that's where everyone else is. It's a lot easier to join them when your vibration is already low because you get fed from that lower energy.

It might have been helpful to do a third scenario where Francesca starts off in a great mood and then to be able to sit with her co-workers allows herself to lower her vibration by connecting to their stories and giving them her energy until she is at their level. If you have heard of the expression, "birds of a feather flock together," that is what happens in this this third scenario. Francesca, wanting to connect with her tribe, gives up her higher aligned vibration, and thus connection to her own intuition, so that she can fit in. The *herd*—her *work tribe*—is happy because they have gotten her to give up her energy and "fit" into what is has been their unnatural state of "normal." This is all happening subconsciously, although they can feel the energy.

Moving Past the Unnatural State of "Normal"

Give yourself the amazing gift of realizing the incredible abilities we all possess because our ancestors were able to conquer their fears of fire and learn how to harness it. In a way, we are at the dawn of a new age. This time it's going past our fears of a different kind of energy. This time it's our inner "fire"—our *energetic body*. Through fire, humans have been able to cook food, heat water, heat their homes and, ultimately see in the dark. Metaphorically speaking, it signifies being able to bring light to where there was only darkness. Harnessing fire is an act no other Earthly "animal" is able to do. It is usually reserved for gods and goddesses. We are entering a new level of being for humans.

The War Against Feeling Good

I don't know if you've noticed it too, but there's a concerted effort to keep things that cause us pleasure to a minimum. For example, sex, in general, is seen as something "icky" to many people, instead of a very beautiful, sacred, exhilarating and a enjoyable act that created your most favorite people!

If we're to be open and totally honest, there are subjects that even I as a grown woman have trouble talking about because it feels "weird." I have done enough energetic work to realize that the oddness comes from my going toe-to-toe with my domestication. Because I've made this realization, I define domestication as blocking out my own internal GPS and following the rules, opinions and wants of others. When I feel this sensation, I no longer automatically move away from it like a reflex. Instead, I explore it even more by leaning into it. I move towards it instead of away because I am open to what it is showing me. I am also open to seeing what part of my life I've let be domesticated, most without my conscious awareness.

The human body is magically designed for many different things. One of them is the ability to self-soothe and self-pleasure. What an ingenious gift to have. In our natural flow that makes perfect sense. If feeling good is the best way to turn on your internal guidance system, then having the ability to increase the level of physical joy would do the same.

Having an orgasm is one of the closest ways that we get on this planet to what it feels like to live in that big, luscious Love-Ball. Other people can feel that kind of human ecstasy simply by deeply meditating or through breath-work. I have taken some breath-work classes that were incredibly powerful. The point is that when you are open, you *get to* experience things that others never do, simply because they are closed to anything they cannot control or label. Living in that closed way, can dramatically limit your joy. Limited joy gives you feedback that you're living inauthentically.

A definite indicator that someone has been *domesticated* is that they tend to shy away from speaking about anything pleasurable. They also distrust people who are "too happy." In the domesticated state, feelings are something that may need to be at the very least cut off, if not entirely dismantled. Instead it's the "no pain, no gain" belief that people believe. What fits perfectly with the Right Now Operating System (OS), is absolutely rejected in the Herd Operating System (OS). Why would this be? In the Right Now OS, you get your information by being in a peaceful constant flow that gives you feelings of happiness. If you get too low you feel it, and can use this built-in system of being able to shift your focus to bringing you back up. It is just another powerful, yet simple, tool to allow you access and alignment with your spiritual DNA.

When domesticated in the Herd mentality, however, all connection to feelings must be eliminated because feelings are deemed weak, unreliable and unsafe. With this kind of goal, anything that would bring pleasure is seen as "bad" because it makes people do crazy, not controllable things. "Control" is a very important part of the Herd OS, because without it all chaos would break loose; that is what the ego leads us to believe.

This reminds me of the quote in the movie, *The Matrix*, where Morpheus says, "The Matrix is a system, Neo. That system is our enemy. But when you're inside, you look around, what do you see? Businessmen, teachers, lawyers, carpenters. The very minds of the people we are trying to save. But until we do, these people are still a part of that system... You have to understand, most of these people are not ready to be unplugged. And many of them are so inured, so hopelessly dependent on the system, that they will fight to protect it."

Sexual oppression is widespread. Whether it's about the act itself or how people identify themselves in terms of gender and sexuality there is a lot of fear and oppression. Society has historically put upon women the task of being pure and chaste, and for men to be wild and to sow their oats. Even today in some societies if a woman is raped, she is the one punished, sometimes even by death. This is complete madness!

For the last twenty years, I've been holding "Happy Me" retreats in places like Vermont, Cape Cod (Massachusetts), Napa Valley (California) Lisbon (Portugal), Estoril (Portugal) and Cascais (Portugal). Most are total strangers to each other. Because I set up an environment that supports a "full of yourself" energy level, the feedback I get is always very similar. Those who come to the retreat cannot believe that by the end, no one knows any of the most basic details about each other. They are all blissed out and joyful because they have had the sacred opportunity to live in the moment. The consensus is that they feel relaxed and lighter. Because most of us live in stressful situations, we forget how hard of an environment that is to live in. It takes a lot of energy to be constantly judging. We think we *have to*, but there is another, lighter, more powerful, easier, more authentic way to live and that is living your life authentically full of yourself.

> *Don't wait for a Gandhi, don't wait for a King,*
> *don't wait for a Mandela. You are your own*
> *Mandela, you are your own Gandhi,*
> *you are your own King.*
> —Leymah Gbowee

Maria Salomão-Schmidt

The ones I pity are the ones who never stick out their
neck for something they believe, never know the taste
of moral struggle, and never have the thrill
of victory.

—Jonathan Kozol

Chapter 8. Calling Your Energy Back

I got the rare opportunity to study directly with the charismatic Carolyn Myss when I lived in San Francisco, California in the late 1990's. She taught me to imagine that each morning, we get 100 energy dollars. How we choose to use our energy throughout the day, by what we think about, determines whether we have made *return on investments* (ROI) that fill us with even more energy (a strong ROI), or bankrupt us (no ROI). I've used this powerful tool almost daily in my own life to clear some of the heaviest of icky energy patterns that were invisible to me prior to doing this amazing exercise. By being able to *notice* where my energy was going, I am still able to this day to stop myself before deciding to use my energy in ways that will give me a poor ROI. The more you do it, the more effortless it is to maintain a full flow of your own authentic energy.

Calling your energy back is about using this same exercise and applying it to pre-existing energy patterns, especially the wounded patterns. In your lifetime, every time something happened of great significance, especially something *icky*, you mostly likely left some part of yourself there. As we discussed earlier in the book, this is called a *stuck point* because the energy stops there. When this happens, your overall energy system begins to lessen because it dissipates your energy. What you don't realize is to stop your energy flow takes a lot of efforting and that eats up your energy. It drains you to maintain just one event that you have created a stuck point for, now imagine a whole lifetime of stuck points that you "have to" maintain. After a while, you feel depleted and you don't know why, because nothing major has happened. Well, it has, but just not all at once or in one place. This becomes your new normal. Because many of us do this, this has also become society's normal too. This makes it even harder for people to notice that it is so very unnatural to being full of yourself.

To bring your energy back to its natural state is to let it be a *flow point* again. This is done by revisiting the troublesome memories and thoughts and asking if this is where you want to invest your energy. Many of these *wound patterns* are not even conscious, but we avoid them consciously because they are usually incredibly painful and uncomfortable. How you know it's a trigger is if you find yourself saying some form of, "I don't want to talk about it." Now would be a great time to bring in a heaping dose of FORGIVENESS.

Just to be clear, forgiveness has nothing to do with the other person at all. No, really. Each of us is really doing the best we can with what we have. Let me repeat that again, EACH PERSON YOU MEET IS DOING THE BEST THEY CAN WITH WHERE THEY ARE. Anyone who does harm to someone else is suffering on some level, even if they do not know or show it. Forgiveness means you're disconnecting your energy from that person or event. Notice it's not the act of ignoring or blocking. It is again using your powerful tool of imagination. Imagine a cord and cut the connection. This might have to be done a few times to a few hundred times as it comes up, but when it shows up at the door of your imagination, begging to come in, simply send it gently on its way by cutting the cord. It's also about forgiving yourself. Freeing the energy from their energetic mortgage, to stop that low energy loop. It's moving from a stuck point to a flow point, which is your natural state.

Maria Salomão-Schmidt

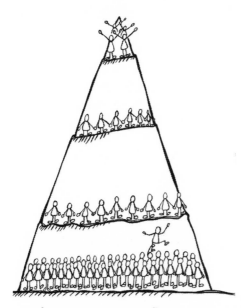

Welcome to Mortal Mountain! You know, what keeps you stuck is not the memories of icky things. What keeps you stuck is replaying (or focusing on) something over, and over, and over again. Think about it. YOU are the one who chooses (through focusing your thoughts) to bring the *ickies* of the past or the *fear* of the future into the now. What a way to ruin a perfectly good present moment.

Most of us have been domesticated into doing this so when this happens, be kind to yourself and let it go. The more you let go, the more energy flows. The more "good" (authentic flow) energy you keep for yourself, the more amazing *coincidences* you begin to have, all because your vibration is growing! You're becoming more full of yourself, more authentic in your unblocked flow. This happens because of how energy works on Earth. I use a simple analogy with my clients that you may love too:

Imagine that all of humanity is on a mountain, let's call it Mortal Mountain (MM) for fun because there is a huge gift in remembering that this life we are on is temporary. A huge amount of people are on the bottom level of MM because they are energetically *heavy*. The lighter you energetically get (which means the more energy you can call back and grow), the higher up on the MM you go! The higher up you go, the more cool experiences you will notice, manifest and magnetize. When you start to see that this happens more and more, it motivates you to clear up more of your shit because it's so very fun! Talk about an interesting life! The characters and experiences that you magnetize into your life becomes the adventure of your dreams! See how it works? This is why I could not wait to share this book with you!

Imagine if everyone lived this way! This is how to reduce suffering, and bring world peace and Love to this planet. *Yes, pain* is definitely part of the human experience. It is vital *feedback, suffering* is not. Realizing this is the natural flow of evolution. We, humans have historically blocked our natural flow through our ego and pain building. We are now evolving from *stuck point* to *flow point* living, which brings everything back into alignment. The more people focus on their natural flow, the more real it becomes!

How Do I Re-focus My Attention and Intention to Call My Energy Back?

Here's an incredibly important tool that you may have not even put any value on... the ability to ask questions. You refocus yourself best through questions. Yup, simple *questions* are one of the best ways to call your energy back. Questions not only give you information, they also give you a direction. The key is to ask a question that help you create a *flow point*, not a *stuck point*. Ask yourself questions that get your attention to what you specifically want, not what you want to avoid. Here are examples of *stuck point* questions: (Warning these can lower your vibration if you connect with these questions. Your brain is a computer and will process the information you expose it to and feed it. Make sure you notice if you are leaking energy as you read these. How do you know? You start feeling "icky," "hopeless" or "heavy.")

First Set of Questions

- What is wrong with me?
- Why am I always attracting mean people?
- What was I thinking?
- How can I put up with this crap?
- Why can't I ever get that?
- Why doesn't it ever work?
- What is wrong with him?

Can you feel the heaviness in just reading those questions? Yuck! OK, dump those questions from your energy field. Once you have done that, take a deep breath and slowly read the following questions. Notice how you feel after reading these questions:

- Where do I want to go from here?
- Where do I see myself?
- What would be the best version of me?
- What do I want/need to let go of to move on?
- What am I afraid to do that must be done for me to move forward?

- What is my superhero power that can help me get through this?
- What other thing did I accomplish that I did not think I initially could?
- What is calling to me? Pulling me forward?

Have a mind that is open to everything
and attached to nothing.

—Wayne Dyer

Do you feel a difference when you read these two sets of questions? This simple process helps you stop spending *energetic dollars* so that you can start focusing more on the things you really want to get or experience in your life. Once you have stopped spending your *energy dollars* on stuff you don't really want in your life by using these questions, your energy begins flowing in the direction you're focused on.

As you call your energy back, you begin filling up with more energy and have a better connection to your intuition—in other words your *internal GPS*. You begin feeling lighter. The lighter you feel in this lifetime the more amazing your experiences will be to you, because they're the ones you're attracting from your highest level of being and your most authentic you. From this more authentic vibration, you'll be effortlessly magnetizing your life's purpose.

 JOURNAL TIME... In what parts of your life do you have a high ROI? Where do you have a low ROI? What *ahas!* are you getting from noticing how you spend your energy in this manner? How do you spend our energetic currency?

*Hugs can do great amounts of good—especially
for children.*
—Princess Diana

Things I Want To Remember/Research/Review:

Maria Salomão-Schmidt

The biggest challenge we face is shifting human consciousness, not saving the planet. The planet doesn't need saving. We do.

—Xiuhtezcatl Martinez

Chapter 9. The Wound Pattern

One of my favorite things to remind my clients is that whatever happens in the *macro* (large), also happens in the *micro* (small). Things reverberate out and into each other. The earth is a macro reverberation of each human being. If it's a *mess*, so are we.

Many people live with a big, fat lie. It's the lie that has brought incredible amounts of heartache and suffering to planet Earth for thousands and thousands of generations. Our culture unconsciously reinforces it. Even though they themselves struggle with it, parents and grandparents still pass it down to their children because they have been led to believe that this is the way the world "is." Many see it as absolute truth.

WARNING: You may have to read this section a few times because your brain might just zone out when you read it. Give it a chance to sink in though, because making this realization, getting this *aha!* will open up your life immensely. Be kind to yourself as you process and digest this information.

"So what is the lie?" you ask. Well, simply put, it is the belief that "to live with an open heart is dangerous." It's the feeling that you cannot be authentic and not share what you really feel until you trust the other person. Be careful. Be guarded. Be safe. Don't share your heart because it might get broken. Take that in for a moment, because you may be tempted to think that this does not "fit" you or how you live your life. Be honest with yourself and check in. *How* do you approach situations? Job prospects? Sales prospects? Love prospects? Dreams? Goals? How do you ask for what you want? Do you go after things with an open heart, or do you pull back because of fear of rejection or of looking ridiculous to others? Notice, without judging. How do you feel? (*Remember to breathe as you read these. You're welcome!*)

The belief that *"to live with an open heart is dangerous"* is first introduced when you were young, very young. In fact, it was there since you were conceived but you were focused on other things. Those around you taught you what to focus on for your own safety. For most of us humans, the human experience involves the fact that somewhere along the line your needs were not met. Your heart broke in some way. It could have been experienced when someone did something unloving towards you at school, in an activity, with family members or at home.

This trauma forms your *core pattern*. Some people call it our "core wound" but our true *core* is impervious to woundology. What gets wounded is your ego. The pattern developing from this comes about from the ego assigning meaning to painful events. The ego tells you that if you don't do what it says you will be what at a basic level all human beings subconsciously fear, to be abandoned and die because they are alone. To prevent this from happening, we begin continuously and constantly attributing meaning to events until a pattern is formed. In other words until we learn how it works so we know how to act around it. Let me show you how very powerful this process is by having you do the exercise below. How much you can let yourself go is how much you will get out of this exercise. Let's dive in!

I took a long time getting ready to exist.

—Fernando Pessoa

Maria Salomão-Schmidt

The Trigger Exercise... Slowly read this list and notice which one of these phrases triggers you. Check off as many as you feel apply to you growing up:

- ☐ No one ever had any time for me
- ☐ I was ignored and did not feel seen as important
- ☐ I was bullied
- ☐ I felt invisible
- ☐ No one really took care of me
- ☐ I was constantly monitored
- ☐ I was put down for not being good enough
- ☐ I felt that what I wanted did not matter
- ☐ I was afraid of being hit, or abused in some way
- ☐ What I felt did not matter
- ☐ I was always picked last
- ☐ I wanted someone to cuddle and hold me, in a safe, loving way

- ☐ I was abandoned
- ☐ I was beaten or spanked
- ☐ I never felt like I fit in
- ☐ I was left alone much of the time and neglected
- ☐ I was sexually molested or raped
- ☐ I was called names
- ☐ I did not feel heard
- ☐ I felt like I was unworthy of being loved
- ☐ I was starving for attention
- ☐ I felt ugly
- ☐ I felt empty
- ☐ I was only loved when I did things the right way, or the way they wanted me to

After reading the section above, take a deep breath here. Stop and notice what is coming up. This can be some pretty heavy stuff. Remind yourself that you are safe. Feelings are not "bad." They are just little packets of energy there to give you feedback. Where do you feel it in your body? The heavier it is for you, the more important the feedback it's giving you that's affecting your life right now. Lean into it. Remind yourself that you are safe. Use whichever of the Helpers from Chapter 3, you need to stay present to the releasing of that formerly trapped energy and those no-longer buried thoughts.

Finally Full of Yourself is helping you move through that being stuck place, and more into the flow of what you came here to Earth to do. This is only found by living through your authentic flavor in the world. Breathe. Journal. Notice. Let go of *shoulds*. Move your body. Release *have to's*. Go for a walk and talk it out. Breathe. Release judgment. Go punch a pillow or punching bag. Release the blocks. Embrace the flow. Create flow points whenever you notice stuck points. Shift, baby, shift! Let yourself fill up with your natural flow!

A Self-Care Note: Honestly, taking a nap after this exercise, even a cat nap for just a few minutes, would do you a world of good, as would drinking a glass of water, or taking a pee break. These three things are important parts of the process. They help you stay in your flow from all this self-discovery.

Unraveling this Exercise Further

 This list of questions is a small sample of how most humans grow up feeling, fearing or avoiding. There's a huge laundry list of things people do to hurt children. The expression, *"Hurt* people, hurt people," comes to mind. I say, *"Healed* people, heal people." Many times people are well-intentioned but because they're dealing with their own wound patterns, it comes out in a distorted, ugly manner. This causes huge amounts of heartache. It's ugly energy creating more of the same ugly energy. So you end up with wounded patterns creating more wounded patterns, passing it from person to person, and generation to generation. You repeat what you know, or what "worked" in the past, and that's how patterns have been passed on for this long.

"When the only tool you have is a hammer, all your problems look like a nail." By reading this book, you're becoming more aware of your innate tools, so you can more easily break your nasty, life-sucking wounding patterns. Because of these ancient, painful wounds, many live a *shadow* life, with their hearts closed off for fear of being hurt. Their life is a shadow, a reflection, instead of full of themselves.

Maria Salomão-Schmidt

JOURNAL TIME... Let's get some movement in your life! What energetic wound patterns are you ready to let go of? What are you willing to release to get more of your authentic flow back?

She kept her LIFE small to protect her HEART,
not realizing that she was actually suffocating both.

—Maria Salomão-Schmidt

Things I Want To Remember/Research/Review:

There is one great truth on this planet:
whoever you are, or whatever it is that you do,
when you really want something,
it's because that desire originated in the soul of the universe.
It's your mission on earth.

—Paulo Coelho

Chapter 10. What Is The Truth?

Enough about the lie, that as J. Geils sang "Love stinks, ya, ya, Love stinks." What about the truth about love? Does Love stink? The truth is that your *wounds* only gets worse if your heart does not open; it's like a suffocation of the energy body. A closed heart means a reduction in energy (LOVE), our natural energy, and an increase in FEAR. Fear-based living is how most of the world operates no matter what mask they show others. Fear, simply redefined, is when we block the flow of our authentic Love/Light/Energy in the world. It's time that I made something clear that you may not have not fully realized.

Contrary to how many people live their lives, living with a closed heart is not only dangerous, but it's also incredibly painful! Why? It is massively painful because we are energy, and energy loves to move, expand and grow. In fact, each generation is born with 5–10 times more energy than the generation before it. That is why most adults are running around after children who seem to have boundless energy telling them to stop or slow down. Children, in fact, do have more boundless energy than you and I, and we have more than our parents did. Understanding this simple concept could cause a lot less stress in households around the world. Just like with the universe, the energy part of us is expanding. With each generation it expands even more.

What Babies Teach Us About Movement

Think about children, even babies who cannot yet walk. What are they always doing? Are they sitting or lying there doing nothing? NO, of course not! In fact, if your child is listless, it is a sign that there is something very wrong. Healthy children are always moving, wiggling, talking, laughing, exploring. This is not only because children have more energy than we do, but also because, unlike most adults, children are led by their energy, with the body complying to that flow. This is the natural flow of how our bodies work. It is our undomesticated, natural state of being and well-being.

 The Lazy Crazy Baby EXERCISE... Access the power of your imagination. Check in with the image you have imagined of these children.

FIRST GROUP: Listless, slumped, not making any sounds, expressionless.

SECOND GROUP: Laughing, jumping, running, singing, smiling and talking.

Can you clearly picture each group? By just describing their behavior can you tell which group is happy and which is sad? For most of us, it is a clear answer. This simple example shows us that when we are closed off we don't expand. When we stay stagnant, it's incredibly painful! Yet, if you think about how we treat kids and even the child inside of us as "adults," we probably think we favor the second group; but as a society we tend to favor the behavior of the first group, especially when in public, like in business or school.

Why is this? Well, it usually comes from not wanting to be embarrassed or judged by others and to have an "orderly" existence. It's usually about the fear of being "out of control" or to do something "wrong." The description of the second group is more about when people are playing. *Playing* has traditionally been seen as frivolous, but how the energy body thrives is by being allowed to flow more as it does in the second group.

 JOURNAL TIME... Use this opportunity to write down your thoughts and feelings so that you can be heard. Check-in with the little kid inside you. What does he/she want you to know? What is he/she feeling? This may stir up some very strong feelings so be kind and patient. Use lots of breath and keep visualizing flow points when you hit stuck points. There is a whole treasure chest of information here. Let yourself go there! Above all forgive and have fun!

An eye for an eye leaves the whole world blind.

—Gandhi

This Is What Growth Feels Like

For many of us it looks and feels like a lot of chaos, misery and suffering in this world of ours. Seems like it's intensifying, and that is because we are on the verge of a massive shift. What's happening to humanity is the equivalent of what happens to the seed of a magnificent oak tree. The seed in non-growth mode sits dormant, uncomplicated and uninspired. When growth is activated by an outside force, such as with the introduction of water in this case, the seed begins transforming.

The inside of the seed begins to expand. Eventually it grows so big that it rips out of its shell. This act of growth is not an act of gentleness. It cannot be because the container, or form that it's in, the outside casing of the seed, can no longer hold this new level of existence. For growth to occur a cellular tearing is an integral part of the growing process. This is a natural part of the growing cycle. Growth simply cannot occur without it. If you know it's a natural part of the process, it can be a lot easier to handle and understand. It also takes away some of the fear because it's expected, natural and makes sense. When you don't know it's coming, that's when it can get scary.

Growing up, one of my younger brothers experienced a similar process. When he was about 10, his body was growing so fast that he had a lot of pain in his legs. This pain was caused from his legs growing so fast that he was feeling the expansion in his body. It was so painful that it kept him from sleeping. He was terrified until the doctor told him what it was. The pain was still the same but there was no longer any fear. Oftentimes fear feeds pain and suffering. The pain was temporary and once he adjusted it subsided. Pain is a natural part of the process.

Part of our evolutionary process is to notice how even *pain* can be a gift. You did not read that incorrectly. I just said that pain can be a *true gift*. Let's be clear that I'm specifically speaking about pain, not suffering. The one thing pain does better than anything else is that it helps you focus on the present moment. Suffering does not have a present moment, it is a vibrational frequency people live in. Pain is more powerful than that. It is pure feedback of a focused area. If you avoid the pain, you avoid the feedback.

We have become a society that runs from pain at all cost, and by doing so we lose the important information it gives us. Instead of using this gift, what we have learned to do is find ways to bury,

Maria Salomão-Schmidt

hide or mask the pain; thus, we have lost the feedback that it brings. When the *message* is not received, the pain grows. The more it grows, the more resistance appears. What started off as a "little" problem has grown into a nightmare because it wasn't first noticed. It would be like covering up your fire alarms when they went off and not checking to see if there is even smoke. By the time you detect the smoke you have a much bigger problem on your hands than if you had dealt with the "inconvenience" when you first noticed it.

> *Do you know that most people that I meet*
> *spend their lives looking for occasions to be offended?*
> *They actually are out there*
> *hoping they can find some reason to be offended.*
> —Dr. Wayne Dyer

Things I Want To Remember/Research/Review:

We'll love you just the way you are if you're perfect.

—Alanis Morissette

Chapter 11. How To Finally Get The Love You Need

One of the best feelings humans can have on this planet is to love deeply and unconditionally, without holding back. Living life mostly as a flow point. It's analogous to living fully and full of yourself. Another way to grasp this concept is to imagine being fully present. You were born this way. It's your natural state, although mainstream society teaches the opposite. We are magnificent beings with a wide-open hearts. Your heart is the brain of your *internal guidance system*, your very own GPS. When you were born, as you entered your body, you were naturally flowing *Unconditional Love*.

Somewhere along your journey, you hit the harsh lessons of *Conditional Love*, which triggers domestication. It's a "please love me" state of mind, begging for Love from the outside world. The Trigger exercise you did earlier demonstrates how *Conditional Love* feels.

Part of the human evolution period we're going through is about reclaiming our intuition. We're learning that what we were labeling as Love is really *Conditional Love*. Conditional Love is dense, heavy, slippery and painful. It's a miserable feeling to go through life this way, closed off to your internal flow, having to look for it outside of yourself instead. You'll never find it there, because our essence IS Love. Our next evolutionary leap is to realize that *we're the Love we seek*.

Conditional Love is based on *what* you do, not *who* you are. You're taught and shown over and over that you're not enough, that you need to behave at a certain level to be loved. Supposedly, if you don't reach a certain expectation level, no one will love you. If no one loves you, in this system of thinking, then you have no worth, and will be alone. The fear of not being loved drives people to desperation, which results in living an unaligned life. We humans take this fear (blocked energy) and create all sorts of painful scenarios. If people feel they're "not enough" they may become super aggressive, or one may go to the total opposite end of the spectrum and become victims. Within these two extremes there are thousands of ways people show up. On a massive scale, this is how wars are born.

If you're flowing with life, you are in alignment, but if you are "fighting" (or in *resistance*), you are out of alignment. *"Efforting" is a sign that you are slapping your own life force in the face.* This may be termed *sabotaging* yourself.

To live with *Conditional Love* is incredibly painful, equivalent to the body living with greatly reduced oxygen. Looking at someone who has trouble breathing can be painful to watch. The same happens with energy. Because they have no energy, they begin doing less and less or becoming more and more aggressive. No matter how you slice it, the body absolutely needs that constant flow of breath to keep it alive and healthy.

Like the *meat body* needs air, our energy body needs a constant energy flow. When that energy slows down, we don't have enough of it to live our full potential. When we live in *Conditional Love*, a fear state, we are blocking our energy and stagnating our lives. People who live in this fear paradigm attempt to increase their sense of control believing it'll ease their fears. They tend to live very small lives because they want to control what they can so they can be "safe." This is a survival state-of-being brought on by the choice to focus on fear. By choosing fear you block your dreams from being realized. Ouch!

 JOURNAL TIME... What are you TRYING to control in your life right now? How is that working for you? Does it feel authentic? Does it feel icky? What do you want to shift?

We criticize and separate ourselves from the process. [Instead] we've got to jump right in there with both feet.

—Dolores Huerta

We delight in the beauty of the butterfly,
but rarely admit the changes it has gone through
to achieve that beauty.

—Maya Angelou

Chapter 12. Deconstruction

Just before our son Christopher was going back to Roger Williams University, he sat down with my husband, Doug, and I to go over his goals. His major, Construction Management gives him classes, that I, with my communications and business background, never even knew existed. As he was describing what he learned in one class, Christopher shared that sometimes structures needed to be *deconstructed* as a first step.

Later, as we were discussing his goals for the second part of his junior year, he shared that he felt stuck in certain classes. I brought in the example that he had described to me earlier, that sometimes the best solution is not to completely demolish, but to *deconstruct* what is no longer working and keep what is. Christopher shared with us that it is a vital part of how he always saw his work, but not his goals. That *aha!* really seemed to sink in. I have since then shared this example with my clients. It is a very simple way to realize that it's sometimes helpful to *deconstruct* the areas in our life that aren't working, even though we had assumed that was how life is.

We humans are going through a period in time where we are in a whole lot of messy situations on most levels: personal, work, local, national and global. Take construction for example. If you have an old house that is no longer viable, building on top of that which is rotting and falling apart, only makes thing worse... In order to have a home that works, you need to deconstruct the parts that are not working. Sometimes that means demolishing the whole thing and starting over; but even then, there are parts that can be salvaged, reused and repurposed.

The massive shifts that are happening on our planet right now can be addressed by using this simple *deconstructing* process that I learned from watching our son Christopher. Perhaps this is a good time to give you an example: A great one is from happiness researcher Shawn

Achor, who addresses the age-old dilemma, is the glass half-empty or half-full? Instead of delving into it, and discussing the merits of both sides, Shawn simply says who cares whether it's half-anything. The important part is that you can get a pitcher with water and fill it when it needs filling. By breaking down the "problem" of having a glass of water that is at half full and then moving immediately to the *stuck* part and labeling it, Shawn takes it to the underlying matter in question by asking "What is the real issue here?" *Finally Full of Yourself* uses this method of evaluating those things in your life where you feel STUCK, SICK, CONFUSED or LOST, and shifting them.

 JOURNAL TIME... Look for places in your own life where you can DECONSTRUCT your life, so that you can begin building on the strong foundation of the *authentic* you, *not* the *artificial* you, that you think others want you to be, in order to feel loved. I will continue to discuss more on this later. In the meantime, start using this immediately in your life so you can massage out the areas where you are in pain, sadness or boredom. Begin where you are. Let go of judgment. You got this... because it's just about letting your natural flow, flow.

> *The true sign of intelligence is not knowledge*
> *but imagination.*
>
> —Albert Einstein

Things I Want To Remember/Research/Review:

It always seems impossible until it's done.

—Nelson Mandela

Chapter 13. The Speed At Which We Are Shifting

I love learning! We recently got a membership at the Boston Museum of Science and go with our children at least every couple of months. I'm amazed at how each time we learn something new, it helps us see the world in a different way. My husband Doug and I think we are going for the kids, but we often end up learning even more than they do.

Learning is expanding. It feeds us to our core! Many adults have starved this part of themselves for fear of looking childish or inappropriate! It is in honor of our child-like energy that I include this section. So many of us have confused *childlike*—having a sense of wonder—with *childish*, immature and narcissistic tendencies. As a society, especially in America, we have gone through a dumb-down period where children can more easily identify corporate logos than historical figures or facts. It is another form of moving away from our natural feedback system. Without crucial valuable feedback, we mistake what is helpful for what is hurtful, and thereby put ourselves in harm's way.

It seems that the majority of modern day society has moved away from connecting to the earth, and instead towards instant gratification and the "need" to constantly acquire *things*. The Fresh Air Fund is a fantastic program that takes inner city kids from New York, many of whom have never been anywhere else but in the city, and places them in suburban homes for a few weeks during the summer. We had two boys stay with us. One of them, Joey, thought that carrots literally came from the grocery store and not the ground. He did not believe it when we told him they came from the earth! We had to literally go to a farm so that Joey could see how things really grew. He thought he was on an episode of Candid Camera or Punked.

Before you judge Joey, how much authentic unprocessed food do you eat? How far away from the authentic food chain have you moved? This isn't a unique occurrence as we move away from the source, of both food and energy, we begin to lose connection to our core. There is *source confusion*, which describes how disoriented we have become to the connection to ourselves and our planet. In order to heal, it's vital to re-establish the sacred connection with our thoughts and focus. Begin focusing on the inside, versus the outside.

 JOURNAL TIME... *Judging* is something that keeps us small. What do you notice yourself judging? Breathe. How do you feel? Breathe. Ask what it has come to teach you? Breathe. What are the hidden gifts it's showing you? Write.

You Want Me to Do What on that Healing Table?

When I was in energy medicine school, as part of our trainings we did *energy healings* on people. For those who are not familiar with the term, *healings* are when you observe, clear, and help replenish another's energetic field. It can happen by touching people with your hands but can also be done long distance. If you want to really blow your mind, energy can even be sent into the past or future to help heal something. I oftentimes send massive amounts of Reiki (Love energy) to myself as a child.

When one first starts out and has never done any energy work, it can feel a little off-putting! It can feel really, I believe the technical term is, "woo-woo." It can take a lot of getting used to, but once you are able to surrender to the process of just feeling what you feel, it's pretty spectacular for both you and your clients. For me it has been some of the most enlightening experiences of my lifetime because it feels great to be able to explore what felt "off" or "icky" in my life. It's allowed me to explore the world of energy in ways I never even knew existed.

To help us practice doing energy healings, the school had open houses for those in the local community who wanted to receive healings. Since we were still learning, we volunteered our time. The very first woman who came to me was Judy. During her healing as I was going to her third chakra, I saw, in my mind, like watching a video, a motorcycle accident where a young man in his 20s had been decapitated. He seemed extremely happy though as he was holding his own head under his arm and wildly waving at me. There were white blood-soaked sheets on the highway covering what I presumed were body parts. It was a very weird thing to "see" on my first "official" healing.

After the healing was over, I did not want to tell Judy what I'd seen because, quite frankly, I didn't want her to think I was a kook! As I started to tell her bits and pieces of the story, she seemed very interested, so encouraged, I continued describing what I'd seen. Judy's eyes widened, her lips drew a smile and she started weeping and hugging me. It turns out that her brother had died 26 years earlier, just as I had described. He was decapitated in a motorcycle accident. Judy shared that she had not felt his presence around her for some time and asked him to give her a sign. Boy did he!

Later that evening, I approached my teacher at the time, Rhys Thomas, and described what had happened. I was so very excited, I could hardly get all the words out. I finished with, "I didn't just imagine it! It was real!!" Rhys laughed, "This is all our imagination. Everything we create is our imagination." Talk about popping my balloon! I was totally confused. How could it be that I was using my imagination? I had always been taught that our imagination wasn't real and not to be trusted. Now here I had this amazing life experience, and it didn't fit into how I understood the world. I was stumped for almost a year, but finally I understood that we're energy first and everything in this world comes from what we believe.

Inauthentic Practitioners

Speaking of "what is real," if you're not very familiar with energy work, you may find this section on inauthentic practitioners useful.

A very dear family member in Long Island, New York asked me one day about the Reiki. He seemed skeptical because of an *icky* experience he had with someone who said she was a Reiki practitioner. Not everyone who says they practice any form of healing, whether it be a doctor, psychologist, energy healer or life coach, is living and operating from authenticity.

As you explore the world of energy remember that many are still performing their jobs from an inauthentic place. Just to be clear, these are not "bad" people. Most aren't doing it with ill will. They may even think they are helping. The thing is that you can only connect with others from the vibration you are on. Some practitioners are on lower vibrations. They think the world has wronged them, so they're just "getting theirs." They are being led by their low energy body and don't even realize it. This is the great awakening that's going on throughout our planet right now. As with many other things in life, it's always a good idea to check out any practitioners or teachers before you work with them, not just from references—but also by slowing down and checking in with yourself. When in doubt—with or without proof—above all trust your instinct.

The Next Chapter

Since this next chapter is background information, you may find yourself wanting to skip it but give it a chance because knowing how things happen is valuable. Having a sense of wonder is so very important for the health of our energy body! Plus, our planet could really use some creative solutions. This section is meant to ignite your passion and curiosity!

 JOURNAL TIME... How do you use your imagination? What do you think of your imagination? Do you think it's valuable in others? In yourself? Are you thankful (and in awe) of your imagination? What would make you appreciate your imagination even more? (Gentle reminder that comparing yourself to others is a great way to lower your energy and live inauthentically.)

Decades of research has shown that play is crucial to physical, intellectual, and social-emotional development at all ages. This is especially true of the purest form of play: the unstructured, self-motivated, imaginative, independent kind, where children initiate their own games and even invent their own rules.

—David Elkind

Only I can change my life. No one can do it for me.
—Carol Burnett

Chapter 14. Deconstruction Since Fire

Timelines

When I was researching *Finally Full of Yourself,* I had a challenging time because new archeological discoveries keep shifting the dates below. Still, I wanted to include the dates so you'd have an idea of our planet's timeline.

- Earth Formed – 4.6 billion years ago

- First Flowers – 160 million years ago

- Dinosaurs First Appeared – 230 million years ago

- Dinosaurs Become Extinct – 65 million years ago

- Our Ancestors (Members of Homo) Use Fire – 2 million years ago

- Controlled Use of Fire By our Ancestors (Homo Erectus) – 400 thousand years ago

- Human Beings Appear – 200 thousand years ago

- Widespread Use of Fire By Humans – 125 thousand years ago

Evolution involves change over time. With the help of fossils and archeological discoveries, scientists have been able to uncover amazing information about our ancestors. Scientists like Dr. Rick Potts, from the Smithsonian's National Museum of Natural History, have so far uncovered 600 different individual fossilized remains of our ancestors. The course of human evolution involves many differences, both physical and behavioral. Physically, the brain got larger and larger, while the face became less sloped and actually became smaller. Behaviorally, our ancestors also changed over time. For example, 2.5 million years ago they smashed rocks into other rocks to make very large, cumbersome tools. Our ancestors also used the flakes that flew off the rocks, to cut meat off animal bones.

Fast-forward to 1.5 million years ago and our ancestors made another huge discovery. They were able to chisel a large rock so that it had one very sharp point, thus inventing the hand-axe. To us that might not seem like a big deal, but to them that was an incredibly useful tool that greatly improved their survival rate. It was actually so big that it was one of the largest known developments for the next one million years!

Think about how slowly things developed. The Earth was in existence for over four billion years before any flowers even showed up, never mind humans! The most up-to-date information, as of the writing of this book, is that human beings first appeared on the planet 200,000 years ago.

According to what we know so far, it took us about 75,000 years to learn how to use fire. Each major shift started happening closer and closer. First by thousands of years, and now in our times things change sometimes within days. The developmental pace on this planet is indeed speeding up at a tremendous rate, and most of us are feeling it. That speed causes us to have to think, act and live very differently from our ancestors.

FIRE – The Earthly Form of Energy

Today, many of us take fire in all of its forms for granted. It is only on those rare days when something breaks down, leaving us without heat or unable to cook for a few hours, or days, that we begin to truly appreciate, from a deep place of gratitude, the gift and importance of fire. Other than those occasions, we turn on lights without so much as a giggle of excitement that we have this truly amazing power to add more light to our world, keep us warm, create things and cook our food.

The control of fire by early humans was a turning point in the cultural aspect of human evolution that allowed humans to cook food and obtain warmth and protection. Making fire allowed the expansion of human activity into the dark and colder hours of the night, and also provide protection from predators and insects.

Today, we tend to be moving at such *busy* levels of living that we oftentimes think life *is* supposed to be this way. When we realize how very slowly things have developed and how very different our lives are now compared to even two hundred years ago, this gives us pause and heightens our perspective on human evolution. If we take human history seriously, we can use this information as a gateway for uncovering a deeper sense of wisdom and happiness.

The Last Two Hundred-ish Years

Fast-forward about two hundred years ago to the 1800s. From where we just read this will seem like a completely different world. Now to be clear, I am writing this as someone who lives in what is called "developed" or "first world" nations. There are still many places around the world, including America, where poverty and lack of opportunity creates situations akin to the 1800s model you are about to read about.

Again things are moving faster and faster. In the 1800s, some kids were allowed to go to school, but many still went barefoot. They got up at 5:00 am to do their chores. Schools were often run by a teacher who was many times no older than 14 years old. The only heat was from a fireplace where the kids would have to take turns bringing wood from home. Because of chores and conditions, many kids had to go back and forth as many as three times a day—and remember, many had no shoes. The kids that lived in the city worked in factories. It was not uncommon to see 6 year olds going to work in places that had horrific sanitary and work conditions. At that time, there were no labor laws like we have today in many countries. Countries, like individuals, develop at different speeds.

The people who lived like this were little more than slaves to the wealthy businessmen of their day, who would use their labor for close to free. Energetically, these men were harnessing the power of many to acquire the fruits of their labor. This is a system of complete unbalance and isn't sustainable for long periods of time. Looking at it now, it seems unfair, but energy isn't affected by fairness or unfairness. What happens energetically, though, is the same thing that happens physically: when the top of something becomes too heavy, it topples over. This was a tipping point for humanity. We have had more and more of these *tipping points*, or *shifts*, as we have moved closer to the present moment and beyond.

Maria Salomão-Schmidt

The Expansion Exercise... As I re-read the above, I realized that the inequities of the last paragraph are still happening today to many in our global family. The truth is that it only happens because the rest of us turn a blind eye to it. Sure, it can be overwhelming if you focus on it all. Start where you are. Notice what inspires you. Focus and use your imagination towards creating a solution. Pick something that you want to improve in our world and go after it one action at a time. The journey is part of the waking up process!

JOURNAL TIME... Being grateful helps you energetically connect back to your alignment stream. It is a focusing tool. This is why looking at your life through energy is so important. By shifting your attention to gratitude, you instantly reconnect to your authenticity. It is the equivalent of being in really bad traffic and instead of being upset, simply getting off the exit ramp, effortlessly by passing all the traffic and immediately moving into flowing again.

Your life is a complete reflection of your thoughts.

—Maria Salomão-Schmidt

Things I Want To Remember/Research/Review:

The opposite of love is not hate, it's indifference.
—Elie Wiesel

Chapter 15. Modern Day Energy Vampires

 WARNING: Make sure you take a lot of deep breaths during this chapter. It will help you better process and shift from stuck points of energy.

One of the hardest things for me to witness on this gorgeous planet of ours is ISMS... RACISM, AGEISM, ETHNOCENTRISM, CLASSISM, ABLEISM, HETEROSEXISM and SEXISM. It especially hurts when the people who are seeing it happen, right in front of them, are so disconnected or fearful that they either ignore it, or justify it, because it may feel too UNCOMFORTABLE to face it.

Feeling good is feedback from your spiritual DNA that you're in alignment. If you avoid what's uncomfortable when you are getting an intuition hit that something is off, you will not feel good. This is where *shame* and *blame* come in. More about those two later in Chapter 31.

Racism, sexism and the other -ISMS are completely *unnatural* states of being (no flow, only stagnation) so they are painful and stifling to our energetic body. A baby is born without -ISMS because babies are born *undomesticated*. In order for them to acquire the -ISMS, they must be systematically taught to block their hearts so they can hate and view others as less than. Once they are taught this block they then re-create that unnatural state of discord throughout their lives. Their -ISMS need to be deep-seated to maintain the hate (blocked energy).

Energy vampires, those stealing others' energy by claiming less-than-ness, feel the *icky* feedback from being out of alignment, but they blame their pain on the very people they have targeted. Energy vampires put the solution/cause outside of themselves, so they stay stuck in their wound pattern. Even though they are the perpetrator, they act like they're the victim, and thus, further lash out at those they are already harming. Many energy vampires feel so victimized that they even go so far to form groups to fight for their -isms, all in the name of maintaining their "way of life."

With their negative belief of what *should be* locked in, it's harder to shift back to their natural alignment of happiness. They are unwilling to NOTICE it so they continue paying a heavy *energetic mortgage* on it. The people who live with -ISMS close their hearts. They are modern day *energy vampires*. They cannot open their own hearts while holding on to the hate, so they put others down through any difference they can identify, to steal their energy. In this unnatural state, happiness eludes them... and they have no idea why.

We are all cells in the same body of humanity.

—Peace Pilgrim (Mildred Lisette Norman)

Start Noticing the World Around You

You'll be amazed at what you will find when you start exploring this world. You have no idea how much you don't know. *You can easily be a part of the solution*, if you just begin *playing* with this information. Think of yourself as a single cell in the human body. The healthy cell is one that fulfills what its DNA has communicated. The unhealthy cell is one that does not live out its purpose. You get  to decide whether you are a healthy cell or a cancerous one. Whatever you decide affects the entire body of the human race.

Healthy humans do not decrease the values of others. They do not blame others for their situation. When human beings are not living in alignment, their out-of-alignment condition is actually hurting the other "cells" (people), just as cancer does. The time has come in human evolution for us to look inside ourselves and remove as many of the -ISMS as we can. The more we do, the more we make room for more of our authentic self to emerge. That is the path towards happiness and joy! The more of us that do this, the more Love we

bring to the world. The less we do this, the more there is pain and suffering in the world. This Finally Full of Yourself movement is about ending suffering on our planet so each of us can access our natural purpose, fulfillment and happiness. This is how we finally reach world peace!

A Painful Time Begins Shifting

Oh, yes! I am going there! For the first part of the 1800s, slavery was still legal in the United States and only officially ended on January 1, 1863, when the Proclamation of Emancipation that Abraham Lincoln signed went into law. Even though it was official, many former enslaved human beings, now free, found themselves without any other options than to continue living under the same conditions as

they had. The lack of education and support system for this population had not been addressed or ameliorated. This type of racism, energetically, can only occur in an unnatural society where the flow of the energy body is blocked.

Like sexism, racism has been prolonged because there is an easily identifiable characteristic which allows people to create another label. For example, the Irish immigrants were discriminated against when they first came to America, but by losing their accent and blending in, they now "fit in," so it's harder to identify them as different. In deep contrast, a person with darker skin or women cannot, nor would they want to, so easily change their most basic characteristics. Because of these easily-identifiable discrimination points, even as I write this in 2016, two hundred years after Lincoln's Emancipation Proclamation, there is still a huge disparity in how people of color and women are treated "less than" white men. This entitlement cannot continue. The planet cannot sustain this disconnected state of living. It is destructive, unconnected and divisive. It's a cancer that is destroying our planet!

Chris Rock Brought Courage To The Oscars

A special hats-off to actor and comedian Chris Rock who hosted the 88th Academy Awards in a year when not one person of color was nominated for the second year in a row. It is rare in my lifetime where I witnessed someone directly speak the truth through humor to so many people who were both squirming and laughing in the audience. Most of the people there would not consider themselves racists, but the fact that not one person of color was chosen means there is an ISM buried somewhere in there. Although incredibly uncomfortable to watch at times, it was also refreshing to see someone be so authentic. Chris Rock took a huge risk doing it, but this is how things shift...Someone finally stands for what they believe. It is an incredible example of authentic courage.

> *Negativity is an anchor that weighs you down and a shiny object that re-focuses your attention on the inauthentic.*

—Maria Salomão-Schmidt

Courage is born from leaning into our uncomfortableness. Being comfortable, what most people strive for, is what keeps us stagnant. The opposite of being comfortable is not being uncomfortable—it's being *whole*. Chris Rock spoke from his core. He was speaking truth to complacency. Chris said what most did not have the courage to say.

 We are at a key time in human evolution where we will see more examples of this. It is vital for those who see any discrimination, whether it is a joke or a quick remark, to call people out on it because it is something that lowers our collective energetic vibration. It's not about conflict, it's about bringing awareness, bringing light to a place or person on this planet who is living in the darkness of ignorance. Ignorance is a form of unalignment from one's authenticity.

We are *one*. We are all from the same *source energy*. Our outside bodies are the vehicles of who we are on the inside, yet some will use what they see to control others. They control them because they want to set up energetic and physical feeding stations. The system of slavery in the physical world is about holding hostage (in one way or another) people in order to use their labor or services for their personal gain. In terms of energy, the enslavers have blocked their energy, and in doing so, have cut off communication and connection to their heart. Because they are energetically drained, they feel completely compelled to take it from others in the form of *energy vampirism*.

No one operating in authenticity, connected to their spiritual DNA, needs or wants to control another. It does not feel good to do that. As Ice Cube's song goes, "You better check yo self before you wreck yo self." Check in with yourself. Does it feel good to be controlled by someone else? Most of us would not want it to be done to us. Whole societies set up horrific systems of energy vampirism that became so entrenched and normalized that they were seen as "just the way things were."

The only way people who are energy vampiring others can justify what they are doing is by lessening the value or worth of the other person or group. When you have a whole society backing you up, it's a lot easier to commit these atrocities. Many don't even question them at all. If someone complains or questions this unnatural system they are labeled as a troublemaker or outsider.

Many who aren't being discriminated don't even think about having this conversation because they don't feel they are racist or sexist. Their thought pattern "this has nothing to do with me because I'm not racist." It's this kind of thinking that prolongs racism and all other -isms. The evidence is all around, and increasing. Until people, who consider themselves not part of the problem, begin to stand up for those who are being attacked, we can't have the shifts necessary to bring long-lasting peace and happiness to our families, neighborhoods, countries and planet. As part of human evolution, ISMS will eventually disappear because people who live in their alignment don't *need* to put others down or steal their energy. When in alignment, you never even think of taking energy, time or things from others because you have what you need.

We can't let people drive wedges between us...
because there's only one human race.
—Dolores Huerta

 JOURNAL TIME... We are obsessed with being the victim, but be honest and write about when YOU were the energy vampire. Notice what you did and how it felt at the different stages of the interaction. What do you have to learn from being in that dark place that most of us *try* to hide? What happens when you shine light on it? What do you feel?

Maria Salomão-Schmidt

What comes up? What do you want to release? This journal is meant to build your vulnerability and courage. As you read on in this book you will see how very important these are!

 Brown Eye/Blue Eye Exercise... I absolutely couldn't end this chapter without giving you an exercise that'll help you better see how powerful this *core wound pattern* is in our society. The shocker is that the excuses for racism, sexism, etc. are made up based on identifiers. Skin color, for example, has nothing to do with value or intelligence. It's all perceived. You might "know" that but this exercise, if you really let yourself play with it, will give you shockingly great information! Plus, you'll free up a lot of your energy dollars! Yessah!

The amazing Jane Elliott... "Internationally known teacher, lecturer, diversity trainer and recipient of the National Mental Health Association Award for Excellence in Education, exposes prejudice and bigotry for what it is, an irrational class system based upon purely arbitrary factors. And if you think this does not apply to you. . . you are in for a rude awakening. In response to the assassination of Martin Luther King, Jr. over 30 years ago, Jane Elliott devised the controversial and startling, "Blue Eyes/Brown Eyes" exercise... labels participants as inferior or superior based solely upon the color of their eyes and exposes them to the experience of being a minority. Everyone who is exposed to Jane Elliott's work, be it through a lecture, workshop, or video, is dramatically affected by it." Your assignment is to go check out her site and see the experiment. You can find it at www.janeelliott.com.

Life is one big road with lots of signs.
So when you riding through the ruts, don't
complicate your mind.
Flee from hate, mischief and jealousy.
Don't bury your thoughts, put your vision to reality.
Wake Up and Live!
—Bob Marley

Painful emotions show you what prevents you from creating harmony, cooperation, sharing and reverence for life.

—Gary Zukav

Chapter 16. Labels Are For Clothes, Not People

We are born without labels. It was only in the 1400s that labels were invented to keep people separate. The people of the time who were in power wanted to find a way to divide people so they invented something called "races." They used the easy-identifiable trait of skin color to separate "races" so that people could be more easily categorized. Why would someone want to label people? When you are organizing your food pantry, labeling the shelves with labels like dried foods, baking supplies, nuts, etc. can be helpful because it keeps things organized and separate. The only reason you'd use this kind of labeling on people would be to do the same thing, hold control of others by keeping them organized (limit flow) and separate (limit freedom).

There's a wonderful visionary, poet, director and teacher named Prince Ea who has an incredible video on YouTube called *I am NOT Black, You are NOT White*. It's so incredibly powerful and inspiring to have someone who is only in his 20s be able to see the world so clearly! He is an example of the *Firsters*, who are very important to the healing of our planet. You can read more about the *Enders*, *Bridgers* and *Firsters* in Chapter 17.

Prince Ea's powerful video *I am NOT Black, You are NOT White* touches many people's core because of its authenticity. It is groundbreaking and new so it will also most-definitely rub some people the wrong way because it's too big of a leap from where they are to where the information is. As I write this, it has almost 10 million views. In it, Prince Ea compares our bodies to cars. He says society is like a dealership that has given our bodies labels of what our outside looks like, but we are not our outside. What matters is on the inside. He asks "Who would you be if the world never gave you a label?"

Expand Your Energy Exercise... This exercise serves as a simple reminder to explore the world. Just as you did as a baby, be curious. Grow your sense of wonder. Step beyond the teeny, weeny, little box that most people try to "live" in.

We're incredibly lucky to live in an age where we have easy access to amazing information! Here's a super fun exercise that'll expand your worldview, just as traveling does. This time you get to travel with your imagination. Earlier I mentioned the amazing work of Prince Ea. He has many videos that are completely in alignment with his core. Watching them helps you get into your authentic flow. So take a moment right now and go have some fun watching a couple of them. Just go on YouTube and look up his name. Expand what your thought was real.

Why are labels so important? When you live in fear, having a label is key for survival because life is seen as mostly dangerous. For this reason things need to be judged, and then, categorized as "good" or "bad." Judging is a key component of being domesticated. Think about how heavy it is to be in a world where most everywhere you go you have people around you telling what you "should" or "should not" do. As you get more and more accustomed to living based on the feedback of others, those voices move into your head so that the level of "shoulds" and "have tos" get taken up a few notches. It's this voice that is directly connected to the ego. It's this voice that must label everything to be able to *control* it. Having no label, or being unable to label someone or something, is very uncomfortable for people who are living in this space. They lead very sad, painful lives that are full of efforting.

For example, there was an experiment by parents in Toronto, Canada, who decided not to tell anyone the sex of their child. No one knows the child's gender but the parents, the midwives who delivered the child and a close family friend. Some call it child abuse because it was hard for them to imagine not being able to label someone. It is very confusing for them because gender-labeling is the basis for how they enter into a relationship with others—Labels help them be able to live in their artificial world. We don't often think about it, but we get thousands, if not millions, of "hits" on people when we first see them. It is from this point of view that we do or don't connect with people. We make assumptions that is just how things are for now; but if we take a moment to notice on a deeper level, what will we find?

Diversity is about all of us, and about us having to figure out how to walk through this world together.

—Jacqueline Woodson

 I (finally) Give Myself Permission to BE ME! Exercise... Notice what labels you put on yourself, as remnants of past voices that still swirl around in your thoughts, directing your focus. Decluttering is not just for things in the physical world. It is also for thoughts. Decide which thoughts you want to keep, and which you don't want to keep. Write yourself out a permission slip allowing you to release what no longer serves you.

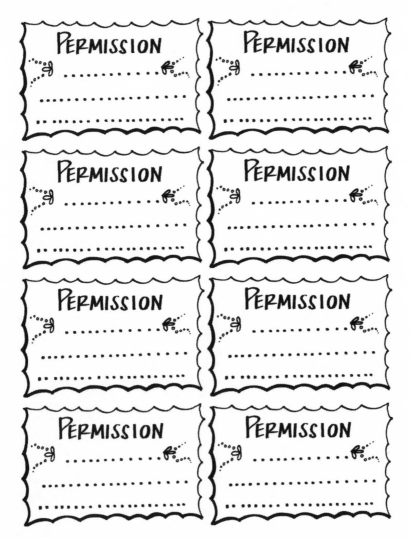

Maria Salomão-Schmidt

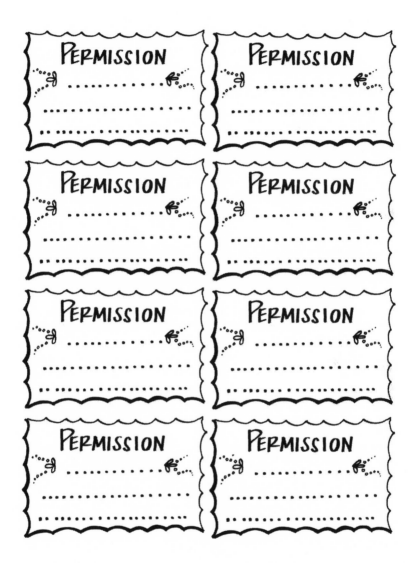

I think we risk becoming the best informed society
that has ever died of ignorance.

—Reuben Blades

Chapter 17. Humanity On The Cusp Of Massive Transformation

The Three Major Generations

In the last three major generations we have seen huge shifts like never before. They have never been more prominent than they are right now. These shifts are happening on all levels, the way we eat, communicate, live, work, mate, marry, etc. The increase in the speed of change that I described earlier can be greatly felt in the people who are alive now, at the writing of this book. For the first time in history, we're experiencing the biggest range of differences among the generations who are alive. By this I mean that the way a child today is being raised is very different from her grandmother's childhood. On the other hand, the grandmother's childhood was, in general, very similar to her grandmother's childhood.

World War I and II was the first time that much of the world was warring together. World War II alone involved a whopping 61 countries with 1.7 billion people (three quarters of the world's population at the time). Fifty million people lost their lives and hundreds of millions of people were injured. This was the first time in human history where such a huge part of our planet was focused on the same wars. People here on Earth began to pray for peace. What that means from the point of view of our energetic bodies is that people for years, kept sending out SOS messages. The response was that more and more higher evolved energies started incarnating to help shift the energy on Earth from fear and destruction, back to our energy body's core alignment of Love (freedom and flow). If you notice, you'll see this is how we've started shifting. The shifts are moving at colossal speeds, compared to how slowly it moved for our ancestors.

1. Born In The 1940s And 1950s – The Enders

The first major shift in energies or "souls" that were born can be seen in those born in the 1940s (plus or minus ten years). Before that time you learned how to be in the world from your parents, who also learned from their parents, who in turn learned from their parents. In order to stay "safe" and do the "right" thing formula, repeating and replicating this through each generation was key. Most changes in the way people did things that did occur during the 10,000 years prior, happened over several generations. Change was frowned upon. If you wanted safety and security you did things the "right" way, which was how your parents or elders taught you. Things shifted quite slowly. When these "kids" who were born in the 1940s and 1950s grew up, they were the children of the 60s with free love and protests. It was a radical time of shifting that had not been seen before.

Old ways of doing things were falling away. Women's roles were beginning to shift, although you could still see ads with a man spanking his wife as part of mainstream culture. Things became more automated. It was now much more commonplace to own cars, phones and televisions. Cities got bigger. The middle class grew and thrived. More people bought homes and went to college. Ideas were shared more quickly than they had ever been with things like FM radio, faxes and mimeograph machines (copiers). Even though there was much change, most of the Enders as young adults still followed certain cultural codes passed down from their parents and grandparents with strong and subtle variations. On the other hand, there was an unstoppable counterculture revolution taking place in the form of rebellion to what was lacking or did not work for them. Although many of the young people of this time eventually "settled down" and got "real jobs" but not without leaving their mark. One way they left their mark was with the music of the time, which is still popular and powerful today. That music carries with it the longing for the freedom and flow (Love) that they were seeking. Something major in the history of humanity was shifting on every level.

For the very first time the young are seeing history
being made before it is censored by their elders.

—Margaret Mead

 Enders Exercise... Music truly fused together all the facets of the counterculture of those who grew up in the 60s. Emerging were things like: the search for equality, the anti-war movement and exploring love. Music was also more accessible than ever before because for the first time teenagers had access to the advanced musical technology (of the time): transistor radios, eight-track car stereos and FM broadcasting. Again taking advantage of our accessibility to technology, go back on YouTube and check out the actual greats of the 60s performing, people like the Beatles, Janis Joplin, the Rolling Stones, Jimi Hendrix, Led Zeppelin, Jefferson Airplane, the Byrds, Bob Dylan, Jim Morrison and Neil Young. Take a moment to connect with them as you listen to their music and watch them move in the world. Notice what gifts they bring you. What do you pick up as you watch them? What messages of Love (freedom and flow) do they give you? Remember there is no test. This is just a fun exercise that expands and connects you to some of the most amazing artists of all time. Technology allows you to connect with them so take advantage of the wisdom that is there for you.

2. Born In The 1960s – The Bridgers

The major shift from how things had been done and life had been lived, happened to the next generation. Those children of the 1940s had the children who were born in the 60s (plus or minus fifteen years). These children are the ones I call the "bridge generation," or the Bridgers because they were the generation that marks the end of how things were done. I am part of this generation. We grew up with one foot in how our parents taught us how to do things, and another in the what made sense in each new situation. For example, we tended to have kids later, much later than our parents by at least one, or even two decades.

In my own family, my beautiful mother, Maria Raquel, who was born in 1937, did not get married until she was twenty-seven. At that time, everyone thought she would never marry because most of her friends by that age already had several children. My mother did not have children until she was 30, which was also considered "super old" for that period. A generation later, I got married and had children almost ten years after the age that my mother did, closer to 40, but in this case it was considered "normal" for my generation to get married and have children much later on. I did not even get married first. We only got married after we already had two children and were pregnant with our third. This would have been unheard of in prior generations but for us no one batted an eye.

One additional interesting point is that many *Bridgers* never lost our connection with our childhood. Even as adults, the *Bridgers* play with toys, while our parents generally never did after a certain age. I have a pair of Mary Jane shoes that people in my mother's generation would have considered shoes for children and not adults. At work we have toys and cute things that we can touch and play with. I do all over my office. No one thinks anything of it. We are the first generation to still have this kind of connection to the things other generations were trained to grow out of.

The Bridge Generation was also the first generation that greatly reduced the amount of spankings and beatings as punishment for their children. We were the first generation to experience the shift in the way we treated and spoke to our children. In addition, Bridgers treated their children more like equals than children had ever been treated. As we were growing up, it was commonplace for parents, teachers and adults in general to be able to hit kids. It was so widespread that it was normal. If you do it now, you would get arrested in most places.

Changes like this extend to almost every part of our lives. One of the biggest changes has been in technology and communication. Cell phones, the internet, roadways, transportation, food availability, social media are all things that have shifted human evolution and growth. For Bridgers, computers were introduced during their childhoods. They remember a time with absolutely no computers, and now they are an integral part of everyday life, a major shift experienced by both the Enders and the Bridgers.

The shift from the perception of the child as innocent
to the perception of the child as competent
has greatly increased the demands on contemporary children
for maturity, for participating in competitive sports,
for early academic achievement, and for protecting
themselves against adults who might do them harm.
While children might be able to cope
with any one of those demands taken singly, taken together
they often exceed children's adaptive capacity.

—David Elkind

3. Born In The 2000s – The Firsters

Children who were the children born in the 2000s (give or take twenty years on either end) have had childhoods that are completely different than their grandparents. I call these children the *First Generation*, or Firsters, because they are the "new" generation of modern day humans. Think of all of the last 10,000 years of human beings in a bucket. Each generation is a layer of water.

The Enders are at the top of that bucket of water so that they can see all the generations before them and they can also see outside the bucket. But the Bridgers are on the *lip*, as though not one more drop can fit in the container. The Firsters are no longer in the *bucket*. They are "on the ground." Being on the *lip*, the *Bridgers* can clearly see the *Firsters* on the ground, as well as seeing clearly the *Enders* and all the generations that came before them. *Bridgers* are connected to both the end and beginning of human evolution. *Bridgers* know both the old ways and the new ones. They can usually just fit in either one and therefore help those on either side connect with each other.

The *Firsters* are being given a world that they don't really understand. Many of them are very sensitive beings. For example, never before have we experienced so many cases of children diagnosed with major food allergies, conditions and illnesses. For a number of reasons, these children are feeling very lost right now. If you ask medical professionals who specialize in adolescent youth, you'll find that Firsters are in deep trouble. They are our wilting canaries in the mine. They are cutting themselves because they cannot feel. They are drinking, having unprotected sex and doing drugs in incredibly high numbers. The teenage suicide rate is the highest it has ever been too. This generation needs our guidance and support.

It's hard for me to even write this but we're handing them a world that is polluted, depleted and depressed. Firsters are here to shift our planet back to Love. Our job (for the Enders and, especially the Bridgers) is to help them with the visionary healing work they have come here to do. We can connect them with the parts that they can't touch or understand and together we will shift back to our natural state of alignment, each doing our intended part effortlessly.

The Firsters oftentimes cannot understand how to even live in that world that was so second nature to their parents and grandparents. The grandparents could relate to the world of their own grandparents because it had not changed as dramatically as it has now. Because of this, there is much disconnect between the generations. Here's a great example that'll help you see the difference in the generations.

Picture a school where what's being taught is pretty useless in terms of practicality. How each generation typically reacts is key. The Enders will keep it to themselves and just do it. Never would they even think of questioning why because they've been trained to respect authority. The Bridgers would verbalize the question, "Why do we need to learn this because we will never need it?" The answer would be something along the lines of "Shut up and do it." and they would do exactly that. The *Firsters* would simply refuse to do it because it does not make sense... and quite honestly, they are spot on.

Many of the things in today's schools and society do not make sense but we tolerate it. Firsters don't know how and it is within that small difference where the hope for our human family to heal is beginning to unfold. This generation makes us question our "why's" at this most critical time in human evolution. Firsters allow us the ability to practice the act of noticing, and acting on that noticing.

It's important to note that not everyone who was born in any one time period took on the characteristics of those around them. I know plenty of people who did not succumb to peer pressure and lived life on their own terms. My purpose for explaining it this way is to show how the shifts that have been going on and increasing as time has marched on is something that is affecting us all. As you get deeper in the book, you'll become more aware of how this is even more relevant that you realize now.

For the first time in forever, we're in that rare position of being able to actually witness evolution happening right before our very eyes. No other humans have ever experienced this amount of rapid change. As you can see from the progress of inventions, evolution and thought on this planet, things have been moving faster and faster and taking less time to develop. Where things took millions of years to shift, now they shift within years, months, or even days. This is what is happening in the physical world on this planet.

Energetically things are also shifting. As part of the great awakening, we are moving from living in the *fear-based* operating system to a *love-based* one. This shift is opening up a whole new world of relating to each other, by way of experiences and inventions.

It's hard to grow when you live in defense (depressed, sad, angry, victimized, used, depleted). Life for many humans has been like that for many years. People who were ahead of their time were those living "undomesticated"—living from their *authentic* selves. These people were seen as not fitting in at this time, and many of them paid dearly for it. Those who survived with their authenticity intact are some of the very coolest people around.

Infants and young children are not just
sitting twiddling their thumbs,
waiting for their parents to teach them to read and do math.
They are expending a vast amount of time and effort
in exploring and understanding their immediate world.
Healthy education supports and encourages
this spontaneous learning.
—David Elkind

 JOURNAL TIME... What generation do you align yourself with? How does that limit you? How does that encourage you? Notice where your *shoulds* and *have tos* appear with this Journal Time. Notice where you have *stuck points* and where you have *flow points*.

Without reflection, we go blindly on our way,
creating more unintended consequences, and failing
to achieve anything useful.
—Margaret J. Wheatley

Maria Salomão-Schmidt

I like to be a free spirit. Some don't like that, but that's the way I am.

—Princess Diana

Chapter 18. Why Do We Tell Stories About Our Lives?

Human beings can use sounds and visuals to activate feelings. If we were to stop and pay attention, we'd realize that *stories* are simply the way we anchor those feelings in ourselves and others. Because we are energetic beings, those feelings help transmit energy to each other. Stories are the conduits for our energetic bodies. These stories can be a way to harness energy that opens up the gateway for even more Love (freedom and flow) to our world or it can be used to lower the vibrations of others.

The Herd Operating System (OS) is the domesticated state in which we choose to live life from what we think others want us to do, instead of from our own internal guidance. When someone is operating from their *domesticated* self, they use stories to **beg or steal energy** from those around them. In our natural state of effortless flow, these stories help pass on information and energetic levels that help all parties involved connect to their own unique *zone*. This creates *harmony*. Much more about this in the next few chapters.

The Trilogy Of Awakening

When you meet someone for the first time where exactly do you begin the conversation and how do you pick what to talk about? Ever think about that? How do we ever pick a starting point with so many choices? Well, if you slow down enough to start noticing, you'll find that both *your intuition* and *your ego* are always feeding you information. You get to choose which one you listen to. The ego is constantly, and if I may be so bold to use this term, "yapping!" It simply doesn't shut down or up. It's the doer doing the noticing. Your intuition is also always flowing but not with words so much as with non-verbal indicators (*noticings, ahas!* and *knowings*) that show up through your feelings. These three terms are offshoots of each other but the subtle differences matter greatly because they help you stay in your alignment.

Noticing –

I would say that the *Noticing* is the first thing that happens when you start paying attention to that "being-ness" inside of you. It's exactly what you're connecting to when you meditate, the energy part of you. To connect to this part of yourself is a form of surrender, in the sense that you're letting go of mistrust and allowing things to flow without blocking, defending or deflecting. In the Herd OS, this is considered absolute madness. Just think about the word *surrender*. When is that ever described by society as a valuable quality? Pretty much never when you are in your *domesticated* state! Being vulnerable is the most jackassy position you can put yourself in because something is going to get you, so you must always be protected and on guard.

The act of *noticing* also happens in the domesticated brain, but it's greatly discouraged by labeling things that are dangerous, stupid, frivolous, wasteful, selfish, imaginary, not real or not important. The reason the *noticing* never really shuts down is because it's your energy's *pingback system* to get back to your energy body's flow. Just like gravity never *ends* or *begins*, your internal guidance system also never stops bringing you back to your authenticity.

When you're operating in your domesticated state, it's like having REALLY bad reception. The more domesticated you become (meaning the harder you try to actually *win* or *succeed* within the un-winnable system), the further away you get from your authenticity (your spiritual DNA). That love beacon, that's your internal GPS calling to you. It never stops calling out to you, sending you guidance. For those who believe in an afterlife, when you eventually pass from this life, it's that *pinging* that guides you back to source energy.

Aha! –

After noticings come the **ahas!** When I lived in Japan, I first learned that the Japanese call these **ahas!** *"satori"* where you don't know something, continue to not know it, still don't know it and POING— suddenly seemingly out of nowhere you know it! It's that specific moment of clarity that births the beloved *aha!* moment. (sigh) Just moments prior things seemed confusing or disjointed and suddenly they're working in complete flow with one another. In sports and business, we sometimes refer to it as being "in the zone." It's feedback that you are connecting to your spiritual DNA.

Clarity comes from engagement, not thought.

—Marie Forleo

Knowing –

The final component to this trilogy of how to connect to your energetic body involves the simple concept of *Knowing*. It's different and less sexy than the *aha!* that has an electricity of excitement about it. The *Knowing* is simply receiving information that you have no idea how you got it, but you know that you know.

A classic example of this, is mother's intuition, where a mother gets a sixth sense *Knowing* that her child is in danger, even if they are miles away from each other. The inauthentic state of being, where you are living the life you think you should, looks at this as a rare occurrence, a fluke or an accident, that just happened without rhyme or reason. When we're living from our core, our zone, it's simply using the invisible communication lines that exist among our energetic bodies.

This might seem weird to some, but think about how the concept of cell phones would have been absolutely and completely impossible to your great grandparents, or even grandparents. How can we listen, see and talk without any wires or tubes to people who are on the other side of the globe! If we went back in time to the 1800s and told people what the future would bring, we most likely would be put into a mental institution because we were speaking of things people could not even imagine. This is how the world has operated, when people don't understand something, it's seen as dangerous and it must either be contained, ultimately, so it can be controlled or monetized. If neither is possible then it/she/he must be destroyed. This is how people live in a fear-based society.

We are evolving on all levels, including energetically. We are in an all-in "game," of sorts, in human history. The things that we've done to our planet while we've been living in the Herd OS has caused massive amounts of damage. As we have lived unaligned lives, we have caused the Earth's natural resources, environment, water, climate and animals to go also off balance. One of the main reasons I'm writing this book is because I'm now as awake as I've ever been. Part of my lifetime's mission is to get the message out so that you can receive this *tsunami of Love* message right to your mind and heart... Time to wake up and live your life's purpose *out loud*! The time is now. The planet, and all its inhabitant need you now! Keep reading so you can continue accessing your spiritual DNA.

 JOURNAL TIME... When is the last time you had an *aha!*? What was it like? How did it feel? If you cannot remember one, write about that. Remember you are journaling as a tool to better access your spiritual DNA so the more you can share in your journaling, the more icky energy you will release, and the more yummy energy of authenticity that you will call back to you.

You don't have to be great to start,
but you have to start to be great.
—Derek Hough

Things I Want To Remember/Research/Review:

Maria Salomão-Schmidt

You come to realize that only one person can tell you what's expected of you, and that's you.

—Jason Mraz

Chapter 19. Dismantling Domestication

 Quick Check-In (Do Anywhere) Exercise... To move past this phase in our human evolution, it is important to activate the first component of the AWAKENING TRILOGY; to start *noticing* where each of us is at in this present moment. Use your breath. Take your time. Drop your shoulders. Roll your neck. Where are you in this present moment? How are you carrying your energy? Are you connected to the LOVE/FLOWING/HAPPY/EFFORTLESS part of yourself or are you connected to the JUDGMENT/SHOULD/HAVE TO/EFFORTING part of yourself?

Once things are *noticed*, the natural tendency of the domestication is to immediately begin *judging*. Nothing shuts a person down faster than *fear* they'll be judged. This is part of our survival DNA when fear is activated. I experienced this big time when our daughter Sophia was born with Downs. Where this massive fear arose from I have no idea, but it was incredibly *cellular*. It was not logical at all but instead like an internal panic attack that flooded my body with feelings of *danger, danger, danger*!

It felt like suffocating from the inside out, like if I did not reject this child, then I would be rejected. It said that she was worthless anyways, so rejecting her was not only "fine" but the only "wise" and "safe" thing to do. I know it may sound irrational now to those of you who have not experienced it, but that's the whole point of fear and ego. It's *irrational*, unless you're swimming in it, and then it just seems like really important information. You begin asking yourself questions that damn you even more such as, "What *should* I do? Is this *right*? Why us? What are people going to think?" All of this type of questioning is direct verbiage from the *herd handbook*, and it keeps you stuck by focusing your attention on only low vibration possibilities. It reinforces that the world is dangerous and that you need to protect yourself, so you don't get hurt.

One of My Very First Major Life *Ahas!*

It was during my senior year at Boston College (BC), with only two more terms to graduate, that I was on my way to accomplishing one of my biggest lifetime goals! This plan to go to college had been deeply ingrained in me by my culture, society and parents. Graduating from one of the top universities in the world, according to what I had been taught, meant that I was doing things "right." In other words, I was on track to have the life that had been dreamed for me. That path, that most of us were taught, is the one that supposedly leads to "happiness," but only if you do things the "right" way.

Be a good girl/boy and you'll get there. Nothing is more important or ingrained than to be "good."

So here I was in my last year of undergrad, trying to decide what would be the best next "right" step. Options were pretty much go to grad school or get a "good" job because, after all, that's why you go to school, especially if you are a middle class immigrant. There's a strong unshakeable sense that accomplishing these dreams somehow demonstrated that one's family is worthy of being in America, by doing the "right" thing, fitting in, working hard and even excelling. While on the road of doing what I thought I "should" do, I received a *gift* senior year at Boston College which I did not fully grasp until decades later.

Classes are chosen by a lottery system in which each student gets a random number. The higher your number, the better chance you have at getting the ones you want. Under this system, seniors are able to pick classes before the juniors, sophomores or freshmen do. As expected, there are certain classes that are so popular that only the seniors with the highest lottery numbers can get in. Professor Dr. Daniel Baer's class was one of those incredibly popular classes at BC.

Dr. Baer taught in the psychology department at Boston College. His classes were as "outside the box" as most of us had ever seen, especially at a Jesuit institution! Each time we met, he blew our minds by choosing topics that no one else was talking about. (Important to share that this was in the late 1980s, so there was no internet. We got our information only from books, encyclopedias, magazines, TV, newspapers, the radio... and librarians. Librarians were definitely the very first search engines in my humble opinion! I LOVE LIBRARIANS!) It's an interesting observation that the sole materials for the class were two massive books of photocopied articles from many different sources that Dr. Baer put together. This information was so new to the mainstream population at the time that it would have been challenging to find books on these particular subjects.

What particular subject? Well, the subjects Dr. Baer brought to us could best be described as topics that would fit into Leonard Nimoy's iconic television show of the time, *IN SEARCH OF*. (Side note: Leonard Nimoy also attended Boston College.) One day we would discuss UFOs, the next time we'd discuss witchcraft or telekinesis or ghosts. You get the point! Every student was absolutely mesmerized by the authenticity with which Professor Baer shared this avant-garde information. While most other professors were trying to fit us neatly into our societal "boxes," Professor Baer was igniting our curiosity and imagination. I was too deeply committed to the belief system I had been taught my whole life to immediately "get" the magnitude of the gift he was giving all of us; but I count that class as having been one of the seeds that helped "download" and write this book, thus making my life's work possible.

My most vivid memory, almost thirty years later, is from the very first days of class. Those are the most powerful for me because of the fact that Dr. Baer was delayed in Spain after the summer break, so he got a psychic to come substitute for him!

Yup, you read that correctly, a *psychic!* Those two classes were one of my major life shifts in this lifetime. It was such a big shift that I would not fully understand it until many years later. So there we were, in a very Jesuit institution, being taught by a psychic! What are the chances? We can definitely call this an extraordinary event! I'm sorry to say that I don't remember her name, but she changed the trajectory of what I thought was possible.

She opened up the world for me in a way that had been closed before. She told us things that I had never heard before, such as just like our bodies, our energy can also get dirty, and needs to cleaned. She taught us that we have an energy field and how to clear it. She also said something *sooooo* intriguing that over the years it has played over and over in my head. She said, "This is one of the most exciting times in our human history. Souls are wanting to be here now because of what is happening, on planet Earth." She reminded us that, "You have no idea how incredibly lucky you are to have been born during these exciting times! Many souls would gladly take your place!"

We are lucky to be here? Huh? At that time I was working five jobs to pay college. Life was exciting but "lucky?" More than anything, life felt like hard work. I kept wondering, "Why are we lucky to have been born now?" "What was she talking about?"

It was information that I needed more pieces of the puzzle to solve. This piece I had didn't make sense in and of itself, so I kept moving in the direction of what I was taught I was supposed to do with my life. You know, that HAPPINESS FORMULA we were given: Get a good education, to get a good job, to get a good mate, to get married, to have 2.5 kids, to get a dog, to get a white picket fence, to have grandkids, to retire, to die and go to heaven... but only if you were *"good."* Only domesticated people call this the *Happiness Formula*. I call this the *Domestication Formula*, and it has been one of the biggest sources of pain on this planet because it's *not authentic*. Things that are authentic flow, while things that are inauthentic have a lack of flow, or are blocked. More about this later in the book.

After I graduated from Boston College, I continued my obsession for living life the *"right"* way because I really wanted the Love and praise from my parents and those around me. I thought that is how to be happy so I wanted to put everything I had into it, of course! I got my first "real" job in Japan. I then lived in Boston, New York City and Atlanta and eventually, after getting my MBA, landed working in public relations in San Francisco. I was extremely focused and worked non-stop because I wanted to attain what society told me was "success." (It was so strongly my focus that the word "success" was my actual password for everything at the time.) To help me attain my goals, I voraciously read books of the masters in the field of self-help like Anthony Robbins, Og Mandino and Napolean Hill.

I was so driven and focused, that by the time I was in my mid twenties, I made my first million. I owned two homes on either coast, one a two-floor brownstone in downtown Boston, steps from the Boston Symphony, and a house with a view of the bay in San Francisco's Bernal Heights. I traveled all over the world. I went shopping a lot. I owned BMW & SAAB convertibles. I went to the theater. I became a philanthropist. I ate out at amazing restaurants. I took interesting classes. I taught university classes. I was invited to speak at conferences all over the world. I was featured in national and international magazines and newspapers. On paper I was absolutely living the dream life.

I was incredibly thankful for this amazing adventure which was in large part possible because my parents had moved from Portugal during the reign of Salazar, a ruthless dictator, to the land of opportunity, America. Because of my parents decision to move, I was given a really amazing gift of being able to make my own destiny. I was able to have and do incredible things because I owned my own communications/public relations firm in Boston and San Francisco during one of the most exciting times in human history, the *dot com* era where visionaries like Craig Newmark of Craigslist were shifting the world in massive ways by releasing their ideas into the world.

Maria Salomão-Schmidt

It was absolutely thrilling working with start-ups and companies like Yahoo, MathWorks and Sun Microsystems, and amazing people like Maya Angelou, Wayne Dyer, Jane Goodall, Jack Canfield, Les Brown and Mikhail Gorbachev! It was exhilarating! I was living "the dream" but incredulously inside I felt disconnected. No matter what I did, it was never enough. The thrill did not last once I attained something. As soon as it faded, it was back to the grind, still having to prove myself, but now to clients, analysts and reporters.

When I traveled, for example, I was so "*not* present" that I literally always made a bee-line to the gift store to buy a local souvenir, so I could find some way to connect to the place I had been. Try as I could, I could not "FEEL" myself there in the moment. My mind was so used to racing, it could not slow down to be present and it felt absolutely horrible—and who wants to feel horrible? I pondered why this was happening when I was doing all the "right" things. I came up with THE answer. It had to be that I was not working *hard* enough, so I dug in even more. If success was supposed to make me happy, I was obviously not there yet, so I started sleeping even less, making more deals and creating even loftier goals. After all, "No pain, no gain," right? That is what I had been taught all my life.

I kept wanting to have more, not for the material aspect but because I thought that was the way to happiness, and to be loved. I was not feeling good even though everything on the outside looking in was almost "perfect." Whatever success I got was not enough, because I was *not* truly happy. The whole time it felt weird, like I was going through the motions of doing all the "right" things, but it was *not* effortless, in fact there was a lot of *efforting*. I was working long, long, long hours. I was exhausted but willing to *keep trying* to crack the code to living a life worth living. "It would be worth it in the end," I kept reminding myself. "This is just how life is."

 JOURNAL TIME... Read the following passage and then take a moment to journal your thoughts on how you can see this in your own life. What are you willing to release? What do you want to shift? What do you want to explore?

One way people get REALLY STUCK in their lives is by blocking their own flow of energy. When you say, "NO! NO! NO!" through your actions or words, you're blocking our own flow. You're 'trying' to make things stop, even back up, so that you can create your 'safe' 'box' of a life. This is not how the energy naturally works. Energy likes to flow so to maintain this block you need to really effort. If you find yourself tired and bored, chances are that you're blocking your natural flow. The ego wants things to stop because it thinks it's 'trying' to help you.

The solution is to simply surrender. If you're tired, put down the food or drink you are using to numb out and go take a nap. If your job won't allow that, check in with where you work. Ask. Seek a shift either within the company or at another company. Another solution is to go to bed earlier. Keep breathing as you read this. I can feel you somewhat being triggered because I suggested a shift from outside of your box. Did you feel it? Lean into that. Remember you are as "safe" as you can be for someone who has an unknown end date on this planet. While you are alive, have the intention to live life to the fullest! Make that dash between your birth date and your death date worth the ride! When you say "YES! YES! YES!" your life begins to flow again.

 JOURNAL TIME... Take a moment to journal about whatever catches your attention from passage above. What came up for you? Could be something you want to process, or something you want to celebrate. Use this journaling invitation as a way to connect to the yummiest part of yourself... which also might be the scariest to you. Keep noticing. Keep breathing. Keep writing. Keep giggling. Keep leaning into the uncomfortable. Keep exploring. Keep playing. Keep surrendering. Keep releasing. Keep shifting. Keep expanding. Keep connecting.

We are always uncomfortable around our false self.

—Maria Salomão-Schmidt

If you don't know the trees
you may be lost in the forest,
but if you don't know the stories
you may be lost in life.

—Siberian Elder

Chapter 20. What's Your Story?

Your story is your vehicle for what energy levels you tend to live in. If you notice, most people tend to tell the same version of the same 10–13 stories over and over again. The stories you tell are a reflective tool for where you are energetically and how you think of yourself. Stories help you hold up an image of what others think about you, and what you think about yourself.

 High and Low Exercise... Activate your imagination for this one. Take a deep breath and do the following:

1. Think of people with low self-esteem. What stories do you expect them to talk about? How do you feel when you are around them?

2. Now think of people with high self-esteem. What stories do they share about their lives? How do you feel when you are around them?

For either of these levels of self-esteem in others, does it matter if your self-esteem is high or low as you interact with them? How so?

Stories Connect Us

Stories are very important to how we connect to each other. They have been around for as long as human beings could talk and will be around for as long as we are. Most people don't realize that stories are vital to how we set the energetic level of our life.

My children LOVE hearing about how they were born or stories from when they were little. I realize now more than ever how I describe their stories literally helps form how they show up in the world. What they hear activates some part in them.

When my eight year old daughter Isabella was about three, she attended Small Miracles Preschool in Holliston, Massachusetts. Bella, as she prefers to be called, separated two kids who had been fighting over a toy and successfully and effortlessly negotiated a win-win solution where both kids were happy. The incredible Ellen Kerstein, who runs this wonderful preschool, called me to share how in all her years she had never seen a small child of her age do that.

I've been telling Isabella that story for most of her life. Do you think that has affected her in how she sees herself? What if I had told her a story over and over again about when she had a huge temper tantrum and how loud and unruly she had been on a visit to Newport, RI? That one is also one of her childhood stories. What if that was the story I kept telling her and others in front of her year after year? How would that affect how she saw herself and the world?

We humans are full of both light and dark, as is each day. Whatever we focus on, we get more of. Stories are powerful tools because they help us do three things:

---

1. Connect with others.
2. Hold a certain vibration by retelling the story.
3. Direct our focus.

Whether the stories you tell center around what's going "wrong" or "right" in your day/life, then you put yourself in that vibration. From that vibration you attract your life's events. If it's a heavier vibration, it will attract heavy events, interactions and occurrences. If it's a lighter vibration you will attract more flow and alignment. Pay attention to the stories you tell yourself because it's one of the most powerful things you can do for your life.

The Story That Kept Me Small and Victimized

During my 20s and some of my 30s, one of my biggest stories was that I was a survivor of domestic abuse. I had a cache of heart-breaking stories I would share with others that exposed how challenging my youth had been and how much I had gone through. Suffering is a key element that pulls people in. In some religions, the more you suffer and sacrifice, the more pious you are, and the more value you have. It fits in beautifully with some of the "good boy" and "good girl" models of how to be in the world that keep us disconnected from our spiritual DNA.

Stories from someone who is already energetically full of themselves is different because they are not depleted and therefore don't need to take energy from others. When they tell the story it's more about connecting. It becomes about sharing a life experience in a way that exposes who they are. They are ok with sharing an intimate detail. They are open and vulnerable in a way that makes both people grow. In this case it becomes a sacred act and both receive more energy. It becomes a beautiful win-win that helps unlock each other's spiritual DNA.

If, on the other hand, the person who's telling the story isn't full of themselves than they need to take energy from another source, usually another human being. Stories from someone who is not already full become an unconscious way to take other people's energy. Many times that's why you so very feel depleted when you talk to them. (see Chapter 15 on *energy vampires*.) Feedback that you've given someone your energy can come in the form of being exhausted or even of feeling sorry for that person. To be clear, having empathy is different than feeling sorry for them. It's important to notice the difference.

At the time I had absolutely no idea I even had an energy body. I think I thought that "my soul" only kicked in when I died and that I did not really have to deal with it until then. As for sharing about my childhood, all I knew was that when I told stories of my abuse, it I felt better sharing it with others.

The fact is that like many things that initially feel good but are not good for you. You initially feel better, because you get energetically fed from it, but if you pay attention there is something that feels a little "off."

The reason is that what I was getting was recycled "poor-you" energy. It's like eating sugar. You might get a really yummy, good feeling initially, but then feel lethargic and tired. Energetically sustaining yourself like this long-term is challenging because it's feast-or-famine. I did all of this unconsciously. I had no idea I was using these stories energetically. Now that I run my energy more from my authenticity, I no longer need to tell these stories of abuse. When I do, it's usually for a presentation so I can help create a teachable moment. From this viewpoint, the story tends to be less from 'woundedness' and more from the perspective of a "deconstructing" or "dissecting" what shows up. Instead of an energy sucking tool, it's now a powerful teaching tool that helps people see how their energy body is working. It is in energy pockets like this one where suffering hides.

Make no mistake, stories anchor us in an energetic vibration by stirring up certain feelings and focusing our attention on those feelings.

One of the key things you can take away from this book is to *notice* your stories because they are another form of FEEDBACK of how you are running your energy. Remember your life is always talking to you! Your stories are telling you what energetic channel, or vibration, you're on (high or low) and if you're leaking energy or flowing in your authenticity. This is how we start creating more happiness in our lives. It comes from our core. We just have not been paying attention to our energetic body's feedback, mainly because many of us did not even realize we had an energetic body! This is a game-changer for all humanity. This is how we bring peace to our world. There is only war or conflict from people when they are leaking energy. Want to know why?

The physical body needs many things, especially oxygen, right? It is one of the key elements that help the connection to our Earth. In high school, I took lifeguard training classes at Centennial Beach in Hudson, Massachusetts. I learned one of the most important lessons of my life. Someone who is drowning is no longer in their brain, the way that you and I are normally. The fear is so great that the drowner goes right into his primitive brain, which is defunct of language, understanding or meaning. It has ONLY ONE FOCUS... SURVIVAL! Both the rescuer and drowner have a lot of adrenaline pumping, but the drowner is in his *reptilian* brain. The only way to get the person to safety is to either approach him from behind or wait  until he stops thrashing. It is not uncommon to have two people drown when there was originally only one. This is because that reptilian brain is only looking for safety. That person will use you for leverage to get that most sacred commodity we need to access to stay on this planet— air. He will latch onto you like super glue and not let go—literally for dear life, even if it means you both drown!

(*Side note that could save your life:* If you ever find yourself in this situation where you're trying to save someone but they are drowning you instead. Quickly before you also go into that reptilian panic mode, grab onto the person very hard and pull them deeper into the water. By doing this it freaks them out even more and they let go of you. I have actually had to use this and it really does work incredibly well. It's useful information if you get stuck in this situation and those who never thought they would.)

Maria Salomão-Schmidt

That's a strong visual story that helps demonstrate just how very important it is to the human body to have air and how "out of its mind" it can be trying to connect to that air. You meat body will go to desperate, unusual measures to stay connected to what it needs. The body needs the constant and continuous flow of air for it to continue its existence on planet earth; that's the deal here. No air, then no life, and the result is that the energy and *meat bodies* separate. We call this death. Now I want you to know that I realize it's a bit creepy calling it a "meat body" but to keep things simple, that describes it perfectly so that is why I am using it. There is better clarity this way. Remember your body is only your vessel.

Noticing Your Energy Body

It's a little known fact that the energetic body also has certain elements it needs. One of them is the constant and continuous flow of energy. Without this flow, the energetic body also can leave this human lifetime. It's that serious.

Let me give you another example to help you better understand where this happens. Ever wonder why sometimes people are mean to you, or you to them? Any time someone is mean to you there's a strong exchange of energy going on. Let's activate our imagination and conjure up an example. Since road rage is something that seems to be flourishing in our society right now, let's say someone cuts you off in traffic. From an energetic perspective, he's on a "mining" expedition, which means his energy is low. He needs to get more, and a great way to do this is to steal yours. It's very important to realize that this happens on a subconscious basic brain level, so most likely this person doesn't even realize that is what he's doing.

This lack of realization that besides the body's needs we also have energy needs, is one of the main reasons there's so much conflict on this planet. *Conflict* is feedback that we're living out of alignment with our nature. It rules much of how humans behave. It's one of the reasons people feel powerless and don't know why. The deal is that the energy vampire can only get your energy if you get triggered by their assault.

Take a moment to check in and notice that even using only your imagination, you can feel how *icky* it feels when someone does that because you're getting feedback that he's there to take your energy. It is important to remember someone behaves this way only because it's a way that has worked in the past. He's not "drowning" at this point, but rather feeling the lack of energy and reacting to it on a subconscious level, since most people don't even think about the energy body existing, much less what it needs to survive and thrive! The more aggressive or angry he is, the more he is energetically suffocating from lack of energy. In deep contrast, when people approach you with Love it feels entirely different. It is in noticing the feedback without judgment that you begin to bring more peace and alignment into you life.

The stories we tell literally make the world.
If you want to change the world,
you need to change your story.
This truth applies both to individuals and institutions.
—Michael Margolis

Things I Want To Remember/Research/Review:

Maria Salomão-Schmidt

We imagine what is possible
and then we build walls around it.
We can choose the palace version of our dreams,
but instead most live in filthy shacks.
We create our own lives. We follow the rules we choose.
Those who don't think they have a choice,
give their power away.
It takes a moment's noticing and a re-ignition of choice
to call your life back.
—Maria Salomão-Schmidt

Chapter 21. His Name Is Bird, Larry Bird

Ever had the experience of driving down a road hundreds of times, so much so, that if someone asked you if you thought you knew the road pretty well, you would answer a very confident, "Of course. Yes!" Okay, what if one day you decided to walk that same street, instead of zooming by in your car. If you do, you realize that not only is the perspective different when you walk, but also, there's so very much you missed in the car.

There's so much beauty and living that exists between the cracks of your day, as you race around from task to task, scattering your energies and cultivating stress. The interesting part is that you don't even realize it until you slow down. This is a clear example of what many who are trying to make a living today feel, as they live in the rat race of trying to make both a living and live a meaningful life. The people who live their lives "fast" don't think they're missing much, until they actually stop—or life forces them to slow down, usually through some form of heartache or illness.

It ain't pretty, but it is beautiful.
—Maria Salomão-Schmidt

Going Back To Basics – Larry Bird Style!

When I was growing up in Hudson, Massachusetts, I loved watching professional basketball. Larry Bird was one of my favorite players! One of our high school coaches used to coach for the Celtics and shared with us how Larry Bird always believed in going back to basics. Larry was always the first one to arrive and the last one to leave, because even as good as he already was, Larry was always practicing shooting the ball over, and over, and over again. In a game when he started missing shots, Larry again went "back to basics" by breaking down the shooting process into tiny steps so that he could find out what part of the process was off and get the flow back. This was simple brilliance. Just as with driving, when we slow down to notice each step, we can correct what is not working in our lives.

 Exercise Break... In yoga there is a wonderful exercise that I'd love to share with you. Close your eyes. Take a deep breath. Now imagine that your face is a clock. With your eyes closed, look up at 12 o'clock. Look up as far as you can without moving your head or neck. Then go to 1 o'clock, again stretching as far as you can look without moving your head or neck. Then go to 2 o'clock.... all the way around until you come back to 12 o'clock. Wherever you notice resistance or lack of flow give it a little attention and flood it with Love (which is just happy thoughts). Go around the entire clock at least a couple of times. Also, do it a few times in reverse, from 12 o'clock, go to 11... 10... 9....

Extra Benefit: This is also a truly simple way to get rid of a lot of headaches, especially when they are the kind that hurt the sides of your head, your temples. Share this with your family and friends. Many times I do this with my kids and then they don't even need any pain medication because the headache is gone on its own in seconds. Just needed a little internal stretch, that's all. Another example that you have most all the tools you will ever need already inside you!

Like Larry Bird, in order for us to get into our flow, we also need to go "back to basics." It's important to know who you are. Your point of reference is key, because if you think you're a body having an occasional spiritual experience, your life will be completely different from the thought that you are an energetic being experiencing life

Maria Salomão-Schmidt

through a temporary vessel of arteries, bones, skin, etc. As you read about in Chapter 2, every human has at least two main bodies. One *meat* body and one *energy* body. It is vital to call it energy and not a soul. Here's an explanation why...

Can you feel your soul? Can you access it in any way? Connect to it? How do you know it's *full* or *happy?* The word "soul," even though it is widely used, puts a block between you and your energetic body. Now if you use the term "energy" and ask the same questions, let's see if there is a difference for you. Can you feel your energy through your *feelings?* Are you connected to your feelings? Can you feel when you are *happy?*

Using the term energy gets you connected to your internal GPS where you get vital feedback about how energetically full or empty you are. It's from there you know whether or not you are flowing from your core or out of alignment. The worse you feel, the more you are away from your natural flow. This is new to us humans, but it is an emerging part of our evolutionary process. It's being triggered by the massive emergency situations we find ourselves in at this precious moment in Earth's history. Never has the world needed us to "wake up" more. We've been living from a reverse state, painfully living our lives as if our energy flows from the outside in—that we need others to feed us love and attention, instead of inside out. This belief system is the key cause to human domestication. When blindly following what others say is the "right" way becomes our focus, instead of what our inner self is telling us, we get painful feedback. Because most everyone is doing it, we all live with suffering at some level. In this way, suffering becomes normal, while not suffering, or being happy, is seen as *unnatural or unattainable.*

The key to stop this crazy lie, is to call our life back. You have been most likely taught that to attain "enlightenment" or to be "happy" you have to do something or get something/someone outside of yourself. You alone are not "worthy." In Catholicism it's even said that you are born with sin and must get it removed through baptism. For centuries human beings have been taught to doubt ourselves, and that things are complicated and difficult.

The truth is that it's MUCH simpler than you think. The very first step in calling your life back is to notice your energetic body and the vital feedback it's continuously sending you. You access this information simply by checking in with your feelings. By slowing down to notice, *without judging*, you're doing the work that'll uncover, not only your path in life, but also your happiness.

What is going back to basics for you? Answer the question, "What is going back to basics for you?" As with all your *Journal Time* sessions, feel free to draw, paint, doodle, write, dance, sing your answer. Play with where/how/when/with what you "journal." Go outside the box and see what meets you. Let yourself be led to the answer versus *trying* to *think* of what the *right* answer is. Play with it. No, really! Give yourself permission to PLAY! Explore what comes up. When you notice JUDGMENT of any kind release it. Use the basics of your *core* to find your own unique answer to create a magnificent win-win exploration play-date with yourself. This is the kind of activity that gives a huge energetic return on investment (EROI).

> *You live either the gift or the curse.*
> *You get to choose which.*
> —Maria Salomão-Schmidt

Things I Want To Remember/Research/Review:

Their life's calling was continuously reaching out to them, giving them clues as to how to awaken, if only they slowed down long enough to take notice.

—Maria Salomão-Schmidt

Chapter 22. The Great, Big, Massively Yummy Love-Light Ball

Every life begins with a story, so let's activate our imagination and explore this one... Here we go!

Imagine a big, no I mean a really, really big, stunningly beautiful ball made up of playful Love and light. This incredible juicy Love-Light Ball is a massive free-form flow, made up completely of the yummiest energy. It is magical with the most magnificent colors you have ever seen, or dared imagined. There is no darkness in the Love-Light Ball. Pain is an unknown entity, as is fear, hate or conflict because those things come from lack of flow. The Love-Light Ball only knows fluidity. There are no angles, only complete flow with no obstructions. The Love-Light Ball feels amazingly safe, delicious, creative, curious, warm, fun and exciting. It's made up entirely of pure energy with no matter whatsoever, and this energy flows abundantly and effortlessly, as it embraces movement. It's akin to the deeply inspiring expression I've heard the beautiful Maya Angelou in her stunning voice say, "Joy Rising." (I get goosebumps just thinking of her saying that!)

To power each of the individual Love-Light sparks that make up the great, massively big yummy Love-Light Ball, there needs to be certain conditions. The most important one is the constant and continuous connection to the larger collective of Love-Light sparks. The individual Love-Lights cannot exist without that connection to source. The connection can be obscured or reduced, but it cannot be cut in any way or under any circumstances because it simply "is." Now use your imagination to visualize that this is where your energy body comes from. You're a magnificent spark from the Love-Light Ball!

Continuing With Our Story...

Meanwhile, on our planet, Mother Earth, feeling creative takes some of the 118 Earthly elements at her disposal to form an absolutely incredible "meat body" complete with bones, organs, veins, muscles, arteries, etc. To power the *meat body*, Mother Earth engineered it so that it would need three of the four observable states of matter:

1. Oxygen (Gas)
2. Water (Liquid)
3. Nutrients (Solid)

The meat body part of us absolutely needs these three elements to survive. The most important is oxygen because it's the one we cannot survive without after only seconds or minutes. Even if water and nutrients are present, without enough oxygen, the body will perish. Next is water. The body can go without water for days, but after that it begins to shut down, even if it has enough oxygen. If it has enough food, however, the body is intelligent enough to get enough liquid from the food. The last observable state of matter is nutrients. Even if the body has enough of the first two elements, oxygen and water, without nutrients, the body will also eventually die because it does not have the raw materials the body needs to function.

Everything with a beginning will also have an ending. The body is a creation made entirely on planet Earth. Everything on earth will follow the same pattern of being *born* or created, a period of aliveness, and then a *death*, an ending. It's a natural cycle, a pattern that is repeated over and over again in every living thing, but also extends to the planet itself. In the popular Disney movie, The Lion King, the concept of the *circle of life* was introduced, especially to our children. Everything has a season. Our planet flows with the beginning, middle and end of each day, season and year.

Maria Salomão-Schmidt

When our bodies, the vessels of this life's journey, cease to hold the energetic spark that brings them life, we call this *dying*. From the energetic perspective to die means to disconnect from the human body. One of the hardest things for other human beings to understand is how people, especially those whom they adore, and even more especially, children, can be there one moment and gone the next. This is harder still, if there isn't a clear warning sign that a person is going to be "leaving" his/her body. It could be a car accident, heart attack, beating, overdose, cancer, organ failure, bleeding, dehydration, starvation, bullet or fall. Many people try to block out death all together because they just don't want to think about it. It takes a massive amount of energy to suppress this natural flow and the result is intense fear. This blockage, like any other, lowers one's vibration by redirecting energy away from wholeness and flow.

Coming from the body's perspective alone, life is incredibly fear-inducing for three reasons. One, because there's a lack of control over when, where and how death happens. To the human brain, in most circumstances, death is an unexpected occurrence that can happen with no rhyme or reason. Two, because of lack of clarity of what happens after death, "where" one goes. Three, because there's a fear of the pain, not only for your own death, but also for the pain experienced by those who are left behind.

Fear is the by-product of wanting to control these three factors even though they may not be controllable. But why? Why can't you control so many things in life? Human beings, as explained earlier in this book, are a combination of energy and meat. The energy body has certain laws of its own. So often we have been living without focusing on the energy aspect. When we operate from this standpoint in the game of life, the only factor that's focused on is the world of the physical. Anything that cannot be measured or picked up in some way by one of the five senses, is immediately deemed as not "real," and therefore less than. Because it falls into the not real category it is given little or no importance. Future generations will look at humans of today and our limited thinking, as we look upon our ancestors, the Neanderthals, who lived 40,000 to 130,000 years ago.

The Adventure Continues...

Now back to our Love-Light Ball story where we're again activating our imaginations to get to a deeper understanding of this simple made-up story... Mother Earth is very proud of her *meat body* creations because she has managed to use the resources on Earth to create something extraordinary. Soon her excitement wanes, because although she has every resource on planet Earth at her beck and call, no matter what she tries, she's unable to activate the lifeless *meat body* she has created. What's missing is *the spark*, the light from within, that will power the vessel she has created. Mother Earth, being extremely resourceful, and not one to give up very easily, pauses to check in with her incredible powers of intuition. Soon her *aha!* moment arrives.

Her magnificent *aha!* unveils the idea to send out a beacon, a request of sorts, to the Love-Light Ball asking if any of its Love-Lights, or "sparks" want to come *play* in these amazing, state-of-the-art, fully-loaded *meat bodies* Mother Earth has created. What she offers them is *contrast* and a way to further spread and deepen love and light in the world. They agree because what energy loves to do more than anything is move and expand! Energy does not know fear or pain because those are things only experienced by the meat body when it is blocking the flow of the energy body.

From then on, an incredible energetic partnership formed. When none of the Love-Light sparks wanted to come on a particular adventure, the body simply absorbed itself back into Mother Earth. Every once in awhile, however, a Love-Light spark agrees and comes to Earth for an adventure. If we were to interject ourselves into this story, then we can say that you and I are Love-Light sparks who both responded, "HELL YEAH!" to this wonderfully wild and crazy adventure. In doing so, we are given the gift of a ticket to come to planet Earth. This book is to remind you of this to bring you back to your core. From there, it's much easier to realize why you are here. YOU ARE A SPARK! YOU ARE ALWAYS WHOLE! ALWAYS! The only time you don't *feel* whole is when you are blocking your energy body's flow.

 JOURNAL TIME... We have been given the gift of this lifetime. Whether you believe in reincarnation or not, you have this lifetime here and now so I ask you directly, "*What are you doing with this one great life?*" Because you are reading this book, you undoubtedly are on a quest to find the answer to that specific question. Keep leaning into that question—even if it feels uncomfortable at first. The discomfort is what fear feels like. It is what has kept you small and depressed.

Maria Salomão-Schmidt

The Other Side of Fear Is Love

What you seek is on the other side of fear. To not let fear control your life takes intention and focus on Love. Love, you may remember is freedom and flow. This is where practicing comes in. When fear shows up, instead of running from it, *lean* into fear. Let yourself feel what you fear. It is absolutely terrifying at first. You are facing 10,000 years of domestication. You'll find, however, that when you do lean into it, FEAR DISAPPEARS—because fear is *not* real. You may perceive it as a block but it's actually the meat body closing the energy body's natural flow of intuition in order to control it. It FEELS real because when domesticated, you have been conditioned to ultra-focus and notice the fear first. You're trained to think of FEAR as a safety mechanism. Anything new and different is labeled *dangerous* first. Things are labeled as "good" or "bad." When we live like that, we create a world of suffering. What you focus on grows, so focus on what you want, not on what you don't want.

The lifetime you're in right now is based on the partnership of energy and matter. For you, the human being, flowing at your best and highest vibration, happens when your energy body, or spark, is leading your life. In this scenario your meat body is the follower and your energy body is the leader. There is alignment because your meat body is operating under the same principles as you, the spark, has always followed—of infinite wisdom, flow, trust and love. Interestingly, the parts of the word "incarnate," *in* means "going into" and *carn* means "meat" so in other words "going into the meat body."

We all know that the body is not infinite. It *will* die. Dying is a term that only exists in the physical world, because it is the name given when the energy loses its connection from its lifetime's vessel, the meat body. This fear of death is so massive that it causes the body, through the brain and ego, to override, or block, the Love-Light energy. This is why people feel stuck in their lives. It's because energetically, they are blocked!

The meat body enslaves the energy, keeping it contained for fear's sake so that a human being begins living the most inauthentic manner of existence, as a body who occasionally has a spiritual experience—instead of being a spiritual being having a temporary body experience.

This is an incredibly torturous way to live which is why many spend much of their lives numbing out. The results to our human family is that a global magnification of fear and inauthenticity. This translates into feedback that shows up as wars, conflict, arguments, rape, stealing, hitting, enslavement, using, yelling, jealousy, violence and depression. You don't have to look far to see it in your own life at work, in your family, with friends. People who are afraid or angry will bully or manipulate others. It happens in all sectors of humanity including government, business and families. It even happens in our own heads when the parts of us that are fearful self-sabotage bliss. Can you remember when you sabotaged your own bliss? Squished your own intuition for what you "thought you should do."

Energetically, things on our beautiful Earth have gotten totally turned around—but it is just an evolutionary step we are now passing through. Instead of living from a place of natural freedom and flow (love), we now live from a place of stagnation and blockage (fear).

It's a very painful time in our history, especially for those who can't understand why there's so much suffering, conflict and sadness. This book was downloaded from *source* energy to help us remember how to go back to our joyous core. Core living (by acknowledging and noticing your energy body) means living your magnificent life in alignment, from the *inside out*, and not as so many are living it now—from the *outside in!*

Only those who will risk going too far

can possibly find out

how far one can go.

—T.S. Eliot

 Grounding Your Energy - A Connection to Love Exercise... Reminder About Your 1st Helper – GROUNDING. As you go through your day, remember to *GROUND YOUR ENERGY*. It'll help you to make a better connection to your internal GPS which guides you in having a more authentic life. Take a slow, deep breath now. Drop your shoulders. Pull in your core by tightening your stomach muscles until you feel your spine shift. Nice and easy. Release your breath if you are holding it in. If you notice tightness in your jaw, gently open and close it and move it from side to side. Take another deep breath. Picture a rock, any size or shape. Feel your "icky" energy fall away from you and feed it to that rock. Rocks like to be hard, but living things do better with *flow*, not hardness. From this day forth give all your *hard* or *icky* energy to the rocks, who need this type of energy to stay hard, so they don't crumble.

For extra grounding, place both your feet on the ground—the more naked your feet, the better as well as a more natural ground to place your feet on, the more grounded you will feel. For example, standing on dirt, grass, sand, moss, even snow, in your bare feet, regardless of the temperature outside is one of the most grounding things that you can do. Keep breathing deeply. When we over think, we tend to cut our breathing down. Deep breathing will help you process information better too.

The thing that surprises me most is, you cannot change who you are.

—Jeff Probst

Things I Want To Remember/Research/Review:

Watch your thoughts, they become words.
Watch your words, they become actions.
Watch your actions, they become habits.
Watch your habits, they become your character.
Watch your character, it becomes your destiny.

—Lao Tzu

Chapter 23. Do You Know You Get A Choice?

What's the point of getting up every day and doing all the things you do, day after day after day? Why do it? Are you moving in a certain direction? Do you know what you're doing? Do you know why you're doing the things you do? Does it feel good? Are you honoring yourself and others in the process? Are you kind? Do you give back...from your heart, or because you "should?" Are you present to your life? Are you living your authentic life, or your *supposed-to-live-this-way-because-that's-just-how-things-are-for-me* life? Are you simply just tired and feel like it's basically the same shit, different day? When you get to your 99th birthday will you have lived each year of your life of the same year 99 times?

Have you ever stopped to think who taught you how to do the things you do? How did you learn to be in the world? How did you pick your profession? How did you learn how to *be* you in the world? How do you know what you are supposed to do and be? Most of us are so BUSY doing what we feel like we should, we don't even stop to think about the *why* of it all. We glorify being *busy*.

With almost every conversation you have with someone who asks how you are, at some point in the conversation one of you will say some version of, "Oh you know... we're so 'busy' with _____." (Fill in the blank with any number of responses that strike your fancy.) Many of us feel like we are waking up to a life in *mid-flow*, as though we are moving in a direction, but don't know why we're doing what we're doing—but everyone is doing the same things so we just go with it... until we can't stand it any longer. This is not new. Even as far back as 469 BC, Socrates was noticing that our ancestors of that period were dealing with a similar pattern when he said, "The unexamined life is not worth living."

What Human OS Do You Use?

If someone talked to you 40 years ago about operating systems (OS), you would not have had a clue as to what they were talking about. Just as human beings have evolved, so has our technology. On our planet, as one thing evolves, a shift happens causing other things to also evolve. "Evolve," simply means shifting. Although it does not always seem like it, everything on our beloved planet is always moving and shifting. For example, the earth, does not feel like it's moving, when in actuality it is in constant motion. Movement occurs in all life forms on earth, even when we don't notice it.

These shifts on our planet are happening on all levels of our lives including food, water, jobs, housing, communications and technology. If you buy a computer and there's no OS, you just bought yourself an expensive paperweight. The OS is a set of rules and commands that allow the computer to do what we desire. The OS is what helps everything run and determines how it all runs. What happens on the micro level, reverberates out into the macro, and vice versa. Humans, like computers, also have OSs. At first, we did not even have the language or concept to understand or describe OSs. As computers came into existence, however, we began to understand the actual concept of needing an OS. This insight helps us see how we function in the world. Most human beings are just beginning to realize that even we have an "operating system." The next step is to realize we are conditioned from a very young age to determine which OS we use.

Remember earlier in *Finally Full of Yourself* when you learned about the Big Love Ball? That is source energy. It is "where" we originated. You can give it any name you want to fit your beliefs.

All of us came here to get the "ride of a lifetime"—both literally and figuratively in the vessels that we call "meat bodies." This is a description that I have never heard put quite this way, but I feel that in order for you to get to your life's core, it helps to relate on this *raw* level. Core work is like that. If you *try* to solve something and don't get to the source, you don't get the change you seek. The work you're doing in this lifetime is sometimes stunningly beautiful, sometimes ugliest of ugly, sometimes effortlessly easy, and sometimes *stuckest-of-stuck*.

What's important is to slow down and notice what feels stagnant. Your life is always talking to you, giving you feedback. Listen. Realize that you determine the volume. Ask. Adjust. Listen again. This is how shifting happens. By going back to noticing your energy body, you make the life shifts you desire.

To refresh what you learned earlier, if you want to have peace and happiness in your life, one of the ways to do that is to realize that you have been living your life through a *human operating system*. You may have the immediate impression that this sounds complicated, but not when you realize that you've been using these human OS programs unconsciously all your life! It's only now that we're beginning to realize that there's something more. We're witnessing human evolution when human beings are shifting into alignment with their unique authenticity, instead of struggling to live the *should life* someone else created for them.

There are two main human OS: the Right Now OS and the Herd OS. We'll talk more about the Herd OS in Chapter 26. For now we'll talk about the one we are all born with, the Right Now OS. Again, you're incredibly familiar with it because you have had it all your life! You just did not know it had a name. It's absolutely you in your core alignment with everything effortlessly flowing and working as it was designed. The result of this kind of alignment is something people call happiness or joy. An easier way to say it is that: The byproduct of living in your alignment is happiness. Examples of these are everywhere on earth.

One of the biggest categories of humans that operate in the Right Now OS are small children. Imagine a child playing with her toes or even playing in poop, for that matter. She is obliviously happy. Younger children are just joyous because they tend to live in the moment—simply being. What they are doing is irrelevant for them to experience the by-product that is happiness. This applies only to children who have not been abused. Abuse is a form of introduced fear. Fear blocks the flow of authenticity. It creates mistrust where there was once trust. This is a big expansion for most people but that's ok. Take your time to process it. We will keep discussing the human OSs throughout the book.

It is finally when you let go of what people
expect you to be and people's perceptions of you,
that you're able to be the version of yourself
that you're supposed to be...
It doesn't matter if you're half crazy, or eccentric,
or whatever it is—that you have to be true
to who you were born to be.
—Gwyneth Paltrow

Another large category of people who also live in the Right Now OS are people who have been labeled "mentally" or "intellectually challenged." Some people are offended by those expressions. I don't like them either because I personally think those labels are what most labels are, *one-dimensional.* For example, I now see people who have Down Syndrome as being incredibly evolved spiritual beings. Much of what they focus on is LOVE. They smile. They live in the present moment. They are authentic. If they feel something, they say it. This kind of authentic behavior and living in the moment of joy are rejected by people in society at large. To "normal" society, these individuals are oftentimes still thought of as somehow *less than,* not whole. Just because people have different mental processing capabilities, does not mean they are any less of a human being. We human beings are just starting to get this fact.

Hard to imagine that just a few decades ago, these amazing people were experimented on, killed and institutionalized. When I am doing my retreats and workshops I often say that if someone is living in their alignment, to the outside world they look like they are "high or mentally challenged."

This insight comes from watching our little daughter Sophia, who was born with Down Syndrome. "Sophalicious," as we often call her, was smart in her own way. Because her brain was unique in the way she processed the world, she could not be "domesticated." Her real brain was her heart. This is what made her so very special. No *overthinking*—just strong *heart energy.* Complete *authenticity!* It was so refreshing to be around someone like that! It did not mean she was happy all the time. It meant that whatever she was processing she did and then went back to the joy of being. Sophia did not block her energy. She simply let it flow. All her thoughts and actions were *flow points*, where the energy did not get stuck. It is that kind of fluidity that is *authentic*. The by-product of that authenticity is *happiness*.

 The Visible Shift Exercise... The following is a great exercise to help you align with the vibrations that you're attracted to. Take a deep breath and have fun picking the words that best represent the level you want to live on. Fill in the blank with words that inspire you and create your own *high-vibration affirmation!*

Here are some examples to get your creativity and authenticity flowing... Magnificent, Fun, Creative, Outrageous, Debonair, Brave, Wild, Intelligent, Kind, Funny, Authentic, Magical, Brilliant, Talented, Resourceful, Radiant, Radical, Sexy, Satiated, Benevolent, Philanthropic, Hysterical, Visionary, Masterful, Abundant, Artistic, Honoring, Courageous, Fantastical, Beautiful, Expansive, Fun-Loving, Adventurous...

I am on the same vibration of the most _____,

_____, _____ people who have ever lived.

Once you have your affirmation, write it down in as many places as you can to anchor and inspire your focus on high-vibration living. (Ideas: In your car, by your toilet paper roll, on your bathroom mirror, at your desk, in your wallet, etc.) There may be a tendency to want to pick more than three words. Focus is important here. Too many words water down the potency of the affirmation. As with everything, do what feels best to you. "Mistake" is a word of the the Herd OS, because it means something was judged as being done "incorrectly." There are no "mistakes" in the Right Now OS—only exploring and getting feedback.

Maria Salomão-Schmidt

For A Bonus... This is a great exercise to do daily, weekly, monthly, quarterly or yearly. As you evolve, you can aim for a more authentic *high-vibration affirmation*. It helps set the intention for your life. Whip out your calendar and schedule it now, so you are using this as an anchor to create your most *authentic life!*

To be unafraid of the judgment of others is the
greatest freedom you can have.
—Timothy Shriver

Things I Want To Remember/Research/Review:

I think she is a genius of the soul.

—Tim Shriver (speaking of Loretta Claiborne)

Chapter 24. The Beautiful Loretta Claiborne

In my research, I came across a woman I had never heard about named Loretta Claiborne. On her website www.lorettaclaiborne.com you will find the following bio:

"Loretta Claiborne is truly an amazing and inspiring woman who has not only touched the lives of hundreds of thousands, but has changed the lives of all with whom she has met. Ms. Claiborne is a woman of faith who shares her personal life story that carries a heart-felt message of hope and tolerance for all people around the world. In 2000, Walt Disney Productions created *The Loretta Claiborne Story*. Claiborne says, 'I figured if my story could change a person's mind about another person, or especially a child's mind about another child, then it was the right thing to do.' Loretta's life's accolades are too many to account, but a few of her most impressive awards include: receiving two honorary doctorate degrees (Quinnipiac University in 1995 and Villanova University in 2003); completing 26 marathons with her best time 3:03, finishing in the top 100 women of the Boston Marathon; the 1996 ESPY Award-Arthur Ashe Award for Courage recipient; Walt Disney Productions movie titled *The Loretta Claiborne Story;* WorldScapes publishing company produced *In Her Stride*—the biography of Loretta Claiborne; a 4th degree black belt in karate; communicates in 4 languages and is fluent in American Sign Language; inductee into the Women in Sports Hall of Fame and Special Olympics Pennsylvania Hall of Fame; spoke to the U.S. Congress, as well as hundreds of other groups and organizations; introduced President Clinton at the 1995 Special Olympics World Summer Games and appeared twice on the Oprah Show. This is just a small snapshot of who Loretta Claiborne is and some of the things that she has accomplished in her life."

Pretty amazing person, right? Well, here's a little surprise for you. There's one line I took out of this bio, which I will share with you now: "Loretta is a world-class runner and gifted motivational speaker who happens to also be a Special Olympics Athlete and a person who has an intellectual disability." Because of the brave work of people like the magnificent Eunice Shriver, who started the Special Olympics, the amazing Loretta was allowed to bloom into her fullness as a person, instead of being institutionalized (energetically and physically shut down) as so many were, and unfortunately, still are.

Eunice Shriver, a member of the famous Kennedy family, started the Special Olympics at a time when mental institutions were growing and the shame of having a child who was special needs could destroy an entire family. Imagine the huge courage and amazing heart of Eunice Shriver to stand up to this kind of ignorance and start celebrating these amazing human beings who have so very much to teach us! Later in *Finally Full of Yourself*, I will divulge from where this deep passion arose in Eunice Shriver.

When Your Name is Brought up on Super Soul Sunday

The following is from an interview on Oprah Winfrey's *Super Soul Sunday* with Timothy Shriver, Eunice Shriver's son, about his greatest spiritual teacher. This interview is a wonderful example of how things are shifting. Shift happens much of the time when one person is open to noticing how they themselves are reacting to a particular event. In this magical exchange, we witness a major shifting point for Tim Shriver.

Tim Shriver

"So I'm racing around the office and the governor is coming to the office. We were working hard to prepare for big games in New Haven. Six thousand people were coming and the governor was coming to inspect everything and I was tense and tight, screaming and barking and (saying) 'clean this up' and 'move this around'. Loretta Claiborne, a person with an intellectual challenge, a child of the housing projects. She's just sitting there helping out in the mailroom and she watches me go by and she says, 'You know Tim, the governor puts on his pants in the morning same as you.' My first reaction was (with teeth clenched) 'Yeah, I know that!' And then I got that one gift of a pause and I thought to myself, 'You know, she's trying to remind me that we are all in this together.' You know? Just relax!"

Oprah

"You know when I read that, I found that so striking because, my goodness—governors. You are raised in the houses with presidents and senators, and... yeah."

Tim Shriver

"Yeah, but we were intimidated by all them. We wanted to be like... we wanted to impress... I wanted to impress him."

Oprah

"Uh-huh."

Tim Shriver

"She was saying don't worry about that."

Oprah

"Don't worry about that..."

Tim Shriver

"Yeah. Relax, because he's coming to our world. She had the audacity to say that you know, you need to come to my world. I'm thinking to myself, 'No Loretta, we are trying to tell these people that we can get into their world, that we belong in their world.' She said, 'No, no, no we are not. Their world is all messed up. Their world is about competition and greed and avarice. They are all unsettled and stressed out. They should come to our world. Everybody counts. Everybody belongs.'"

 Mind Movie Exercise... Activate your imagination again for an exercise to see if it's in alignment with what you have experienced on this planet. I'm using this as an excuse to have fun, so let's even pick the characters to play out this exercise. You can pick any actors you wish. I'm including some of my favorites here.

Characters in our Mind Movie:

Two Friends

- First Friend - Emerson: Frank Langella
- Second Friend - Harry: Michael Capozzola

Emerson was driving his friend Harry to Boston on the Massachusetts Turnpike, affectionately known by locals as "the Pike." On the way, a black SUV cuts off an eighty-something year old lady in a white Mercedes S-class. This causes Emerson to have to swerve, narrowly avoiding getting hit by the Mercedes. As he regains control of his car, Emerson witnesses the feisty white-haired woman screeching to a stop. Her face beet red, as she pumps her fists yelling at the SUV.

Once the men began breathing again, Harry spoke, "Man, that guy deserves some sort of payback for what he did! What a jerk!" Emerson looked at his friend and responded, "Lots of people would look at it that way, but what does that really do." Harry laughed, "What it really does is make me feel better. That is what it does. That guy shouldn't have cut that poor old lady off. We could have all gotten killed."

"So it sounds like you have a need to get even," said Emerson after a long contemplative pause. "EXACTLY!" exhaled Harrison! "That's it, exactly."

The Lesson:

Think about the expression "to get even." In this case Harry is what can be described as being in a *low-vibration state*. What does "low vibration" mean? Well, the further we are from our flow, our happiness, and our connection to love, the emptier and heavier we become. This heaviness is something that we feel in our *meat bodies*, just as we feel heat and cold. It is simply feedback that can help bring us back into our alignment.

When we use the expression, "To get even," it has generally referred to when someone has wronged you, and you get vengeance of some sort. It might not even be anything you've done yourself per se. It could be something that just happened. "To get even" usually means you want to lower them to your level, and you're not feeling so good, because you've been wronged. Once they *fall* to your level then you have achieved satisfaction and can now rise above them, because it feels so good to *get even*. Usually the response is, "Well good, because what goes around comes around." Growing up we learned the philosophy of "an eye for an eye." This is not how the universe works. As Mahatma Gandhi said, "An eye for an eye makes the whole world blind."

From the point of view of your energy body, *vengeance* and *revenge* are simply forms of being an energy vampire. Think about it. They mean you want someone to suffer. Many times you can hear people in movies say some version of, "I want them to hurt as much as they made me hurt."

Deconstruct that for a minute.

So what that person is saying is that they want them to lower their energy vibration to match the icky one you have. When many people in our society do it, it becomes the norm. This is where we find ourselves today as a human family, not wanting others to feel good when we think they have hurt us. Even if that person did do something to hurt you, hurting them just adds more suffering, keeps you stuck in that lower vibration and lowers the overall vibration of our whole human family. Enlightenment means each of us starts realizing that how we see what happens in our energy bodies helps us make choices that will bring more light into the world.

 JOURNAL TIME... When someone cuts you off on the road or is mean to you how do you react?

WARNING: If you have issues with being a *good girl/boy* you may find yourself *trying* to give the *right* answer, or justify your response. To find your flow simply remind yourself there is no *good* or *bad*, just feedback of how you are using your energy circuits. Remember to be as authentic in your response as possible so you can get the most out of this Journal Time!

Kindred spirits are not so scarce as I used to think.
It's splendid to find out
there are so many of them in the world.

—L.M. Montgomery (Anne of Green Gables)

Maria Salomão-Schmidt

If only life could be a little more tender
and art a little more robust.
—Alan Rickman

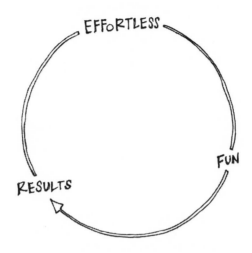

Chapter 25. Shifting From Doing To Being, No Really!

The Key Factors For Alignment

At one of Dr. Deepak Chopra's training sessions, he said something so BIG that I needed several days to really digest the impact of his words. It got my attention because of how different it was from how I was raised to think. He basically said the following three factors need to be present in my actions for me to be in alignment with my joyful, fulfilled, authentic self. Things have to be:

EFFORTLESS   FUN   RESULTS-BASED

While absorbing news and information from the media, fellow humans and the rest of the world, you subtlety and consistently "shift" into the vibration of the status quo. In other words, if you are not full of yourself, you'll align your energy with whom and what you spend your time with. If you don't set an intention, you basically connect to "normal."

The term *normal* can shift depending what group you're in. What is *normal* for one group, might not be for another. The standard *normal* for our world right now is vibrationally low and inauthentic. It's the equivalent of the mob mentality where people disconnect their choice and follow the crowd. *Normal* means you're usually decreasing your energy by being around other unaligned people. This isn't a judgment. It's noticing so you can set your intention. Connecting to *normal* is why wars, violence and conflicts are so prevalent. Those who plug into this channel can expect pretty much the same as everyone else connected to that vibration. *Unhappiness, is normal's feedback.*

To have an *extraordinary* life, connect to your authentic vibration, your Right Now OS. Manifesting becomes easier when you're operating in your zone, guided by your spiritual DNA. There are certain activities that activate the Right Now OS. One of these is as simple as listening to a great song when you completely get into it and don't care one iota who's watching you dance like a "crazy" person. Dancing has such a powerful attraction that when you see others do it, it often draws you like a magnet into that same alignment. You notice yourself smiling, clapping your hands, laughing out loud, connecting to others around you, shouting, tapping your feet, swaying—creating movement and connection to the music. It's pretty powerful when it happens. This is one example of how it feels when the Right Now OS is activated. It's naturally drawing you in. It's effortless, fun and results in happiness, as feedback.

And it's not just music either. Think about when you're on a relaxing vacation or watching a sunset. You can feel yourself breathing differently. Your shoulders drop. Your smile lights up. It feels good. It involves a form of surrendering. It feels peaceful. It feels amazing. When people go on vacation and feel this way, they say, "Why don't we do this more often?" Why indeed!

The Right Now OS is built-in so there's nothing to do or learn. That's why babies live it automatically and naturally. One of the hardest things for people to *get* is that there's absolutely nothing you have to do. Just be you. This sounds too simplistic to those who want to connect with the flow of their energy body, but this is where the effortlessness comes into play. YOU are the Right Now operating system. The only way you are not operating in it, is if you've blocked it.

Remember when we talked about the *Happiness Glass Ceiling* in Chapter 7? If you're too happy (which is feedback that you're living in your alignment) others begin to think you're on drugs or that there's something wrong with you simply because you are joyous. This is because energetically, you are on a different vibration. If they connect with you they are more likely to start letting go of blocking their energy flow. That takes trust but they've been told their whole lives that listening to their intuition and imagination is irresponsible.

Yes, it's not just in your head. There's a reason why you block your happiness. It is so you can try to "fit in." To not be ostracized and excluded, you're told to follow other people's rules. By doing this, you decrease your own flow. In other words, you take the energy that's helping you get information from your internal GPS and use it to feed things and people outside yourself. You know you're in alignment because being in the Right Now OS feels good.

Wait... What? If it feels this good, why in the world would you block it? That's a great question! It might be the most powerful question of your lifetime... *Why would you block your innate pleasure and joy on purpose?* One word—LOVE—because you are taught that if you follow the rules of what is "right" you will be LOVED. If you are loved, you will be whole. If you are whole, you will be safe. Ladies and gentlemen, welcome to the strategy of the Herd OS, where the whole point is to get you not to be you... without you realizing it! By the way, if you are wondering how it can be the end of the chapter with still so much to understand and deconstruct, no worries Love, the entire next chapter is about the Herd OS! I've got your back!

 JOURNAL TIME... Your journal topic for this chapter is short and sweet... Answer the following question: What activities do you like to do that make you smile and lose track of time? Give yourself plenty of time and make sure you write it down.

Right Now Exercise... Once you have completed the Journal Time above, whip out your appointment book/calendar and schedule in some of those activities that you listed above in your journal. So many times we look at what we want, almost as if we were separated by a window. We can see what we want but we seem to not be able to *grasp* onto it. The prior Journal Time is a wonderful exercise, but without follow-through it never leaves the *dreaming* stage of development. Magnetize your dreams and inklings by putting some of the specific things that light you up from the list above. Incidentally, this is an example of calling your power back.

The reason you are here is because you've been called.
Your real job is to hear what that is and honor it.

—Oprah Winfrey

Things I Want To Remember/Research/Review:

Maria Salomão-Schmidt

Now we all have a great need for acceptance,
but you must trust that your beliefs are unique, your own,
even though others may think them odd or unpopular,
even though the herd may go,
[imitating a goat] "that's baaaaad"
Robert Frost said, "Two roads diverged in the wood and I,
I took the one less traveled by, and that has made
all the difference."
—John Keating played by Robin Williams, Dead Poets Society

Chapter 26. What Exactly Is The Herd Operating System?

OK then, so you are that *spark* that came into a *meat vessel* to have the ride of a lifetime, right? You get here and for the first few years, as a baby, you're having a ball playing in the world. At a certain age, for some it's much earlier than for others, you finally get what most of the adults have been trying to "teach" you. You begin to understand that this world is dangerous, that you need to prevent death for as long as possible (even if your quality of life is horrible), that you must follow certain rules or you'll have a "bad" life—or worse, be a "bad" person, then no one will love you.

Some studies show that children hear the word "no" an average of 400 times a day. To put that into perspective, if you did anything 400 times a day what effects would it have? What if you ate 400 times a day, or did push-ups 400 times a day? That is a massive amount of energy and focus on one activity. You would have some major shifts in your life to get past this. Now, imagine you as a little kid hearing "no," from the people you love the most, 400 times a day daily. This would (and has) definitely affected you. This is the beginning of what the beautiful Don Miguel Ruiz, in his incredible book *The Four Agreements*, speaks about—*human domestication*.

Human domestication is simply the systematic introduction of fear. Fear is a block of our Love or light connection. The Herd OS is what it means to be domesticated. We block our own internal guidance or flow of intuition because it is seen as "unsafe" and "not real." Well then, what is real? What is real to those living under the Herd OS is to *follow the rules*. What you are told by most people, including those who love you the most in this world, is that if you just follow the rules, you will be happy, safe and loved. Now it's important to know that this is simply a part of human evolution.

We are evolving like our ancestors did. They were learning how to use their external fire. As we have evolved, we are now learning how to use our internal fire, our energy. We are then just learning how to play in this world, as we shift from SHEEPLE back to PEOPLE. Those who raised us did not know any better. They learned how to be from their parents, who learned how to be from their parents, who learned how to be from theirs... and so on back to the very first humans. You will miss the *aha!*, if you activate the blame game here. Blame just creates blocks. It is not about someone having done something to you or not giving your what you thought you needed. As the beautiful Maya Angelou said, "When you know better, you do better." It is as simple as that. Everyone is truly doing the best they can with the information they have, the coping skills they have developed (or not developed) and with the energetic vibration they are on.

When our precious little daughter Sophia was born with Down Syndrome, a whole new world opened up to me about people whom I had been kind to in the past, but had treated as *less than* because I did not know any better. I thought I was being "enlightened" by having pity on people who were intellectually different from me. Society solidified that belief. To this day, Sophia continues to teach me things that I never could have learned had she not entered my life as my beautiful little girl. My hope is that I can honor her by passing these gifts onto you, so that you also can spread them into the world by being authentically you in the world. This is how you find your happiness, which is vital because feeling happy is feedback that we are full of ourselves. It means we are living in alignment. The more of us realize this and act on it, the more it spreads to our human family. The more it spreads, the faster we heal the planet! How very sweet is that?

All the freaky people make the beauty of the world.

—Michael Franti

Little Background Please

For a long time, the last 10,000 years in fact, there has been one predominant Human OS, which I call the Herd OS. This operating system controls people by controlling their focus from the internal flow of intuition to the rules of the outside. In other words it's about living guided from the outside in, versus the inside out. The evolution of humans is about remembering that our natural, most-effective flow aligns us with our happiness when we connect to our source.

It's our effortless birthright just as it is for grass and flowers. The divine intelligence guides plants to grow in their natural alignment. They don't need to take any classes, create goals or have meetings. They are simply connected to the flow. People living in the Herd OS have been taught to disconnect from that flow. Their flow is their very own internal guidance system (GPS). It's innate and built-in. People operating in the Herd OS, block their own GPS; and instead give themselves up to the ideals that their family, culture, company or society has created for them. The feedback they get of being unhappy, they translate, with society's help, into being about their self-worth. This shifts to a self-esteem issue when in reality it's a focus issue. When you focus on the wrong problem you never get the correct solution.

In the last century, as we humans have been suffering with living in an unnatural state of affairs under the Herd OS, we've been out of alignment. This misalignment has caused much destruction, suffering, conflict and pain. It is only very recently that the great awakening is occurring. It's the next phase of human evolution! We are so very lucky to be alive during this exciting time in human history!

Our whole world is one big feedback loop. When something is off, everything is so interconnected that it starts affecting other systems.

As the misalignment continues to grow, so do the ramifications. It's the same as if your foot is on fire. The faster you notice, the less damage there will be. Our human "foot" has been on fire for a long time and we have been too focused on other things to notice. Some of us have just started smelling the smoke, others have been feeling it intensely for a long time, still others are still completely oblivious and blindly compounding the damage. This is the state humanity finds itself in right now. This is why things have felt "off" for you, even when everything around you seems "fine."

Getting Back to Yourself, Your Core

The Right Now OS connects to a different *flow point* than the Herd OS. In the Right Now OS, people develop and follow their own internal GPS instead of shutting themselves down and following the rules of society. The concept is simple, but when you have lived marinating in the Herd OS, it can be so embedded in who you think you are that you don't know what the blurred lines separate. I am taking time to talk about these two systems throughout this book because I believe these are such very important concepts. Many of those who feel disconnected or stuck can finally understand why, and can create a viable plan to get out of the endless rotary of pain and suffering they have been in. This is what this book is about, after all. It was written for you, for this specific time in human history which is why it's feeling so good to read it!

Even More Background, Please and Thank You

Whether we notice it or not, from the time we are conceived we are being molded to fit into what society has deemed "appropriate" and "safe." It is so deeply embedded in our culture that sometimes it's hard to notice. In direct and indirect ways, we are given a "success" formula for how our lives are supposed to unfold. We are taught the classic rules of conduct for the LAND OF SHOULD—what is "right" and what is "wrong."

You can see this clearly in our own lives when we are figuring something out we oftentimes ask, "What *should* I do?" Many of my coaching clients often start off their sessions asking this. This is an indicator to me of which operating system they are in. Can you guess which one?

Most of our ancestors, including our own parents and grandparents, have not only followed specific, cookie-cutter rules based on their gender, ethnicity, religion and culture, but also passed them on, over and over to each following generation thinking they were doing the "right" thing. Many of these rules have been so clearly embedded into our behavior that we see them as "normal" and no longer even question the *why*.

Let's take a moment to de-construct the Herd OS so you can really see what it looks like written out. Here is the basic "successful" life formula under this operating system. In order to have a "good" life, this is what you are supposed to do. We all know it by heart. Some families might have slight variations but in general it goes a little something like this:

The Herd OS: Living a "Good" Life Formula

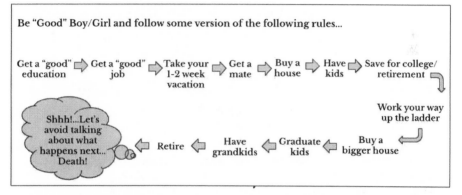

Somehow human beings over time have determined that because the world is such a dangerous place, following these rules will keep you the "safest." The people who do not follow these rules are considered to be "abnormal," "weird," "strange," "off," "dangerous," "undesirable," "a rebel," "a maverick," "black sheep" and "unreliable." Traditionally, if you're a woman, your *Good Life Formula* is even more complex and limiting. This was all done in the name of keeping a "moral," "safe" and intact working society.

What I have discovered after over two decades of working with clients, is that no matter what life issue you are going through, the disconnect, or trouble, comes from when you disregard your intuition and place this Good Life Formula above all else. How about an example from our body's perspective? Following the "Good Life Formula" is the equivalent of disconnecting your nervous system from your brain and connecting it to a *central brain* outside your body. The authenticity of the information is now no longer aligned. The information is corrupt. If the body is being hurt or experiencing pleasure, it cannot give the proper feedback to its own brain in order to correct or even enjoy a situation.

Activating the natural checks and balances system is vital to the organism's health. This is what it would be like from the level of your *meat body*. In a Human OS, we are talking about our *energy body*. The Herd OS is what happens when we disconnect from spiritual DNA and connect to another GPS, but one that is artificial. There are many versions of the Good Life Formula that we are familiar with. We have just never seen it that way until now. Here are some examples of other versions:

- Good Girl/Boy Formula
- Good Mother/Father Formula
- Good Student Formula
- Good Worker Formula
- Good Martyr Formula

- Good Boss Formula
- Good Daughter/Son Formula
- Good Victim Formula
- Good Supporter of Others Formula

Mixed in this equation is a strong underpinning belief that there's a "right' and "wrong" way to live life. Most of us may have not broken down our lives like this, but this is a vital step to help us realize where we are. Especially in Western society, we don't like to acknowledge this model for living, because we like to think we are unique. The truth is that YES, we are indeed unique (See Chapter 46 on *Ice Cream, yup you read that right.*), but that uniqueness is only unleashed when we live our lives from our spiritual DNA. In other words, let our authentic self lead our life.

Just like with any journey, to find our destination, we have to first know where we are starting. Within each journey are an infinite amount of beginnings. Each moment there is the potential to begin anew.

On the other side of the coin, when you live your life based on the Herd OS (not being authentic) you repeat a lot of patterns, many of which no longer make any sense. But, because it has been done that way for as long as people can remember, it is now labeled as (get your fingers ready to do air quotes) "just the way we do it." When you connect to the energy of this OS, what your life is going to look like is mostly determined by three main factors, and those factors show up from the moment you are conceived. These factors are:

Maria Salomão-Schmidt

- Who you were born to (Nurturing)
    - Financial Stability (Abundance)
    - Self-Esteem/Open Heart (Love)
    - Education (Knowledge)
- Where Were You Born (Geography)
- When Were You Born (Environment)

The truth is that, whether or not you are connected to your spiritual DNA, these factors still affect you. The difference is that those who connect to their core energy, use these factors as the weights to build up the *muscles* of their life's purpose. Those who attach to the Herd OS, on the other hand, will live trapped by their limitations of these factors because they are not connected to their authentic power.

Look around you and you will see that examples of who you were born to, in combination with the Herd OS, leading you to a life of being a *drone* or *zombie*, following someone else's rules to gain acceptance by the whole. Acceptance comes from the *outside in* and not the *inside out*. Bottom line is that no matter how you slice it, who you are right now has been largely determined by these originating key factors.

The first one, *Who You Were Born To*, is one of the most important factors of the equation. Within this factor are three key elements: Financial Stability (Abundance), Self-Esteem/Open Heart (Love) and Education (Knowledge). How much financial stability, how much self-esteem and how educated your parents are especially in the ways of childcare, largely determine how your life will be shaped. This three-pronged equation is like a three-legged stool. It needs all three parts to work. If any one of these factors is "off," the stool will topple over. Depending on the educational and financial level of your parents/guardians, the geographic location and the era in which you were born, this formula will vary; but in general, it follows the same path.

The second and third elements are very similar in their explanation. Both *Where Were You Born* and *When Were You Born* determine much of the way you will be treated, and therefore how you will allow others to treat you. There are many places, even today, that still limit the ability of a human being based on any number of factors that have very little to do with ability. Things like gender, color of skin and sexual orientation are still used to keep people in the small boxes pre-determined by large pockets of society. Over the last few decades, things have been shifting from this herd thinking and more into a world that's open to all the different flavors of people. I'll expand on this a bit later because it's another tool for helping to get to our authentic selves.

To feel like they have done a good job, many have a strong vision firmly implanted in their mind of what is 'right' and 'wrong.' Most of the people around us want for their kids to grow up, find a job, a mate, a home and then procreate in the "right" way. To some working hard is considered one way to determine an individual's worth. We have gotten so good at this herd way of thinking, that we pretty much not only do it UNCONSCIOUSLY, but we also pass it on to others mindlessly. By others, I mean that we hold our children, our neighbors, our friends, and our co-workers accountable too. Those who veer from this way of being get quickly and consistently reminded that they are not on track. Over the last three or four generations, this formula has shifted greatly, although its basic structure is still intact—for now.

You aren't the only one reinforcing the rules of the Herd OS on yourself. There are HUGE industries built around supporting this basic path, like the wedding industry, for example. As we have become more UNCONSCIOUS IN OUR LIVING, weddings have grown exponentially more expensive and extreme. It is one day of ego with a lifetime of paying for it. I know a couple who spent the money they had been saving for years for a house down-payment, just to have an extravagant rehearsal dinner! Not for the wedding reception, but for a rehearsal dinner for the tune of $75,000!

This kind of example happens often enough that it's become a bit of a joke in our society with reality TV programs like "Bridezilla." Under the laughter, however, there is a lot of pain with attempts of desperately trying to be seen as important, again a lack of self-esteem. Whether it's the wedding industry or some other institution, one of the symptoms of the Herd OS is *unconscious living* and attributing the quantity of money as equal to the quality of love. You don't have to look too far to see it manifesting all around you. It is simply living in what people commonly call "The Rat Race." (Our apologies to rats because they are too smart to race.)

Let's Take A Gratitude Break

Here's one thing you have probably never heard, but it's incredibly important to remember as we continue on this journey. Just so we are on the same vibration... please allow me a moment to deeply thank you for being born! Thank you for picking up this book! Thank you for your beautiful energy and your magnificent heart! A hearty thank you because all of these elements are what you need to help shift our planet before it's too late. Here's to a magical shift back to our hearts, and back to our Love-Light selves running the show, so we all again may *effortlessly flow*! Onward and inward maties!

 JOURNAL TIME... (As always, feel free to write or draw) What is your first memory? Think of smells, colors, sounds, shapes... What do you remember? Lean into those images and feelings and see what comes up. Give it some time. Let yourself go there and remember details that will help you learn even more about that part of you that you are just now getting ready to know.

> *If you're going to make a significant change in your life,*
> *consider making a big move like taking a trip*
> *to a different part of the world,*
> *or at least to a new location within your country.*
> *This helps you to get out of your comfort zone*
> *and take a different perspective. After all,*
> *"if you do what you've always done,*
> *you'll get what you've always got."*
> —Natalie Sisson

Things I Want To Remember/Research/Review:

We didn't come to earth to get anything. We came to awaken our full potential and infuse this dimension with divine light.

—Derek Rydall

Chapter 27. The Most Powerful Kennedy Of All

Earlier you read about Eunice Shriver and her son Tim who are part of the Kennedy family. The Kennedys have been a very influential family in the history of the world, but especially in the history of the United States. As more and more of us are shifting, there's a greater awareness of how some are helping us shift faster. Since the main goal of the Herd OS is to be able to control (safety) and add value (worth), the people with the most value are those who work. Being "powerful" within the herd mentality is directly linked to being able to make money, because on Earth, money is a tool that can be used to alter human behavior.

People will do things they don't want to do if the amount of money is right, especially if they are desperate. Under this way of living, the most powerful are those who can make money; the more money, the more powerful. Those who cannot generate money are considered the weakest. In our society, children, women and elders are historically not as valuable as a healthy working, usually younger, man or woman. For a long time, and even today, within some poorer families, the main reason people have children is to have more help to work the family farm or to go work somewhere to feed the family.

Historically, people who were born physically or intellectually challenged in any way were considered less than. When my daughter Sophia was born we had no idea she was going to have Down Syndrome. I was in total shock. I am saddened to share that I initially did not want my own child. I had rejected her because what she represented was "too uncomfortable." In those first few hours I reacted as though her being born was the worst thing that could ever have happened. This reaction occurred because my domestication process had taught me that having a "mentally retarded" (the term used when she was born) child was bad, *very bad, almost worthless.* This belief can be so strong that people actually demote others to *less-than* status. In this Herd OS, I saw Sophia as less valuable because she was not the child I had envisioned. I felt shame. I felt disconnect. I felt betrayed. My beautiful mother, Maria Raquel, was key in helping me to unlearn this lesson. I will explain why later in the book, when I honor a number of angels in my life.

Once I got over the shock of our Sophia having Downs, I started focusing on providing her with the best life possible. It was my "SNAP OUT OF IT" phase. Most of the times it felt like feeling around in the dark. It turns out that much of what the experts told us was based on what Sophia would not be able to do. They focused on her limitations. We focused on helping her to *thrive*. I started *deconstructing* what that meant. I leaned into my fear and took it from fear and ignorance, to movement in the direction of what felt good.

In our house, languages are important. I grew up speaking Portuguese and English mainly, but also some French and Spanish. I love languages and the ability to communicate with others. I have taught all my children English and Portuguese with a mishmash of other languages including Italian, Mandarin, German, Japanese and American Sign Language. This might sound like a lot but we have fun and play with it. It's a gift we choose to give our children.

With Sophia, however, we were told that speaking more than one language would confuse her. That did not feel right to me so I ignored their advice. It turns out that language did not confuse her. For example, we taught all our children to sign as infants, because I read that kids can communicate much sooner than they can talk. At eight months Sophia was making up her own signs such as combining *drink* and *milk* together. We love that we have her on video doing that sign, which we delight in watching. The "experts" said she would not be able to speak until she was five years old. At 13 months she could already say about thirteen words.

When we went to specialists and doctors, many but a precious few told us what she would not be able to do, based on what they had seen others not do. What they were not adding to their equations, however, was the fact they were comparing our Sophia to the Downs kids who had grown up in a world that rejected them. Many of these amazing people were drugged and mentally, physically and sexually brutalized in institutions—to be forgotten. In some situations, these beautiful beings were even used as medical experi-ments. They were not considered even human enough to some. I could relate because my reaction when she was born was from that fear pool. The difference was that I was open to shifting thanks to the perfect storm of love surrounding me at the time. My heart breaks that I thought that of my beautiful little girl but I believe it's important to share my reaction because that information could help someone else who is feeling *stuck* by their life's surprises. Again, going back to one of my all-time favorite quotes by the beautiful Maya Angelou, "When you know better, you do better."

This pattern of placing different values on people has happened consistently throughout human history to those who are seen as the weakest, by the strongest in our society. *Strength* in the Herd OS comes from survival of the fittest. It comes from being able to *dominate* and *control* others. Those who have been controlled include: women, children and other men (of color or the elderly). These are the consequences of human domestication. People are re-trained to go away from their natural core, basically forgetting they already are Love in its most pure form. Without that vital flow of energy coming in, the *energy body* begins to energetically "suffocate." The only way it can survive is by either stealing or begging for energy from others. This can only happen when a society has dehumanized its people by judging and ranking worthiness, the natural by-product of this system is the formation of hierarchies. This becomes part of the domestication process.

There are many people who suffered greatly as a result of almost the entire planet living in the unnatural Herd OS. If they had lived in the Right Now OS, they would have been able to unfold, without the outside interference. What has happened on a massive scale, (and in many places is still happening), is that when those in the Herd OS realized others were not doing things the "right way," they did their best to "correct" the situation. Sometimes the people operating in the Herd OS had ill intentions, but many times they had the best of intentions. You can hear these people say things like, "I'm doing this for your own good." "This is going to hurt me more than it hurts you." Regardless of intention, there was a rule, or a way, that things needed to be done. If they did not get done that way—fear helped fuel insanity. Our human family has plenty of those horrifying stories, but even in the darkness there is hope.

Our world is filled with the most magical teachers. Here's a true story you may have heard about before, but probably only in shadows and in bits and pieces of rumors.

Ladies and Gentlemen, the beautiful
Rosemary Kennedy...

An example of when people living in the Herd OS tried to reign in someone they deemed that needed to be saved is this one. It was not often talked about, especially in its day, but today we have evolved enough as a society to be able to begin to see the gifts.

Rosemary Kennedy was the oldest daughter of Joe and Rose Kennedy. Her brothers were President John F. Kennedy and Senators Robert and Ted Kennedy. Rosie, as she was called, was sent at the age of 15 to the Sacred Heart Convent in Providence, Rhode Island where she was taught separately from the other students by a special team of instructors. Her reading, writing and math skills were reported to be at a fourth grade level, although Rosie studied hard. She felt like a huge disappointment to her parents whom she desperately wanted to please.

Although her IQ level was tested at falling between 60–70, her diaries in the late 1930s reveal a beautiful and engaging young woman whose life was filled with a full and jaw-dropping social calendar that included tea dances, going to the opera, dress fittings and meetings with incredible people including President Roosevelt, King George VI and Queen Elizabeth. Below are some excerpts directly from her diary, which was only finally published in the 1980s:

"Went to luncheon in the ballroom in the White House. James Roosevelt took us to see his father, President Roosevelt. He said, "It's about time you came. How can I put my arm around all of you? Which is the oldest? You are all so big."

"Up too late for breakfast. Had it on the deck. Played Ping-Pong with Ralph's sister, also with another man. Had lunch at 1:15. Walked with Peggy. Also went to horse races with her, and bet and won a dollar and a half. Went to the English Movie at five. Had dinner at 8:45. Went to the lounge with Miss Cahill and Eunice [her beloved younger sister] and retired early."

Her father, Joe Kennedy, a very driven man, wanted all his children to be successful. He had very focused goals, and he went through extraordinary circumstances to make sure his family was exceptional. As Rosie hit her late teens and early twenties, she started acting in a way that was against the mission her father saw for her. She was fighting against membership in the Herd OS. Now we know that she was most likely dyslexic with perhaps some mild mental retardation, but mostly just a young girl who was part of a very demanding family and was trying to find herself in the midst of going through the hormonal stages of puberty. There was a huge fear that people would find out. It was under these conditions that Rosemary became a big family secret.

Unbeknownst to her mother, Rose, her father Joe Kennedy, in order to "fix" her behavior and lack of mental ability, took their 23-year-old daughter to get a prefrontal lobotomy. It was one of the very first lobotomies ever given. Historian Doris Kearns Goodwin said that to Rosie's father, Joseph P. Kennedy Sr., a lobotomy—a brain operation then regarded as a miracle treatment—"was an obvious solution" to the frustrations she experienced in trying to find a place for herself in a hard-driving family. However, according to Goodwin's account, "something went terribly wrong," and she emerged "far worse" than ever. It left her permanently incapacitated. She reportedly never spoke again.

Rosie was immediately moved to the institution that was chosen for her, St. Coletta of Wisconsin, where she lived out the rest of her life. Reports say that Rosie liked to send letters to her nephews and nieces, and she visited relatives in Washington and Florida. She also loved visiting the Cape Cod home where she and her sisters and brothers grew up. When she died at the ripe old age of 86, Rosie Kennedy was described by her younger brother Senator Ted Kennedy, in this manner: "She was a lifelong jewel to every member of our family," and from her earliest years, "her mental retardation was a continuing inspiration to each of us, and a powerful source of our family's commitment to do all we can to help all persons with disabilities live full and productive lives."

Indeed the thing that's so crazy about this planet is that judging helps no one. Her father, Joe Kennedy, did the best he could with what he knew how to do at the time. Many of us get tripped up on *trying* to do "better." "Better" is a matter of who is judging. Not judging or letting go of our judgment is what forgiveness is all about. Forgiveness is letting go of our expectations so we can fully bear witness and then release it. Feelings were not meant to hold onto. They were meant to be felt and released.

When something like this story happens, we on Earth get very sad because we imagine what Rosie's life could have been IF... Every person who loses a loved one or makes a decision that hurts others plays the "what if" game. What if I had made a different decision? What if I had done this instead of that? Or that instead of this? The one thing that is important to remember is that this is the Earth School. We are here to play, love, learn and let go. Without being cold, you would never know what being warm is. Without being hungry, you never truly appreciate having enough food. Without being wet, you never really appreciate what being dry feels like. One of the biggest gifts we get on this planet is the gift of *contrast*.

What happened in the Kennedy family was something that caused a deep sense of heartache. It gave her family a deep experience of contrast, especially to her sister, Eunice Shriver, who took that love and heartache and created one of the world's most beloved organizations, the Special Olympics. This global non-profit has dramatically shifted the lives of people with disabilities, and how the world treats them. Eunice found a way to unwrap the gift-side of the equation of her sister Rosie having gone through this ordeal and change the world by focusing on the love. It was a Love gift that she passed on to her son, Tim Shriver, and that he, in turn, is passing on to his children, as well. The love reverberations keep flowing throughout our planet. This is a truly deep example of LOVE RISING!

The Love and Lessons Keep Reverberating...

Eunice Shriver's son, Tim Shriver, is carrying on the lesson of Love started by his beloved mother, not only because he is now the chairman of the Special Olympics, but also because of the powerful messages he shares with the world. In his memoir, "Fully Alive: Discovering What Matters Most," and in interviews he's done, Tim is picking up on the lessons that first started with his Aunt Rosie, and is spreading that message of Love to all of us.

In a National Public Radio (NPR) interview, NPR's Scott Simon talks to Shriver about his book, *Fully Alive*. This part of the interview captures how things are shifting:

SHRIVER: I think we'll look back and people will read what we've written in these days and listen to talks like this and they'll hear us say disability and they'll cringe. We are so limited in our understanding of ability still. I mean, the idea of intellectual disability comes from the construct that intellect is one-dimensional. We already know that there are multiple intelligences, we just haven't discovered that many of them. Maybe we know about eight or 10 or 12, but my guess is there are a thousand so I love the idea of thinking of a world of different abilities—I use the word diffabilities, some folks don't like it, but I think it invites us to rethink.

SIMON: I tried it. Spell Check won't accept it.

SHRIVER: Spell Check doesn't accept it. I know, my editor tried to correct it many times in the book. I said, please—just trust me, leave it in. I think the horizon of finding what matters most will impart, for all of us, lead to the discovery of a great, great array of gifts among the human family and a much bigger appreciation for the gifts that different kinds of people bring.

SIMON: Timothy Shriver. He's chairman of the Special Olympics and his new book is *Fully Alive*. Now that we are moving towards a great awakening where we are seeing some major shifts in regards to people, whom society threw away. This is a great accomplishment for humanity!

Rosie did not have to prove that she mattered or that she was worthy. You don't either. None of us do. We are already whole.

 JOURNAL TIME... This is incredibly powerful stuff and very subtle in nature until you let it sink in. I invite you to journal about what you are feeling right now. What's your experience with people whom society has shunned or deemed as "not as valuable as?" Share from your heart. Let it rip. Feel it. You might just remove an *energetic hairball* or two. Here's an invitation to call your power back.

> *Between two evils, I always pick*
> *the one I never tried before.*
>
> —Mae West

Things I Want To Remember/Research/Review:

What are little girls made of?
Sugar and spice
And everything nice,
That's what little girls are made of.
—Robert Southey

Chapter 28. The Good Girl/Boy Trap

 Why You? Why Here? Are you a rat race participant without even meaning to be? So "What's the point, eh?" Better yet, "What's your point? What's your reason for being on planet Earth right now?" You may not have DIRECTLY asked that of yourself—but how you live your life, the things you spend your time and energy focused on, determine YOUR LIFE's LEGACY. Each thought and action you take designs your life for you. Let's dig in and see what we find!

The Good Girl/Boy Syndrome

There is a depth of awareness you find when realizing just how very afraid you've been in the world. This fear has been maintained from having been constantly reprimanded and put down within these three areas:

1. For how you are feeling
2. For what you are doing
3. For what you are dreaming

It's a very unfulfilling way to live. It feels icky because it limits the freedom and flow (the love) in your life. We have been taught subconsciously to ask the questions above of ourselves and others as a way to maintain the size of the box we live. I love the quote by one of my dearest mentors, Dr. Wayne Dyer, who said, "If you change the way you look at things, the things you look at change."

Where to Begin in Our Own Lives

Even though this is where it originates, we are blind to it and many times pass it on to the next generations. So let's break it down. Now what are you really saying to a child when you place them inside the world of judging them as *good* or *bad*? This might take a while, because for so many it has been ingrained their whole lives. Give yourself the gift of breath here. Keep taking long breaths, because it's one of your most important Helpers you have. It gives you inspiration and connects you to the energy you need in this present moment, the only place you are truly alive.

"Transformation is my favorite game and in my experience,
anger and frustration are the result of
you not being authentic
somewhere in your life or with someone in your life.
Being fake about anything creates a block inside of you.
Life can't work for you if you don't show up as you."

—Jason Mraz

Helpful Hint: It's much easier to process a thought when you are breathing deeply. When you feel "stuck" notice how you breathe. Is your breath barely there or too shallow? As you continue to read this book remember to really breathe. This is a gentle reminder to breathe in a way that flows and frees you up.

In order to peel back the layers, simply start with the key words *good* and *bad*. If you take a moment to think about it, you may find that what you're really addressing is their value. You're basically asking if they are *valuable* or *discardable*. What the Herd OS teaches us is to see everything through a *good/bad lens*. We have learned this from our most beloved people in our lives and we have, in turn, taught it to our children, and reinforced it to those around us. We thought we were helping but now we know better. This has been used to separate people. Under this good/bad view of the world, being loved is based on what they do, and *not* who they are. Unless they do the "right" things, then they're deemed to have no real *value*.

This is a hard concept for many adults to learn because we were also raised this way. There's a part of us that sees it as "normal." It is sometimes hard to see there is a forest when your face is so close to the tree. *Conditional Love* is classic Herd OS. The simple truth is that most of our parents loved us, but they still used this way of treating us to help us fit into the world. They did not even see it as a self-esteem issue. They were completely blind to it. What it did for most of us, was disconnect us from ourselves.

The message was loud and clear. Being *good* was incredibly valuable collateral because it was your ticket to be loved. You are only "good" *if* you:

(a) Do your homework	(e) Respect your elders
(b) Clean your room	(f) Say "please" and "thank you"
(c) Get good grades	(g) Wash behind your ears
(d) Do what I say	

It's such a part of our culture that even jolly ol' Santa Claus reinforces this stress-based concept by having a NICE and NAUGHTY list, which is just another version of "good" and "bad." This way of thinking is so ingrained in our system that people don't even realize it's harmful. The classic movie, *The Matrix,* is a wonderful example of this concept in action. If you  have not seen it, I highly recommend you do. It's a trilogy and all three movies illustrate the points in this book.

 The Dis-Ease Exercise... As we as humans continue to move through this part of our journey, we'll continue to question more and more. We'll also begin deconstructing what things we've taken for granted. The more you are open, the more you will be able to process the magnificent information that is always just right there for the taking. It is very exciting! In the next paragraph I'm going to use the word "disease," but I will write it as "dis-ease." Why? Well, because the word is telling you something more. As we talked about earlier in the book, by slowing it down, or in this case, breaking it down, you have a new perspective of the word that may allow you to be more present with it. The intent is to place emphasis on the natural state of "ease" being imbalanced or disrupted. Now here comes the word... Notice how you read the word now. Again, gentle reminder not to judge, just notice and play with what you find.

One of the biggest *dis-eases* that plagues human beings today is a dastardly syndrome that almost never gets diagnosed. You may get it mainly from your parents and those closest to you, but you also could get much of it from society, as well. One of the biggest spreaders of this is our beloved Santa Claus! If you check with the Centers for Disease Control they don't even have it listed! How can this be when we have reached epidemic levels?

What I'm speaking of is the *Good Girl Syndrome* (for females) and the *Good Boy Syndrome* (for males). If there is ONE overriding program from your childhood that's messing with your life being happy, it's almost certainly this one! Let's dissect it so that you better understand how insidious this negative energetic pattern can be. Once you start really noticing, the *ahas!* will come more easily.

Remember, an *aha!* is simply the awareness that you suddenly connect with in the Right Now OS—which is why it feels so good! Cool, right? To get the hang of this just remember to be open and curious, as you were when you were very young. For most of us, that was the last time we were our *authentic selves* for longer than a song or a vacation.

Our society, as a whole, in order to keep its children "safe," bombards them with phrases that are designed to keep them from being hurt, or even dying. When you subscribe to the "keeping them safe" mentality as your number one goal, then you will also feel the need to control them. In order to *control* them, most parents, for thousands of years, have used one simple word, "NO." As I mentioned earlier, I average child hears "no" 400 times a day.

Another form of controlling parents have used is incessantly judging behavior that can be easily seen in phrases such as:

"Be a good girl and get me that pie pan."
"Little girls are sugar and spice and everything nice."
"You are such a good boy for helping with _____."
"You are a bad boy! Stop that!"
"Have you been a good boy today?"
"Be a good girl for your Vovo." *(grandmother in Portuguese)*

Again, if you read this section too quickly you might miss it, not because of your lack of intelligence, but rather because of how inundated we most often are with this kind of social conditioning from parents, relatives, books, stories, magazines, neighbors, TV shows, teachers, newspapers and coaches. So inundated that it seems "normal" to do, and so to question it, may take examining it a bit longer than you normally would. This inundation happens from the time we are born. You can hear moms lovingly talking to newborns saying things like, "What a good girl you are! Yes, you are! What a good girl!"

The intention is to nurture and it does to a certain extent, but the action can lead to a focus away from self and thereby train children to focus on other people's judgments. The main issue is that instead of correcting the action, people often focus on the worth of the child. For example, a parent may say, "You are careless!" instead of "What you did was careless."

This is a subtle shift, but it rubs up against the very powerful I AM statement, transforming the meaning completely. The damage of judging what is "good" or "bad" with children from an early age accumulates into people's psyches, wreaking havoc for much of their adult life by disempowering them with the feeling that they are not good enough. It's a classic case of a subtle focusing on something that makes a human feel powerless, rather than learning how to correct the behavior and moving on. Instead, they are taught that they *are* the behavior.

This misaligned I AM statement scenario is one of the openings in the underbelly of the Herd OS. This is a place from which a lot of adults are STUCK in their lives—all because they don't feel *Unconditional Love*. They have forgotten that they ARE LOVE and don't need it from others. Why? Because if they already automatically get it from source energy, the "place" their energy came from and will completely return to when it's done with this Earthly ride of a lifetime.

JOURNAL TIME... Take a deep breath. Wiggle your "toesies." Turn off your brain by focusing on your breath. Drop your shoulders. Take another deep breath. Now, without "thinking," read and write down 11 answers to finish the following statement,

"I AM _____"

(your answers here determine the direction of your life).

"I AM _____"

"I AM _____"

"I AM _____"

"I AM _____"

"I AM _____"

"I AM _____"

"I AM _____"

"I AM _____"

"I AM _____"

"I AM _____"

Maria Salomão-Schmidt

It is hard to fight and heal at the same time.
—Maria Salomão-Schmidt

Chapter 29. Why Leaving Your Tribe Can Feel Icky

Discovering Where We Are

When I was getting my MBA, I felt a strong pull towards Simmons College, the only all-women business school in the world at the time. The program was actually started by two women I greatly admire, Deans Anne Jardin and Margaret Hennig. These visionaries were the very first two women to graduate from the Harvard Business School. When they addressed our class, the Deans explained that we were entering an elite group of women on planet Earth. They explained that the number of women who are educated around the world is relatively very small, and the percentages of those who have bachelors' degrees are even smaller—and as far as those who have master's degrees... well, miniscule seemed too big of a word for how they described it. In doing a little research recently, I found out that according to the U.S. Census Bureau, only about 22% of the women twenty-five and older in the United States have undergraduate degrees, and only about 4% of the women in the US have masters degrees, obviously the number of women with MBAs is even smaller than that.

What the Simmons College deans said next at the time, was a shocking discovery. The deans warned us that our own families might butt heads with us and put us down simply because we were getting our master's level program. What Dean Hennig explained was that our families were basically our own individual tribe. The job of our tribe is to protect and care for each other under the rules of that herd. Societally speaking, because girls are raised to be "sugar and spice and everything nice" and to be—one of my least favorite terms in the world—"good girls," they traditionally were seen as those who needed to be taken care of.

Growing up, my younger brothers were given liberties I was not, such as having no curfew for prom, for example. The female child and her virginity is a matter of "honor" for many families. My getting pregnant, or even being seen as promiscuous, would have looked really "bad" for the family, and so my freedom was more limited because of that fear. I was familiar with the concept the Deans were talking about, but having an MBA was unmarked territory.

To some families, although they were proud on one level (as was mine), this "rise" into a higher, unknown realm of education and position might also activate that need for "protection." It's the ol' "don't get too big for your britches" philosophy, which is basically another way of keeping people at the same level as the others, so that the group stays intact. If the family saw it as *unsafe*, instead of helping out the female family member, her own family members might actually do the very opposite, all in the name of keeping her "safe."

The way Dean Jardin described a tribe was unlike any I had ever heard before. She said that a tribe is a group with thousands of rules ("shoulds") of how to behave. When you fall down they pick you up, but when you try to rise above them, they will break your legs to bring you back down. Sometimes they simply cut you off from the family. This also happens in work situations. An example is when you leave a job. Even if you left under wonderful circumstances, when you go back to visit something has changed. You are no longer a part of that group and you feel it. It feels uncomfortable somehow to be there.

Why Trust Your Instinct

You cannot *fake* energy. You cannot *force* it. You cannot *manipulate* it. The millisecond you bring ego into it, your connection lessens to your source. *You* are your source. The only way in is by being as authentic and present as you can be in that moment. No mask, just the rawest form of you. Energy has its own laws, and to work with and within it, there is a certain amount of surrender that must occur. It was in this surrendering that I realized that I felt the closest to my beloved daughter Sophia. I feel that she guides me in some way on my path.

There is a part of me that feels guilty about that, because I'm her mom and I'm "supposed" to take care of her. The more I give into these thoughts, the more I lose the connection to the energy; so I've learned to let go of the guilt so that I can swim in the Love and connection. I have a new and ever-changing relationship with Sophia. It keeps unfolding deeper and deeper. I trust her completely—and in this trust, I am able to surrender to what I am feeling in the "now."

She is my inspiration as are our living children Christopher, Mialotta, Olivia, Isabella and all the amazing foster children and exchange students we've had including Mariana, James D., Vanessa, Laura, Bea, Ali, James, Tehya. All of these master teachers have been instrumental in my learning to be me in this human world.

The Evolution of the Word "Manifest"

Living deeply focused on our everyday lives, it's very easy to forget the basics of who we really are. No one can tell you this. You must discover it for yourself. This lack of focus on who we really are is the basis for how we get "lost" in life. Regardless of how many bills you have, no matter how much drama, tragedy, joy, good luck or money you have—when it all boils down to it, all that "stuff" that we spend our time worrying about means nothing, compared to the basics of how energy *affects* our lives. Essentially we are not made of matter, as was once thought—but rather we are made of energy, which defines us as "energy beings."

In order to know how to operate in the world, it is incredibly important to remember that what we are made from are atoms traveling at high speeds. The speed at which the atoms are moving give us our vibrational level. The higher the vibrational level, the higher you go up the chakras—our *energy centers*. What is happening now, for the first time in the history of Planet Earth, is that a larger number of us than ever before are operating more and more from our energy side, our *authenticity*.

Because sometimes we think we know a word, but don't really understand it, I feel it's important to go over one of most popular words that we are hearing more often in the world. Now is a good time to explain the concept of "manifesting." When the book and movie "The Secret" came out, many more people were exposed to the world of energy. Overnight, the term "manifest" became a household word. Even though it's become a mainstream word, what does it really mean?

If you look up the word "manifest" in the Merriam-Webster Dictionary, it will give you the following definition:

> man·i·fest – (verb): to make *evident* or certain by showing or displaying

Some of the examples the Merriam-Webster Dictionary give are:

- Both sides have *manifested* a stubborn unwillingness to compromise.

- Their religious beliefs are *manifested* in every aspect of their lives.

These examples are based on the old version of the word. Clearly the evolution of the word has not reverberated to them. If I had to give a definition from an energetic point-of-view I would describe it as:

man·i·fest – (verb): to bring from formless to form

Some of the examples are:

1. Olivia manifested her very own family.

2. The power to manifest your heart's desire starts with your thoughts.

Manifesting is a word and an action that also is evolving as we are evolving. It's a great activating word for attracting what you want. Eventually, I realized that the word "magnetizing" is an even clearer way to express this *energy in action*. Manifesting has within it the embedded feeling of *efforting*. In other words, you *need to do* something to bring it to yourself. In the word *magnetizing*, you simply *attract* things you want, as long as you are in the same or similar vibration. Have you ever held two very strong magnets near each other? Once they get to a certain proximity, you can feel the pull. That's how it is for your energy too.

The Secret Movie Stars & Olympic Athletes Use to Reach their Dreams

Some of the highest paid people on our planet are those who entertain us. If you de-construct what the concept of "entertaining" means, it is something that focuses your attention because it engages you in a way that is interesting, funny, sad, meaningful, scary, exciting, deep, strange, etc. A good entertainer focuses your attention and keeps it there to a point where you might even momentarily forget who or where you are because you are so immersed in their acting, singing, dancing and playing. If we break down the actual word entertainment itself you get a very similar description of what we just deconstructed from it:

Enter- (come into, enter)   -Tain- (possess, hold)   -Ment (a state of being)

Maria Salomão-Schmidt

On one level it is entertainment, which can also be a form of escapism—but there's also a deeper level. The entertainers who really surrender to their craft, are the most magical to watch—especially *live*. I'm a big fan of going to the theater. Watching live plays and musicals is one of my very favorite things to do in the world! While in the audience, if you pay attention, you can "feel" the energy of both the actors, as well as the audience.

The two sides are like energetic waves playing with each other. Some of the greatest performances happen when the audience gives the actors a lot of energy and love in the form of great big smiles, loud repetitive clapping, standing up and perhaps even some yelling of words like "bravo" or sounds like some form of "WHOO-HOO!!!" I have taken an informal poll with many actors over the years. They shared with me that it completely raises their performance a few notches when the audience is really into the show.

I am a big believer that the audience has as much of a job of creating a magnificent performance, as do the actors. Most people still see it as one-sided and that simply is not how energy flows. Your actors will burn out much more quickly that way, if they are responsible for holding the energetic space for performances. It's a much healthier, more vibrant *win-win* situation, when you realize that you are part of the equation. Your energy matters. If you need proof, just ask someone who works in front of an audience if the electricity of a crowd affects his/her performance.

BEING "NEUTRAL" IS NOT POSSIBLE: This brings up the fact that many people believe they can be "neutral." If they see something in life that they don't really like, they can just say, "If I don't get involved, then it has nothing to do with me. I'm neutral." There is *no* neutral. When enough people take on this perception, this is a recipe for some of the biggest horrors our planet has ever seen, such as the Holocaust, or the complacency as millions of children were raped and abused by the Catholic Church. I know that some reading this will cringe. As a former Catholic, I also cringe. The conditioning is so strong, from the time I was born really, that to say something that is "against the church" is incredibly uncomfortable or "forbidden." It's also necessary to *feel* that *uncomfortableness* and speak out regardless of what others may say, to initiate and continue humanity's shift in the direction of Love and light.

What Can You Imagine?

Imagination matters. The brain and body have no ability to know whether you made something up, or whether it really happened. This is where visualization comes in. How you use your energy is through your imagination and focus. These two factors are *critical* to your energy body. Many celebrity "A-Listers" have learned to use their imagination intentionally to guide their lives including Oprah, Will Smith, Bill Gates, Tiger Woods and Arnold Schwarzenegger.

Olympic and other professional athletes use visualization as their main tool for training. There's a wonderful video on YouTube with actor, Jim Carrey, who tells a fascinating story of how he wrote out a check to himself for $10 million. He carried it in his wallet and visualized getting it every day. Five years later he got his role in the movie *Dumb and Dumber*. His payment was that exact same amount he visualized: $10,000,000.

Many people also use *vision boards*, which is any size paper, usually a poster board, that has cut out photos from magazines of your goals or things you want in your life. I used a vision board to get me on as a guest of *The Oprah Show;* it worked so well, that I even met Rosie O'Donnell without meaning to but she happened to be in three pictures on my vision board. Vision boards are powerful tools for keeping your imagination focused on what you desire. It is pretty powerful stuff!

Everyone has the perfect gift to give the world
—and if each of us is freed up
to give the gift that is uniquely ours to give,
the world will live in total harmony.
—Buckminster Fuller

PIONEERS OF THE AGE OF ENERGY

Over the years, as we evolve into realizing that we are energy, more and more people have been called to write about energy work. *Energy work* is simply *how* to use your energy. Seems like one would know this, but because many of us have not seen our energy body as something important and real, then it was deemed unnecessary to pay attention to it. In other words, if it were not focused on or acknowledged, then no one could even address it because we were not even really sure how to deal with it. The authors who write about energy have provided invaluable information to help us learn about how our energy field operates and how we can best use it.

Anodea Judith

What she teaches us: How your energy body works.

I could not publish this book without mentioning the incredible work of author Anodea Judith. Reading her books was part of my coursework at the three-year program that I took at the Rhys Thomas Institute of Energy Medicine. Anodea's books are one of the best ways to learn about your energy body.

In her book, *Eastern Body, Western Mind*, Anodea informs the reader on the two directions that energy flows in your body. When it flows from the top of your head to the bottom of your feet you have a "current of manifestation." This is incredibly important to know because it is ultimately how things are created in your life. They enter as ideas (from the top of your body), and then channel downwards into a more solid form, where humans can more readily see and experience life (in the lower part of your body). The energy current from top to bottom is when you get a lot of ideas and as you *pull* them down, you start seeing them show up in your life. The more the energy flows into the lower chakras, the more your five senses begin to notice it. When you meditate you begin to notice the idea at the higher chakra levels, while still grounding yourself.

The other way your energy body's current runs is from the bottom of your feet to the top of your head. When it runs in this direction, you have the "current of liberation." Things that flow in the ascending direction are when one takes the practical, everyday stuff one is doing and plugs into inspiration. This is where *ahas!* come from. Thank you beautiful Anodea Judith for all the amazing material you teach the world!

Wayne Dyer

What he teaches us: Connect with the wisdom of those who have lived extra-ordinary lives.

As I mentioned earlier, Dr. Wayne Dyer has been one of my biggest mentors. He taught me that the word "inspiration" is translated as "being in spirit,"—or doing things from your energy body, which he called the *soul*. That is a wonderful place to experience things from, because this is your point of authenticity. Time and time again, his work on this planet has invited us to dig deeper into what matters most. He once picked me out of a crowd of thousands in Atlanta, GA and gave me a CD. He and I have lots of serendipity including the St. Francis of Assisi and Lourdes connections.

I'm not alone, many people feel the same way about Wayne Dyer—that he was incredibly approachable and easy to connect with. His focus was on being as fully present in each moment as he knew how to be. Although he died suddenly in 2015, I still feel he is teaching and connecting to those who want to keep learning and expanding during their Earth School experience.

Jane Goodall

What she teaches us: Connect with nature.

Jane Goodall is one of those whom I call "glow in the dark people." Her light is so beautiful and authentic. I have had the pleasure of working with her on two different occasions and both times it was as if she had "the peace of the forest" within her. Being around her raises people's vibration. Jane Goodall attributes this to the decades she spent living in nature, simply being.

Jane Goodall helps bring attention to how we are treating the planet. Her love and respect of chimpanzees has created a huge awareness of nature. She is a beautiful siren calling us back to connect with nature through her amazing organizations like Roots & Shoots and The Jane Goodall Institute. You can get more information at www.janegoodall.org.

Paulo Coelho

What he teaches us: Stories are wise teachers.

The beautiful Paulo Coelho is a warrior of the heart. Through his pen, he channels the timeless philosophies needed by humans right now.

He takes this wisdom and puts them into the most amazing stories. These are stories that realign us when we read them. They are power love packets that are unleashed into the world every time you read them. My favorite is the classic The Alchemist. I recommend it to clients all the time.

Julia Cameron

What she teaches us: When we unleash the art within us, the art unleashes us.

Before Julia Cameron dared to write her amazing book, most of us thought art was just for artists. Her series of books includes one of my favorite books of all time, THE ARTIST's WAY. For decades her work has helped people shift back into their natural state of being full of themselves. The way Julia Cameron presents the materials helps the reader see both the light and the dark inside ourselves.

Oprah Winfrey

What she teaches us: Always feed your curiosity.

Oprah Winfrey is one of my very favorite people of all time! She is a whirling dervish of sorts, weaving Love (freedom and flow) everywhere she goes. If you have every heard the expression, "the tide raises all ships," well Oprah Gail Winfrey is the tide!

I call her the godmother of this planet because the ripple of Love that she has been creating for decades is palpable. She has masterfully used television, print, workshops and radio to spread the message of authenticity. Oprah Winfrey is the perfect example of what happens when someone decides to live as completely full of themselves as they know how to be in each moment.

The beloved Oprah Winfrey is a true visionary teacher at heart and her lessons have helped many of us who have watched her shows, first as a newscaster/morning talk show host, then as the host of The Oprah Winfrey Show, then her own channel and, finally, her own network. She has the gift of finding those who are leading our planet in their area of knowledge and she introduces us to them. If you have not watched episodes of *Super Soul Sunday* and *Oprah's Master Class* you are missing out on some of the most amazing wisdom on this planet!

Energetically, through her programs, she has continuously created a space where emerging taboo subjects can be addressed. Oprah Winfrey has always had the courage to speak about the things that others are suffering about in silence. She has explored different ways of being in the world that fit the way she wants to live. Her intentions are strong. The magnificent work she has done with her school in Africa shows the rest of how much of a difference one person can make. Oprah Winfrey's work has deeply affected the fabric of our society. The world is a much brighter place because the spark we call Oprah was born!

Esther Hicks & Abraham

What they teach us: There are non-meat (non-physical) teachers too.

Esther Hicks is a normal woman with an extraordinary talent. She channels a group of sparks called Abraham. If you get a chance pull up a Youtube video on them. I could listen to them for hours. The information shared by Abraham is incredibly freeing and insightful. I have listened to them for years. They have definitely been a strong influence in how I see the world and how I have learned what is possible.

Even though this concept of someone channeling energy that speaks through her is strange to some, Abraham is growing in popularity now more than ever. The information being given is about how we are using our energy on the planet and how we can shift how we use it. One of his biggest lessons is to flow downstream. Let the flow take you. Efforting is no good to anyone! Finally, Abraham and Esther teach with a lot of insight, but they also use humor as a tool to connect and teach us about how our energy systems flow.

 JOURNAL TIME... Ask yourself: "What do I tend to focus on? What energetic benefits do I get from repeating this energy pattern? Does it help me live more or less authentically? Who in my life is dependent on me not shifting?" Who inspires me?

You are already using it every day, every minute in fact. It is your natural power of imagination, the basic creative energy of the universe, which you use constantly, whether or not you are aware of it.

—Shakti Gawain

Maria Salomão-Schmidt

I used to think freedom meant doing whatever you want.
It means knowing who you are,
what you are supposed to be doing on this earth,
and then simply doing it.
—Natalie Goldberg

Chapter 30. Dissecting The Herd World

Just Do What You Are Told And Everything Will Be Fine

The way the Herd OS works basically, is that if you followed the rules, you are rewarded with social acceptance, food, water, shelter, protection, love (sometimes) and ultimately, safety. If you did not follow the rules, you were ostracised or cast out. Unfortunately, the Herd OS drives how people treat each other. You can see it in anyone who uses fear-mongering to get what they want. People put common sense aside and act based on the popular social opinion or culture of those around them. The incredible work of husband-and-wife-team Nicholas Kristof and Sheryl WuDunn who wrote *Half The Sky: Turning Oppression Into Opportunity For Women Worldwide* gives an incredible perspective of what many of us in the Western world find inconceivable. It's a very powerful book that I highly recommend that you pick up and read. It will give you a wonderful perspective on your life.

Over the last three generations, we have been emerging from the grips of the Herd OS, and back into our core operating system, the Right Now OS. The Right Now OS is about letting go of all your programming of what others told you to do, and start listening to your *own* internal guidance system—your *own* internal innate GPS. You can do this when you want. There is no should or have to—only succulent adventure when you are finally ready to *stop* efforting and start *playing* with how good it feels to be the real you. A wonderful example is Caitlyn Jenner, formerly Bruce Jenner, who finally gave herself permission to simply be *authentic*. It is truly a beautiful thing to behold.

To live authentically, just being yourself, all may sound easy, but it's a wee bit challenging at times because of how ingrained the domestication process is within us all. To better help you see what I mean, take a long look at the list of words that are associated with the Herd OS:

Words & Actions Associated with Herd Operating System

- Should
- Conditional Love
- Have to
- Right/Wrong
- Try
- Memorize
- Good Job
- Others' Opinions Matter
- Closed
- Fear-Based Living
- Very Attached to Things
- Very Sedentary Lifestyle
- Forces Things
- Controlling
- Numbing Life (through alcohol, TV, drugs, shopping, affairs)
- Perfection
- Need to
- Always Busy
- Good/Bad
- Stress
- Security
- Doctors Heal
- Mindless
- Judgmental
- Perfection
- Live to Work
- Lives Mostly Inside
- Drives Everywhere
- Passive Aggressive
- Feeling Stuck
- Someone Wins/Someone Loses
- Lack of Sleep
- Never-Ending "To Do List"
- Labels
- Fight-Flight-Freeze
- Need Middleman to Get to God
- Imagination Not Real & Not Important
- Time Passes Quickly
- Value Based on What You Do
- Living in the Future and/or Past
- Eats Quickly and Mindlessly
- Chases
- Lack of Trust
- Depression

Maria Salomão-Schmidt

Don't ask what the world needs.
Ask what makes you come alive, and go do it.
Because what the world needs is
people who have come alive.

—Howard Thurman

Four Main Differences Between the Herd and Right Now OS

1. Happiness can only be experienced when you are in the Right Now OS.

It may be shocking to realize that you cannot *feel* HAPPINESS in the Herd OS. It simply does not exist in that operating system, because the energy in that OS runs completely differently. Happiness is feedback that you are connected to your source, that you are in your zone. I call that operating in your Right Now OS. Think about that for a second. Most of the planet is being domesticated into living in the Herd OS and so they are being groomed for unhappiness. This answers the profoundly painful question the Beatles ask in *Eleanor Rigby*, "All the lonely people, where do they all come from?"

2. To live in the Herd OS is to struggle constantly.

The Herd OS is unnatural, and must be learned. It takes a lot of effort to learn, maintain and run, but that is part of what keeps human beings stuck because all their attention is in keeping up this facade, what some call the "mask," or the inauthentic self. The Right Now OS is innate and effortless. You don't have to "do" anything because it simply is who you "are."

3. The Herd OS is about holding on tight, efforting, pressure, shoulds, judging, rules.

Imagine herds following each other off a cliff because they are just following the ones in front of them. In a fear-based world, there is mistrust and lashing out before being attacked. There is a formula and you must always follow it if you want to be "safe" and "good." To not follow the rules is to be "bad." The Right Now OS, on the other hand, is about letting go, surrendering, being open and even vulnerable. There are no main formulas that someone else set up to follow. It's simply about connecting to your intuition and following your instinct. Being *present* gives you your next GPS reading. There is a trust and flow that effortlessly guides you from an innate, deeply connected space and place.

This is the same energy that you followed when you were growing in utero. When you were inside your birth mother's womb, there was a certain level of trust and surrender that happened because you had not yet been domesticated. This is also the same energy that guides grass to grow. It's that divine intelligence that is called by many names... Universe, Cosmos, Goddess, God or Allah... is the natural energy flow that guides everything on this Earth. It cannot abandon you because it is you. You are energy. When you don't block your innate flow, you live in your natural state of the Right Now OS.

4. The Right Now holds the power of the present moment.

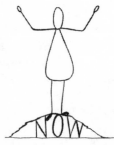

Each Human OS works best in different tenses. The focus of the Herd OS is on the future or past, where one has very limited power. The focus of the Right Now OS is to be in the present moment, which is the only way you can access the information from your spiritual DNA. This is the only place where shifts happen that align to your authenticity.

JOURNAL TIME... Take another look at the word chart in this chapter. Read over the words slowly. What words from the Herd OS have you used frequently without even realizing they set your energetic vibration? How does that feel now? What are you learning about yourself?

It's better to light a candle,
than to curse the darkness.

—T.S. Elliot

Things I Want To Remember/Research/Review:

Our society sends us a lot of messages that imply
we're supposed to be ashamed when we fall short.
But I think we should be throwing each other failure parties!
—Reshma Saujani

Chapter 31. Why Is Shame So Widespread?

Helpful Hint: *Shame* is one of those toxic vibrations that can be incredibly painful so now would be a really good time for you to go back to review the Helpers in Chapter 3. Those who have *shame*, which is most of us at some point of our lives, have spent huge amounts of energy holding on to it. People mistakenly have thought that the pain was coming from outside themselves but it is their holding on to the judgment and *mind movie* *(playing the event over and over again and flooding their body with all those icky feelings)* of the event that's the pain source. Whether yours or someone else's, in reading this chapter you're calling forth the transformation of pain in your life. Please make sure you drink lots of water (Helper #2) and take deep breaths (Helper #4). Doing these in your meat body will help you process things in your energy body.

Shame can only be found in the Herd OS, because it's a vibration that only exists on lower, heavier and darker energy levels, those that are out of alignment. *Shame* cannot exist in the Right Now OS, just as an ice cube cannot exist on the sun. *Shame* exists as one of the more toxic feelings for anyone to energetically hold.

For the sake of your freedom, it's important to note that no one can give you *shame without* your permission. Let that knowledge sink in because one of the biggest lies that unconsciously spends your energy is that people take things from you. That belief puts the power (and the solution) out of your reach. That belief sets up the energy pattern of being a victim.

I define being a victim as someone who believes their energy, or power, is out of their control. YOU ARE THE ENERGY, not the meat body you are wearing. What the Herd OS has you believing as part of human domestication is that you're a meat body with and an occasional energetic experience. It's easy to control and dominate physical matter like a body. It's impossible to control the energy of another. If you feel  ashamed you're getting feedback. You effort to hold on to shame for yourself in order to have it be part of your energetic make-up, because it is not part of your flow. Once you hold onto it, *shame* is incredibly powerful. It can feel so utterly draining to such a degree, that in some scenarios some completely lose their will to live.

The other feeling that's similarly crippling is *heartache*. To help you understand what I mean, I would like to do an exercise with you. Where your focus goes your energy flows, so I want to make sure that you're grounded and full of yourself before you accidentally take in *icky* energy that does not belong to you.

 Simple Grounding and Protection Exercise... First, take a deep breath. Slowly imagine roots coming from your feet going down into the earth and wrapping around the center. This simple visualization helps ground your energy, like people do with car batteries, for example. They are not the only things that need grounding. We do too! Grounding, as you will recall, is also one of the Helpers from Chapter 3. One of the best ways to do it is through this simple visualization. Next, image a great, big beautiful ball of light surrounding you. Again, you're calling upon your imagination to help you. This ball of energy has a permeable surface that allows you to control what comes into your energy field. In life you'll find that if you feel grounded and whole (full of yourself), you'll live a much freer, lighter, richer, deeper, happier life!

This is the most challenging exercise so far. Remember to notice. Focus on the gift instead of the curse of this painful situation. So there is movement through the experience instead of staying stuck in it. Remember that you are whole and safe as long as you stay *full* of yourself. Once you have done your grounding and protection exercise, activate your imagination. Imagine a young girl who has been molested by someone who was supposed to take care of her. She feels confused, sad and in deep pain. As she tries to "make sense" of the situation, she might feel *guilty* that her body reacted in ways that are even more confusing. The tsunami of confusion grows. Most likely the perpetrator has tried to cover his tracks with added *guilt* and *shame* tactics that will isolate the young girl. She most likely will enter into a deep *shame* spiral, believing that she is *bad*, that she must have attracted this on some level because of who/what she is. Check in with yourself to see if you still feel whole. Check-in and see this as an icky occurrence that you can move through so the experience gives you valuable info in the form of contrast. Many who stay stuck think they put it behind them because they buried it. That only makes it fester and hurt more. Being able to confront the situation, while realizing you are absolutely whole allows you to move through it. I take a deep breath here as this can be heavy stuff, but I use this specific example because sexual abuse is at epidemic levels! It is a waste of human energy to have so much of our collective energy on this destructive pattern.

The Three Blame Targets

In the Herd OS, *shame* is often a by-product of *trauma*. *Trauma*, from your energy body's perspective, is a sudden stop to the flow and abrupt drop of your energy. It is vital feedback but living in the Herd OS we have learned to ignore the feedback. Instead we point fingers to try to explain why so we can "make sense" out of what happened. Why do we need it to make sense? Human beings have been living a very limited existence. In the Herd OS everything unnaturally gets processed through the body. The body's main center is the brain. The brain can only function on limited information based on the five senses. I love using my brain! I'm NOT saying the brain is "bad." The brain just works best when it flows from the natural flow of your authenticity. For the human system to function optimally the brain gets to serve the heart, not the other way around. Both are happier that way. It is unnatural for the brain to lead. We are energy beings and our natural center is our heart. To feel means to get feedback. To not feel means to be flying blind. The more you realize this, the more you see why you and those around you have suffered so much.

Note: I get the sense that many people will have a hard time with this but let it sink in because for many they think of their brain as the captain of the ship. You might not know what to do with this new information. That is totally cool. Keep exploring. Keep leaning into it. Keep asking questions. Remember that you are designing your life and you can make it look any way you want. This is just information that you can use or discard, as you wish. Just be ok with playing with the information.

Maria Salomão-Schmidt

Since the ultimate goal in the Herd OS is "safety," whenever something icky happens, the result is *blame*. *Blame* unattended turns into *shame*. There are three main directions people tend to blame.

Blame 1. Another Person

The first and most common way to place blame is *towards another person*. Once the targeted person who allegedly caused said event is chosen, then the *blame* becomes a "curse" bestowed upon that person. If that person is operating under the Herd OS, they accept the *blame* and turn it into *shame*. They are then designated as being "bad," which becomes one of their "labels" in life. The label is "convenient" because it allows that person to go right back to that icky feeling whenever someone brings it up. To those experiencing blame, shifting from this perception feels impossible because how they see the world is often from this viewpoint. On the rare occasion that someone does shift out of their label, words like *rehabilitated* are used to describe the shift. This does not happen very often. Think about it. *Rehabilitated* is not a concept that many people trust because it can seem that most people don't or can't be.

Blame 2. Yourself

The second is towards yourself, which shows up in self-destructive behaviors, especially addictions. This is one step closer to living in the Right Now OS because you have brought the power back to yourself. When it is outside yourself, you feel completely powerless because you continue to give your power to others. The natural human energy flow is always wholeness (full of yourself); but because most of us operate out of the Herd OS, we give our power away and spend the rest of our time searching, looking and begging for it back.

We have forgotten that we spend most of our energy every minute of every day subconsciously giving it away. When I coach people, they are shocked at how easy the solution is, but there it is. You have been waiting for yourself your whole life and there you have always been. How wonderfully refreshing is that? Again feel free to play with this information. If you find yourself going through a major energetic furball, rejoice! It's awesome that you are starting to pay attention to your flow again! Learning that is what takes a bit of focus, and re-focus.

Blame 3. God (or some higher power)

The third possible *blame* target is God. This last one is usually hidden because many are afraid to get angry at God. The way it often comes out in this last level is through *anger* and *rage*. One of the best examples of this, is in the movie Forrest Gump when the captain who lost both his legs in Vietnam, climbs up the mast of the ship and screams at God. It is only after he does this that he can clear his massive *shame energy leak* and have enough energy to move out of depression and into living again. If you find yourself in this category, be ok with exploring where this trapped energy hides and release it. Beware of activating programming that judges any part of the process. It does not allow you to be full of yourself, but rather makes you bleed your precious energy.

Maria Salomão-Schmidt

SHAME's CLOSEST COUSIN

Enter *guilt*. It is amazing how much human energy is spent on *guilt*. *Shame* and *guilt* are so very close in energetic vibration that it's hard to

tell them apart. *Shame* tends to have one level. Once you enter into the *shame* arena, it's pretty much a one-size-fits-all model, but for *guilt* there are many levels, from mild to extreme.

How people deal with *guilt* fluctuates depending on their tolerance for the reward. *Guilt* is usually over an act of something where there was a choice, but the "wrong" choice was made. For example, whether or not to eat that second slice of cake, or to sleep with someone else's mate.

Guilt can destroy you. Those who go to war are a perfect example. Soldiers have seen and done things they deeply regret, like killing children. When they come home to their own children, they serve as reminders. I once saw a documentary of a soldier who shot and killed an innocent child whom he mistakenly thought was throwing a grenade at him.

When he came home, his excited son asked him to play catch, something they had both dreamed and talked about for a long time. As his son threw him the ball, the painful image of the boy he killed suddenly flashed in his mind's eye. The father freaked out. His son most likely translated the event as, "My daddy doesn't want to spend time with me. He does not love me. I am unlovable." How long do you think that little boy will carry that? To whom will he spread that anger and sadness? Guilt is a virus that reproduces.

It seems like many people are going through life almost completely ignoring how much of a toll shame, blame and guilt are taking from our life's joy! Does that half matter? Take a look around. Many of us are like cavemen playing with fire but not understanding how it works, meanwhile scorching the planet with their ignorance of such a simple and useful necessity. By looking at these pain points and breaking down our assumptions, we create an amazing opportunity to call our energy back and connect to our spiritual DNA. Imagine how much sweeter life is when you are full of yourself!

JOURNAL TIME... Where have you felt shame, blame and guilt in your life? Do you feel you still carry some? What will it take to get you to release it? What benefits have you gotten from it? What benefits have you lost from it? What would life look like if you released all these pain points for yourself? Have you used shame, blame and guilt on others? What would life look like if you released all these pain points for others? How would it affect how you see the world?

You can't live a perfect day without doing something
for someone who will never be able to repay you.

—John Wooden

Things I Want To Remember/Research/Review:

Maria Salomão-Schmidt

Do not stop thinking of life as an adventure.
You have no security unless you can live
bravely, excitingly, imaginatively;
unless you can choose a challenge
instead of competence.
—Eleanor Roosevelt

Chapter 32. The Power Of Contrast

One of the most powerful tools we have on planet earth is "contrast." I first heard about this concept while listening to Abraham Hicks. Since then, I've been testing it out with clients, and it's an incredibly powerful tool. If it were not for contrast, you could not truly experience alignment, or what also can be called "living in your zone." You must have the experienced *cold* to feel *warm*. One of the gifts of having had a very chaotic, varied and intense childhood is that I "get" that amazing life experience—that *contrast*, which when I fully appreciate it, awakens me to a life of bliss and gratitude. Here's a fun analogy many of us can relate to.

The Flip Flop Analogy

Many more people wear flip flops than ever before, so this is a wonderful analogy that I use with my coaching clients. My four daughters actually call flip flops "flippies." In homage to them that is what I will call them here too in honor of what my girls have taught me. It's an honor to be their *māmā*.

Let's say you love wearing your *flippies* and wear them every day. You have a certain level of appreciation for having them... at first. As time goes on, you start taking them for granted. You just assume they'll be there and don't appreciate them in your life. They become your "normal." We do that with a lot of things in our life, don't we? Our focus has shifted from noticing and connecting to that item (or person) to ignoring it (him or her). When this happens, we start taking things for granted. When we take things for granted, we begin looking for more stuff to fulfill us and the same cycle begins once again, but now with more clutter coming out the other end. Anyone else experience this, or see the people around you doing it? It's never enough when you don't have the three main ingredients here that create happiness in our lives. Want to know what they are? (cue music—in your own head)

THE "FLIPPIE" EQUATION
SLOWING DOWN (S) + NOTICING (N) + GRATITUDING (G)
= LOVE/ALIGNEMENT (L)

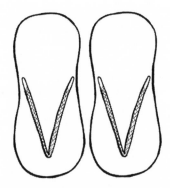

$$S + N + G = L$$

It almost looks like "snuggle" doesn't it? Well, this simple and fun equation will give you more to *snuggle* in your life, that's for sure!

We were built for LOVE (freedom and flow), and when we are in our energy body—in alignment connected to our spiritual DNA—we are fully living/shining out from LOVE. Love is our core. We are Love. We are that spark. There's nothing we need to do or say or be. You may not have viewed these things as tools, but that is exactly what they are. They are tools for aligning with your internal GPS. We already have everything we need. There is nothing to learn, get or acquire. If

Maria Salomão-Schmidt

anything, it's more about letting go of all the domestication, which is really us blocking ourselves, and embracing our natural state of Love (freedom and flow).

Go be that starving artist you're afraid to be.
Open up that journal and get poetic finally.
Volunteer. Suck it up and travel.
You were not born here to work and pay taxes.
You were put here to be part of a vast organism
to explore and create. Stop putting it off.
The world has much more to offer than what's on
15 televisions at TGI Fridays. Take pictures.
Scare people. Shake up the scene.
Be the change you want to see in the world."

—Jason Mraz

Society often teaches us that more, bigger and faster is the best! Speed can be intoxicating. By going fast, we lose something too. Many people have developed a habit of rushing through life, always "busy," running from one appointment to another. Living life at 100 miles an hour, they are stressed most of the time. The feedback they get is in the form of irritability, memory loss, weight gain, advanced aging, food cravings, insomnia (to name a few).

It's incredibly important to slow down. Part of the slowing down is about grounding and connecting to the present moment. From this point of being centered, you'll begin to notice things around you, things that were invisible to you when you were going fast. Although those living in the Herd OS think slowing down is boring, the feedback you get by slowing down is pretty spectacular. Initially, it may feel a bit weird or off, but the more you slow down, the more you will feel like the *effortless flow* that is you. It's just like riding a bike. At first it seems impossible and scary, but once you get the hang of it, you don't even think about it. You just go! It's the same thing with the *noticing*, which is really just listening to the energetic information coming in from your internal GPS. It's always on, always gently guiding. All we need to do is learn to connect to it. This is one of the main reasons you're being drawn to this book. Your intuition is calling you.

The amazing Brazilian author Paulo Coelho, said in an interview with the "Godmother" of this planet, Oprah Winfrey, that we only learn by making mistakes. He says that no one can teach us unless we learn it ourselves. That is absolutely true. You do need to learn it yourself; however, a teacher can help give you missing parts of the puzzle, so you can make sense of how life flows. The intention of this book is to be your teacher so your journey can be even sweeter.

 EXERCISE... Time to again activate your imagination...on purpose. As we do this fun exercise, I ask that you remember how very important the tools you read about in this chapter are.

Now think about wearing heels or shoes that look good, but don't feel good, and that you "have to" wear them for business or a special occasion. Imagine that you have been wearing them for 8 hours straight and that your feet are incredibly sore. Can you feel it?

OK, now imagine getting home and taking off your shoes. AHHHHHHHHHHH! Wiggle your toesies for a few seconds to let them stretch and "breathe." Roll your ankles. Massage your feet. Feel free to take a deep breath here (never a bad idea, no matter what you are doing).

Now slip on those flippies. AHHHHHH! How does that feel? How much do you appreciate the flippies now? THAT IS THE POWER OF CONTRAST! Contrast brings us back to the present moment and helps us appreciate what we have been neglecting. Contrast is happening all the time but we miss this precious gift when we *notice* that it's not even happening. Begin taking NOTICE BREAKS in your life. Stop wherever you are and NOTICE THE CONTRASTS going on around you and in your own life.

My definition of love is freedom and flow.
—Maria Salomão-Schmidt

Feelings are the muscles of intuition!
—Maria Salomão-Schmidt

Chapter 33. Why Are Feelings So Important?

Feelings are one of the of the world's most precious natural resources. They are a vital part of your energy body. Why? Because, as I share in my coaching, *"Feelings are the muscles of intuition!"* Whenever you allow yourself to "feel," you are opening up to that way of receiving a "communication" of sorts from your spiritual DNA. The more you do that, the more you are strengthening your intuition.

Your intuition is your life's GPS. It's what some call the "sixth sense," "a hunch" or "mother's intuition." When people are labeled "psychic," this is what they mean. This is also why you might have heard that *everyone* is psychic, which is true. Some people have this ability to notice energy right from birth, but everyone can develop their awareness of the world of energy because we are energy.

It's incredibly important right now in the history of our planet for us to demystify, and better define what being "psychic" is. People who were born noticing their energy were often considered weird or even dangerous. Some of them were labeled as connected to the devil because being psychic was seen by many as "against god." Many were put in mental institutions or disowned. Some were even killed. Most buried their talents for fear of being castigated. As we are evolving we are starting to realize that feelings are a vital part of this earth ride. Take the following analogy as an example.

Ticket To Ride

What if you were going into outer space on a spaceship. You could communicate with Earth to get advice and directions when needed so you can complete your mission. Now, what if a group, we will call them *the bullies*, takes over the spaceship by spreading fear and rumors that connecting to the Earth is dangerous. The rest of the people, the *I-Don't-Knows* (IDNs), in the spaceship don't know who to believe. In their confusion, they do nothing. By doing nothing, the bullies acquire more and more power. The IDNs lose more and more connection to the Earth and begin to depend more and more on what the bullies dictate. Eventually, the bullies completely take over and control everyone by the messages that get distributed and by rationing air, food and water.

Although the bullies cannot destroy the Earth connection because it's linked to the life support systems, they declare that it is "bad" to connect with Earth. They label those who try as "weak." The people who can figure out how to connect to earth, we'll call them the *Connectors*, are imprisoned or killed. This lasts generations. The IDNs live a lulled life where they mostly believe what they are told. If anyone is found communicating with Earth, they are reported and ostracized.

Some *Connectors* still do it in private but, in general, most of the communication with Earth stops. Because of the lack of connection with Earth, there is no feedback or wisdom being passed. As supplies run out, things get worse and worse. The IDNs begin looking for a solution, but the bullies won't give up their control. People become so desperate that, even though they're afraid of breaking the rules, they begin looking for ways to connect with Earth for help and resources. They change from IDNs back to Connectors. As more and more people do this, those few who were in control can no longer stay in that hierarchy. That archaic system that the bullies created is no longer sustainable and begins to crumble and eventually the natural connection back to the Earth is established.

This is a parable for where we now find ourselves right here on Earth. We're at a critical point in human history. The stakes are very high. Will we keep leading our current lives that are just uncomfortable enough to tolerate, or will we rise and use this occasion to become the most amazing version of ourselves that we can be?

You are feeling uncomfortable for a reason. The more you bury it, the bigger the *ickies* will grow. What is happening right now is a gift, but it feels like a curse. Which one will win depends on how you play out your life. Are you choosing to stay small, as someone else's version of you, or are you choosing to *live* authentically, exploring what is possible and what is calling you? It may be a faint call, but so very *important* to listen to. The more you notice, the more you can hear it. It's your spiritual DNA revealing itself to you. The time is NOW. You may start by learning the lessons in this book and applying them in your life. Share them with your friends. Journal. Meditate. Feel your life shifting back into your unique authenticity because it's why you were born!

Want To But Feeling Stuck?

This one's a *biggie*! You may want to shift back into your alignment, but you don't know which way to "go." After thousands of years of human beings doing things the same way over and over again, finally things are starting to shift dramatically... How we talk to each other, dress, how we work, what our roles look like, what we are allowed to do.

Do you realize that even though Louis XIV was one of the richest men of his time with palaces, land, servants, riches, power and authority... he was not as "rich" as you and I, in the sense that we have access to an incredibly large selection and freedom of what we can do, access, eat, travel, own, live, experience, buy, etc. Louis XIV, as powerful and wealthy as he was, could not have his servants go to the local shop and get whatever he desired from anywhere in the world like we can. Louis The Great, as he was called, could not travel as far, fast or as comfortably as we can. He could never even have imagined the amazing access to airplanes, helicopters, scooters, boats, etc. we now have. Although he had one of the biggest book collections in the world, it was nowhere near what we can access today from our hand-held portable devices. Louis XIV had the brightest minds of his time to advise and entertain him, but again, that pales in comparison to the almost instantly access in oral, written and video formats we have. Even as non-royalty, we can connect to a world that he could not even dream of. That is simply amazing!

Feelings Versus Control

When it comes to burying your feelings, Comedian Billy Crystal said it best back in his days on Saturday Night Live. "You know, my father used to say to me, 'Nando, don't be a schnook. It's not how you feel, it's how you look!' He was *mahvelous!* But you, dahling, hmmmm, you look mahvelous! Absolutely *mahvelous!...* It's better to look good than to feel good." Nando helps us see how we have been taught to discount and block feelings. It was supposed to be a funny skit but within it is much wisdom.

I am a big believer in using humor to shift back into our alignment. When something is truly funny you release part of yourself to the joke. Laughter is a form of surrender. It is absolutely wonderful for your energy body! The iconic Billy Crystal gives us a huge gift in noticing how we have been taught to devalue our feelings. For those willing to activate your curiosity, it might make you wonder if everyone has feelings, why would people hide them? Let's explore that.

For much of human history, indeed for basic survival, our ancestors learned that how things *looked* to others was more important than how they felt. The main reason was that if you were different it might affect your survival. People who were different were often seen as a liability. I learned an expression when I lived in Japan that explains it perfectly, "The nail that stands out gets hammered in." For many cultures, the result is that people buried their feelings, thus greatly reducing their energy body's intuition flow. In order to compensate for the lost energy, people operating in the Herd OS started running their energy from the outside in. They got energetically fed by how others thought about them, so other people's opinions mattered. This became the norm. Exposing one's true feelings became dangerous. Having different ideas or thoughts could even get you and your entire family killed.

The world is often seen as a very dangerous place because of one basic fact... Every living thing on this planet, including the planet, will eventually die. The fear of dying is what many humans have been attempting to deal with. One way people have tried to stay "safe" as long as possible, and prevent death and suffering, has been by doing their best to *control* things.

Humans have become masters at controlling most of their world including food, housing, nutrition and environment. We are hitting a fine line where we are genetically altering our food and other beings, including human beings. This is a form of control that could very easily come back to bite us in the butt, especially if those in charge are operating out of the Herd OS and putting money above all else.

What We Control

It's important to break down what it means to "control" one's feelings. Both our meat and energy bodies have a natural flow of systems to help maintain and run them. What the people, who want to control their feelings are doing, is essentially wanting to stop the actual physical sensations/reactions from happening and just be able to "think" the feelings. "Thinking" your feelings is *not* possible and wasted because it's not connected to your source. *Thinking* your feelings is only connected to your brain, which is not directly connected to *source energy*. The energy contained in a feeling does not translate to the brain, only to the heart.

What goes through the brain can be filtered, processed and manipulated. Energy does not work that way. It cannot be created or destroyed, only shift form. Because feelings cannot be controlled, what ends up happening is that people get cut off from their feelings. They get cut off from their heart and connected to more fear. If you want a stereotypical visual think of the dads who were all about the rules and had no empathy. Those were the ones from the school of thought that real men don't cry.

Without connecting to your feelings you have no feedback and the world becomes a scarier place, much like it would be if you lost your eyesight and had to find your way home. This is how humans have been living, feeling scared and lost, shut off from their natural guidance/feedback system. The state of the world today and your life is a direct reflection of this massive "energetic constipation."

> *When your fear touches someone's pain,*
> *it becomes pity,*
> *when your love touches someone's pain,*
> *it become compassion.*
>
> —Stephen Levine

Even today in some families or cultures, feelings are not given much value or importance. These are oftentimes the same cultures that view women and children as having lesser importance than men. These societies tend to have very rigid rules and be incredibly conservative.

It is a tell-tale sign that, in cultures that hold this hierarchical belief, they also hold the parallel belief that feelings are attributed to women and children. They rationalize that because women and children are more open to feeling, then they have lower cognitive abilities and importance, so their job is to serve the males, who are superior in their eyes.

Being unable to control one's feelings in the Herd OS is considered demonstrating a lack of worth and intelligence. Those who are ruled by their feelings are deemed weaker. It takes a lot of blocked energy to maintain this type of society, which is always very repressive and painful. The only way for this unnatural situation to exist is by distorting the natural flow of our energy. Violence is always involved because things must be *forced* to go out of alignment and blocked. We have been fighting our energy's natural flow that's why many of us feel like we are both suffering and stuck in our lives. It feels and looks overwhelming because it is an unnatural state of being for us.

Why do we *try* to control others? We do it for a number of reasons. See Chapter 15 for examples. In the Herd OS the norm is to disconnect from your feelings... because feelings link you to your intuition... which links you to spiritual DNA. We experience suffering in our life when we block this natural flow, just like we'd suffer if someone reduced our blood supply.

To control a group of people through rules, you often have to get them to turn off their internal GPS because you want them to follow you, not their spiritual DNA. *The opposite of control is trust.* Trust comes when you connect to your spiritual DNA. The more you try to control, the more you must disconnect from your feelings, which reduces your access to your internal GPS and your heart. The heart is the "brain" of your energy body.

Imagine a baby in diapers. Yup, you get to activate your imagination again! If she is warm, well-fed, healthy, well-napped, feels loved and has a dry diaper, there is a very good chance that this beautiful baby girl will be sitting there cooing happily, playing with her "toesies." The natural state of humans is *freedom and flow (love)*. Babies only cry if there is something *off*. Something has to be *missing* for the baby to move from a happy state into one of discontent. Notice that even when upset, the baby is still in alignment because she is being authentic. It's not about being happy all the time, but rather about noticing the feedback you're getting through your feelings. It tells you if you are in or out of alignment.

So, if you want to cut someone's natural joy, you start blocking the flow of feelings and make it incredibly dangerous for them to connect to their internal GPS. You make them focus instead on *rules,* and in doing so, they override their own feelings. "Why in the world would anyone want to cut off someone's happiness? How does that even make sense?" you ask. Well let's get to the bottom of this and find out shall we?...

When a person doesn't have gratitude, something is missing in his or her humanity. A person can almost be defined by his or her attitude toward gratitude.

—Elie Wiesel

Things I Want To Remember/Research/Review:

Love is my gift to the world.
I fill myself with love,
and I send that Love out into the world.
—Dr. Wayne Dyer

Chapter 34. Re-Categorizing What Feelings Mean

Having A Stiff Upper Lip - The Easiest Path to a Shitty Life

As you have learned in earlier chapters, in the Right Now OS, feelings are important because they hold valuable information as to what your energy is doing. If you take a moment to remember when you felt embarrassed, for example, there's an energy to that feeling. It's so strong, in fact, that you can even have physical reactions, such as your cheeks getting very red. What you're feeling is the energy pulsing through your body, giving you information on many levels, so that your entire being can receive feedback as to what is going on. The act of being human is ultimately all about choice. We get to choose. If you forget this basic fact, then by default the choice is made for you.

Oh, and for those who think they can be neutral and not choose, just so you know, there is no neutral. To be "neutral" your energy would have to be *non-moving* or *disconnected*. Neither of those are possible. Energy is always in movement and it is always connected to source. We are energy. As energetic beings, what we do have is *choice*. Even when we think we are still, we are always moving. With our constant movement comes continuous opportunities to make choices. Choices are constantly being made either consciously or unconsciously.

Did you ever wonder? This is why setting your intentions, writing down your goals, making vision boards, creating visualizations and saying affirmations are so very important. They help you make a choice by directing your energy. The friends you keep also keep your energy at a certain vibration. The gift and power is that every moment you get to choose. If you don't like the direction or feedback you can shift it because how you work your energy is through *imagination* and *focus*. That may sound far-fetched to some but if you look at your life, all that you are and do is based on what you have imagined is possible for yourself. I find it interesting that sometimes I will meet someone who will tell me how much they wish they could travel. "One day when I win the lottery, they say." When I explain that they can do it now if they start planning, they can be as creative as they need to be to fit whatever timeline they want. Almost always when I'm in that situation, the people say, "Well see." Their dream is more of a hope, than an actual burning desire. Dreams, like children and pets, are not to be neglected. This book is about helping you realize you have a choice, and then showing you how you can direct your life in the direction of your dreams. It's a really amazing system once you get how it works. One of the key ingredients is access to your feelings.

Feelings tell us if we are building our energy (getting lighter) or leaking our energy (getting heavier). In the Herd OS, feelings are considered to be a negative thing and the goal is to suppress them. Historically speaking, those who demonstrated feelings, such as women, were considered weak. Men were considered "strong" only if they could overpower/control/mute their feelings and do what had to be done. Men who were effeminate often were (and unfortunately still often are) beaten up, or even killed. Hard to believe when you read it, but this is how far we have come from our natural flow.

In order to stay in the Herd OS, your intuition must be completely disregarded and ignored. Since our flow is our natural state, it takes a lot more effort to block it than to flow with our natural energy. It's hard work to block yourself. As the human body needs oxygen, our energy body needs a *flow of our energy* to keep the connection to our body and this planet, in other words, so we don't die. Not living in the Right Now OS is an incredibly disconnected and dangerous way to live, because it completely eliminates any system of checks and balances. It's like our ancestors playing with fire, except it's the "fire" within us. Without understanding how it works and what it needs, we have kept making other "stories" and reasons why things

are as hard (damaged, sad, violent, depressing, horrific, scary) as they are. Society often backs us up in our beliefs of fear and aloneness. This is why the unnatural state of the Herd OS thrives.

If we start noticing and learning what our energetic body needs, virtually all of the conflicts on this planet would cease. Why is this? The biggest hurts people have inflicted on each other over the centuries were because people—both men and women—were operating through the Herd OS. They were domesticated into cutting off their own innate flow of energy and instead gave their personal power to a leader, parent, teacher, priest, police officer, etc., whoever was "in charge." Someone, or group of someones, chose some "shoulds" and established the "right" way to do things. Those who don't comply are punished in some way. Once domesticated, people no longer need a leader or teacher, mainly because after a certain amount of repetition and conditioning it feels absolutely "natural" to follow these rules unsupervised.

A key part of this is that the Herd OS establishes a *conscience*. It acts as a "prison guard" who lives in your brain 24 hours a day. It's constantly creating commentary so you are always being re-focused back to it. Think about it. Your conscience continuously judges whether things, behaviors or people are "good" or "bad." Here's a helpful hint: every time you judge anyone, you are in the Herd OS. Judging usually means looking for safety and feeding the ego.

The reason meditation works is because it unhooks you from the Herd OS by disarming your "prison guard" and instead connecting you to your energy body's natural flow. What does your natural flow feel like? It's the same feeling you experience when you surrender to watching a magnificent sunset.

Feelings (Energy) Decoder

 Decoder Exercise #1... Words are incredibly powerful. Sure we all know that but have not known what to do with that information. Most think it's just about using alternatives to curse words. Notice what comes up for you when you read these words...

- Jealousy
- Shame
- Heaviness
- Cheating
- Defending

- Gossiping
- Praying (the begging kind)
- Sitting for Long Periods
- Following Others Blindly
- Sabotaging

- Yelling At
- Controlling
- Getting Sick a Lot
- Torturing
- Tolerating
- Binging
- Suffering
- Agonizing
- Deceiving
- Judging
- Depression
- Disconnection
- Lack of Trust
- Blocking
- Not Open
- Possessing
- Whining
- Hoarding
- Degrading
- Stealing
- Squishing
- Denouncing
- Leeching

- Not Listening
- Forcing Others
- Eating Processed "Foods"
- Destroying
- Complaining
- Closed
- Flooding
- Denigrating
- Ignoring
- Anger
- Blaming
- Lying
- Sneaky Behavior
- Lashing Out
- Uncaring
- Meanness
- Stress
- Hating
- Demeaning
- Raging
- Suffocating
- Defeating
- Annihilating

When you read the words above, if you connect to them at all, you will notice how "heavy" you start feeling. They are all *Actions/Feelings/Things That Leak Energy*. What you are feeling right now matters so do take a deep breath and release that heaviness, unless you want it to stay with you. Actually, it would also be an interesting exercise to notice how your day unfolds if you hold on to that heavy vibration that those words align with. Remember there is no "right" or "wrong," it's all about choice. You get to design your life by choosing what experiences you want and how you will react to those experiences you don't have control over. If you do want to play with the icky feelings do not do the following exercise.

Aha! Point Exercise... This is one of my absolutely favorites! If you are ready to do this next exercise read on. Gently roll your neck back so that you're looking up at the ceiling. Roll your head from side to side up to your shoulders. Do it slowly. Feel the tiny cracks and stuck points. Snap. Crackle. Pop. Do this for as long as you like. You may also find it helpful to smile and roll your shoulders forwards and backwards. These simple stretches that you can do almost everywhere are as powerful as they are simple. The back of your neck is the *aha!* point so when you release the tension with this type of exercise, you energetically open yourself up to more intuitive hits.

Decoder Exercise #2... Now take another deep breath and read these words. Notice how you feel as you read them...

- Happiness
- Laughing
- Compassion
- Asking
- Listening
- Courage
- Appreciating
- Not Holding On
- Consoling
- De-Cluttering
- Exploring
- Slowing Down
- Releasing Old Patterns
- Watching the Sun Rise
- Whistling
- Noticing
- Swaying
- Yelling for Joy
- Receiving
- Gratitude
- Connecting to Nature
  Giving to Others
- Paying It Forward

- Smiling
- Kindness
- Being Open
- Random Acts of Kindness
- Embracing
- Setting an Intention
- Cherishing
- Praying (not the begging kind)
- Connecting to Community
- Punning
- Listening to a Great Song
- Creativity
- Thoughtfulness
- Looking Up (At The Sky)
- Setting Your Intention
- Play Fighting
- Walking
- Humming
- Laughing
- Giggling
- Welcoming
- Acknowledging

Maria Salomão-Schmidt

- Hugging
- People Watching
- Affirming
- Loving
- Singing
- Winking
- Dancing
- Learning
- Self-Care
- Examining Breathing
- Skipping
- Being Near Water
- Floating
- Writing
- Surprising

- Crying for Joy
- Connecting
- Releasing
- Inviting
- Volunteering
- Playing
- Meditating
- Unleashing Joy
- Gifting
- Seeing Babies
- Being Present
- Kissing
- Jumping
- Reading Poetry
- Noticing

Did you notice a difference in how you felt reading one versus reading the other group of words? These words are *Actions/Feelings/Things That Build Energy*. How did it feel for you? Where did you feel it in your body? What images came up? Did any smells, tastes or sounds come up for you? Let your imagination guide you. Let it flow and share what it wants with you. Feel free to draw, write or record what you are feeling because this can be extremely powerful.

Words are like little *energy packets*. When you use them, you activate the energy in them so that you lower or raise your vibration. This means words can help align you with your spiritual DNA. As our society is shifting, so too are the meanings of words at a faster rate than ever before.

Many people don't slow down long enough to realize this, but indeed words are tools, not just in the physical world for us to be able to communicate with each other with sound—but also in the energetic world with *vibration*. The other side of communication is vibration. The vibration helps you get to an energetic level, while the communication is then the connecting point to your audience. That audience could be you, another person or even billions of people.

 JOURNAL TIME... After reading this chapter how do you feel right now? Notice what comes up and write it down. Feel free to write, draw, paint or even sing what you discover. Give yourself permission. Establish a safe space from which you can let go, unpack, get loose and freely explore the feedback you have been getting in this specific chapter. Connecting to that part of you that's your natural state. It's what happy babies do. You are re-learning how you can connect to your spiritual DNA, which comes to you in the form of your imagination and your dreams.

> *As a culture, we are so scared,*
> *we're not just making ourselves miserable;*
> *we're making ourselves sick...*
> *By all measures, we are the healthiest,*
> *smartest, richest, safest people in human history.*
> *And yet, we have never been more afraid.*
> —Lissa Rankin, M.D.

Things I Want To Remember/Research/Review:

Stop. Close your eyes
and send Love from your heart
to everyone in the world
it will change everything.
—Marianne Williamson

Chapter 35. What Happens When You Slow Down?

In this new age of human evolution, *slowing down* helps clear the vibrational clutter. It's a wonderful tool that has often been invisible or neglected by human beings because the focus has been on "progress." Sacred and Progress do not co-exist in the same OS. Although it's one of those words that seems to be a "good" word, something we strive and sacrifice for, the word "progress" is language that belongs to the Herd OS. Our goal for attaining the idea that we need more progress, has allowed all sorts of atrocities to this planet, including displacing communities of indigenous people, annihilating beautiful trees, animals and other living beings. Director James Cameron beautifully explains this concept to all of us in his incredibly powerful movie *Avatar*.

In the movie, Colonel Miles Quaritch, chief of security, is the main antagonist. He's a military man who has no regard for indigenous life forms and considers them all expendable. Col. Quaritch is the poster boy for the Herd OS. Interestingly enough, for the sake of (perceived) power and control, he has blocked the connection to his heart, where his real warrior lives. It's in authenticity, listening to your energy body, that you're most potent. Nothing is more powerful than you completely full of your essence, full of yourself.

Col. Quaritch wants the destruction of what is sacred to those indigenous people, including the Tree of Souls because it stands in the way of "progress." Energetically, because he has cut off his sacredness, Col. Quaritch wants the world to match his vibrational state. This is because it's much easier to hold an inauthentic vibration when others around you are doing the same thing with you. People in this state of the Herd OS, see those in the Right Now OS as incredibly weak. This is the same vibration of violence and abuse as in the sections about Rosemary Kennedy and Sophia. When people are seen as "less than," then they are deemed disposable. Money becomes the goal above all else, even other living things. This especially happens if those things are seen as separate and different. Today, those who put money and corporations before our planet and people, are on the same vibration as Col. Quaritch. Here's an example of his disconnected approach to life:

Col. Quaritch: "So since a deal *can't* be made, I guess things get *real* simple. [*Sarcastically*] Jake, thanks. I'm gettin' all emotional. Might just give you a big wet kiss! I'll do it with minimal casualties to the indigenous. I'll drive 'em out with gas first. It'll be humane. More or less."

"Progress" is not a concept that exists in the Right Now OS because that enters into the world of *judging* if something is *better* than it used to be. Judging brings one out of alignment. It also has a slight "man conquers nature" vibe that is low vibration ideology because it is about separateness and disconnection. It is the thinking that WE KNOW BETTER than nature, that we are in the state we are in. We still have much to learn.

There's a whole world that has been unnoticed—because the only way to realize it's there is to s-l-o-w d-o-w-n! The deeper we get into *noticing* or *becoming aware*, the more we see that there is such an incredibly rich and fantastic world to discover. Going inside ourselves is one of the most amazing magical trips anyone can take. As we move more and more into this area of discovery, the happiness quotient and the number of aligned humans will greatly increase. Once in alignment, the solutions that will pour in are simply incredible! Just look at all the amazing information in this one little book. This is just a smidge of a smidge of a smidge of what there is to learn.

Some of the most grateful people in the world get that they will never know everything, but they can swim in pools of endless self-discovery, experiences and play! This is why we bother to incarnate in the first place. Are you wasting your ride? Well, don't! Keep being open to the feedback and adjust as you get new information. Feeling bliss means you are on purpose. Warning, your intuitive hits may oftentimes clash with what others think you should do.

Maria Salomão-Schmidt

From the movie *Avatar:*

Selfridge: "Look. You're supposed to be winning the hearts and minds of the natives. Isn't that the whole point of your little "puppet show?" If you walk like them, you talk like them, they'll trust you. We build them a school, teach them English. But after—how many years—the relations with the indigenous are only getting worse."

Dr. Grace Augustine: "Yeah, well that tends to happen when you use machine guns on them."

Selfridge: "Right. C'mere. You see this?" [shows Grace the sample of Unobtanium on his desk]

Selfridge: "This is why we're here. Because this little gray rock sells for $20 million a kilo. That's the only reason. This is what pays for the whole party, and it's what pays for your science. Those savages are threatening our whole operation. We're on the brink of war and you're supposed to be finding me a diplomatic solution. So use what you've got, and get me some results."

When things get too intense, too hard to handle, some people zone out. They go into an almost limbo, zombie-like state where they leave their body as much as they know how without severing the life-death chasm. They are not full of themselves, and many times they become energy feeding stations for others. This happens because whole industries are built around people escaping their lives. They want to escape their lives because all they know is the Herd OS, and living in that OS is incredibly painful. There's no solution in that state of living so people feel hopeless. They feel hopeless, honestly because in the Herd OS, people can have hope but there is no hope, unless people shift into the Right Now OS. Those in the Herd OS enter some form of the "life sucks and then you die" way of seeing life. There's very little joy or happiness because they don't know they have a choice. Here are some examples of activities people use to zone out:

Activities That Can Be Used For Escapism

- Sex
- Drugs (Legal)
- Drinking
- Movies
- Binge Watching
- Shopping
- Smoking
- Social Media
- Never Home
- Playing Solitaire
- Drugs (Illegal)
- Overeating
- Traveling
- Texting
- Vacationing
- Watching Television
- Playing Video Games
- Collecting 'Stuff'
- Gossiping
- Retiring
- Gambling
- Eating Chocolate
- Constantly "Doing"
- Reading

Now as a caveat, it's important to share that many of these activities simply can be earthly pleasures too. Part of the gift of having a body is to be able to enjoy what only beings with bodies can feel. *Light beings* with bodies are also another term for human beings. Human beings are a combination of light and relatively dense matter; without that light, they go back to being simply a "corpse." All the elements of that matter can be found on planet earth, which is why it's the playground for humans. By having "bodies," we're able to enjoy the activities above. These activities are not abusive if done in moderation, or while you're in your natural flow of the Right Now OS. It's fun to play video games or read, but when you're trying to hide something or from something, doing any of these in excess is what people tend to do. It's the repetitive action and the not wanting to deal with what is going on that causes issues.

When operating in the Right Now OS, the activities above are in flow with happiness and joy, the byproducts of alignment. Since, at the time of the writing of this book, most people are mostly operating out of the Herd, then many of the activities are used to *numb out*. Numbing out is one of the most popular ways that people on earth currently use to mask the great discomfort they feel about their lives. They are led to believe that is just how life is, but it is only that way if you believe it is!

Understanding why is a key component in getting you back, connected to the wisdom of your energy body. It's simply about looking at your life as energy. You can start off by noticing where your focus goes. Also notice when you listen to others over your own

Maria Salomão-Schmidt

intuition. The current popular method of being guided is by asking and answering what you "should" be doing. This method just blocks your spiritual DNA from reaching you. These two contrasting life coping strategies are the key to everything!

Just as your physical body needs nutrients, food and water to sustain itself, your energetic body needs a constant flow of energy for it not only to survive but also *thrive*! In the Right Now OS, that naturally happens. There is *no* thinking involved. It is a feelings-based system that allows you to receive your *feedback* as to how to proceed. Life is in a *flow*. In the Herd OS, people live how they think they "should." In order to do that, they have to block their natural energetic flow.

At the writing of this book, it's 2016 and gay people still need to fight to get married in many states in America. In many countries throughout the world, simply being homosexual means that you will be executed. These are perfect examples of how people who have a belief of what marriage "should" be, are using whatever means necessary, even violence to keep others from living their natural flow. Essentially, what those who are blocking gay marriage are doing is closing their hearts. They have a rule they believe that they want everyone else to follow. Energetically, this means *blocking* their natural flow of energy and light, so it can temporarily conform to the "rule" of what they have deemed is "right." By doing so, they are creating a huge energetic block—not only to others, but also to themselves. Those in the Herd OS block their hearts and embrace their "shoulds" with all their might. They see themselves as right and they fight for it to become a "reality." They truly believe they are doing the "right" thing.

The laws of energy that I'm speaking of here are as innate as gravity is to Earth. Let's just say we wanted to suspend or alter the laws of gravity. Yes, this can be done, even on Earth, but it takes a lot of focusing, planning, money, time and resources. A special container would have to be built, energetically fed and maintained. It would keep working only with lots of resources and efforting. In other words, it needs a lot of outside effort and energy. Once the outside effort and energy stop, gravity again takes over.

That is how it is with the *Land of Should* behavior discussed above. People's hate (closed hearts) can be maintained only with effort, and those holding that space are expending more energy than if they were just flowing from their innate Right Now OS. The interesting part, though, is that if you were to ask those who think they are doing the "right" thing by defending their definition of marriage, they would most likely tell you that they are doing *what God wants*. What they are doing, from an energetic point of view, is *not* allowing the natural flowing energy that is their birthright, to flow through their energetic body. What this means is they are being *energetically depleted by living in the Herd OS.*

In being depleted, they need to take energy from others. This is why you see lots of hate groups being angry. Provocative anger is a way to take energy from others. The anger is feedback that they are *trying* to use you as an energetic feeding station. The term "energy vampires" comes from these kinds of behaviors. In old black and white movies vampires say " I want to drink your blood." (man I wish I could do the vampire accent for you right now. If you don't mind just use your imagination for now. I'll do it in the audio book.) What energy vampires do is they are energetically saying, "I want to drink your energy." When your energy levels get too low, you automatically reach out to others to take theirs.

Sometimes it's with their consent, and other times it's not. Those who are against people they view as "wrong" see themselves as "helping" when they are hurting them by taking away their most basic rights. They are not looking at what is, but rather what "should" be. This is exactly why there are *wars, suffering, crime, violence and hate*. People are so used to those being the norm that peace on earth may seem impossible to some, but impossible when you slow it down can also be "I'm possible." After so much violence for such a long time how can I say with such certainty that peace is possible?

People don't like to think that sometimes we are also energy vampires, but sometimes we are. All of us are sometimes. Have you ever seen people laughing and having a good time, and it felt annoying to you? Well, this an example of a very low level of energy vampirism. When you are giving someone a dirty look, that is another example of low level energy leaking which can activate your stealing energy from others. This only happens if you are not full of yourself. Noticing and acknowledging when you are being an energy vampire, specifically without judgment, is vital. For some, using others as their energetic feeding stations is the main way they *energetically breathe*. This is how they are able to survive without connecting to source energy. (Remember the Love-Light Ball in Chapter 22?)

When someone is mainly just feeding off of others for any length of time on an energetic level, what the feedback looks like on the physical (meat) level is *wars, suffering, crime, violence and hate*. Remember seeing those in the prior paragraph. Remember now, being an energy vampire is not *good* or *bad*, just feedback that we are not full of ourselves. When we are not full of ourselves, there are consequences. If you want those consequences to stop you now know how. Start paying attention to how you are energetically feeding yourself. This is why learning how to use your energy body, as well as you already know how to use your meat body, is so very important! Ladies and gentlemen, the solution for peace is finally at hand!

 JOURNAL TIME... What activities have you traditionally used to escape your life? Have they shifted over time? Did they help you cope or drown? When do you notice you use them most to escape? How do you feel about what is coming up for you after having read this chapter? When have you been an energy vampire? How did it feel? How do you energetically feed yourself? In other words, how often do you put yourself in positions of being inspired? How can you add more moments of inspiration and creativity in your life?

Focus on the fact that
the universe is always rising
or lowering itself to meet you.
You choose your level
with each thought, choice and action.
—Maria Salomão-Schmidt

Things I Want To Remember/Research/Review:

But you can only lie about who you are for so long without going crazy.

—Ellen Wittlinger

Chapter 36. Hide It Under The Rug Of Humanity

Hiding under the rug of humanity are a number of things that because we don't talk about them, they grow... and fester. When we do talk about them, we do so with a lot of closed judgment and fear, leaving very little room for light and Love to enter. I say "light and Love" because that's what brings flow. It's by opening back up the flow that things lose their stagnation and effortlessly slip back into alignment. If we are to survive—and eventually thrive—as human beings, we can no longer afford to keep cramming *ickies* under the rug of humanity. It's time for some major spring cleaning for our species!

Here are some examples of actions that cause massive amounts of suffering. There's nothing on this list that'll surprise you because they are all too common on this planet of ours. They are all acts that can be committed only by people who've been domesticated into the Herd OS.

The level of fear needed to commit most of these acts must be so absolute that it blocks out most the love and light; in other words, disconnection from the energy body. It's common that once someone commits an act at this level, they then work extra hard to block further any connection to their heart. This is because to do so would mean realizing what they've done and dealing with how to release all those uncomfortable, heavy, icky emotions to clear it up. It can seem overwhelming and impossible, which is why so many people block it. The pay-off of calling your energy back, however, is bigger than anything else anyone can do in his or her lifetime.

- Committing Incest
- Robbery
- Murder
- Mentally Abusing
- Kidnapping
- Stealing
- Shooting
- Yelling
- Blackmailing
- Beating
- Child Abuse
- Rape
- Bullying
- Infidelity
- Conflict
- Verbally Abusing
- Destroying
- Sabotaging
- Molesting
- Maiming
- Shoplifting
- Trolling (online)
- Torturing
- War
- Belittling
- Violence
- Police Violence
- Scamming
- Denigrating
- Mob Mentality
- Cheating
- Stalking
- Physically Abusing
- Mocking
- Fighting
- Hitting
- Intimidating
- Deceiving

In neuro-linguistic programming (NLP), an approach to personal development and psychotherapy, it is well known that people will do more to avoid pain than to get pleasure. The pain and fear of what they have done is so great that they create a big seal around their heart. *What they think is protection, ends up becoming their own tomb.* By effectively cutting out the connection to their heart, they're cutting out the connection to their authentic selves. People who have chosen this method of coping lead very sad, angry, judgmental, lonely lives, and oftentimes end up using the activities listed in the section of "ACTIVITIES USED FOR ESCAPISM" as methods of coping.

In this section, I touched upon some really challenging topics. They are topics that we human beings *ignore they happen,* or *assume they will happen, so nothing can be done.* Either thought results in prolonged stagnation within our human family. These thoughts present a huge problem for our energy body. This happens for several reasons. One, the topics are too uncomfortable to even talk about. Two, if you're running your Herd OS, you simply don't feel like you have enough energy in your system to take this on. Change is seen as hard and undesirable. Three, we have so many things coming at us and we are so busy, that it's challenging to focus on one more thing—especially when it seems so painful and huge. Finally, we don't want to rock the boat for other people because then what will they think about us? This is because many of our relationships are based on *Conditional Love*.

Our planet is at a time when we are more than flirting with disaster. We are way past that... we're more like already "engaged and pregnant!" At this point we're looking at a shotgun wedding! All kidding aside, our Mother Earth is at a very critical point! Almost every part of our planet, as pertains to our physical world, is giving us feedback of how very unaligned and fragile things are, especially with Climate Change! For some reason, many of us seem to be almost completely ignoring it, so things continue to worsen. Now would be a great time to start exploring solutions, don't cha think? Little steps lead to big journeys. I'd say start now but you've already started. You listened to your intuition when it told you to read *Finally Full of Yourself*. Well done!

 JOURNAL TIME... What secret are you hiding? What's it costing you to keep this secret? What could you do with the energy you would get if you did not have to hold that block of energy in place? Write your secret down. Burn it if you want afterwards but get it down and out of you!

WARNING: *May cause freedom and flow (which is how I define Love)!*

If the first casualty of war is innocence,
then perhaps with each bullet fired, bomb detonated,
leader overthrown, wall built,
economy destroyed and family member killed, we are
not creating goodwill and harmony,
but rather another child who believes violence
is the only means to bring about change in the world.
—Michael Franti

Maria Salomão-Schmidt

The ability to take a conflict
and end it with Love
is one of the most powerful things you can do.
It has been a great lesson for me.

—Dr. Wayne Dyer

Chapter 37. Shifting From The Department Of War To The Department Of Peace

Conflicts and war have been a part of human history. A significant amount of time, effort, focus and money goes to the military budget of a country. If we take a moment to remember that whatever we focus on grows, then we can see that the more we focus on war, the more war we get. The other day my beautiful husband, Doug, shared a war statistic he had learned that day that blew my mind! It did not seem like it could be possible, so I checked it out. How would you answer the following?...

Quickie Quiz:

Many people consider the signing of the Declaration of Independence as the point when the United States became a nation, which was in 1776. Assuming it's 2016 right now, that's 240 years. How many years has the United States been at peace since it was formed in 1776?

a.	125 years	c.	110 years
b.	53 years	d.	21 years

You may be truly surprised and disheartened as I was, to find that the answer is "d." We, in the United States have only been at peace for 21 years, which is only 11% of the time the United States has been in existence! War is such a part of our culture that Wikipedia even has a category called "Military Budget of the United States."

In digging just a little deeper, I was shocked to find that even though our roadways and infrastructure are in desperate need of so much repair, schools are in disrepair, public transportation is unaffordable, as are housing costs. Some cities are even giving poisoned water to children and covering it up—all because they don't want to pay for it. Government officials tell us there is no money, but what they really mean is that the money is going to other things.

The truth is that the United States still spends a large part of its budget helping other countries' military budgets. In one particular case, the amount of aid given was for billions of dollars, with the explicit understanding that this country will spend it on buying from American-owned defense companies. How can we not have more war when these are the seeds that are being planted? I am not disclosing the name of the country because it's really irrelevant. It doesn't matter which country it is, because it's not the only one. Violence is a perfect weapon of the Herd OS because it feeds the fear.

In a fear-based society, *by any means necessary* to achieve an outcome becomes the norm. Human lives, dignity, love, connection, legacy and respect fall by the wayside in the name of protecting their own. They are putting "protection" and "safety" above all else, but only for the things they and their special interest groups want.

As a mother who has lost a child and niece, my heart goes out to all those women and men (brothers, sisters, aunts, uncles, cousins, grandmothers, grandfathers), who lose children to needless stupid and senseless wars and gun violence. So strong is the power of the gun corporations that they've made it against the law to sue a gun company! There are actually more restrictions in America on toy guns than on real guns that kill people. This is madness! It simply does not have to be this way!

Wars follow the same energetic patterns as the individual conflicts that we have within our own lives. We can end wars altogether. It is possible, just like it is possible to bring peace into our own lives. *Finally Full of Yourself* is my contribution to the world to move us into peace. I deeply thank my Sophia for guiding me here to places I was afraid to explore, but that held the secrets to PEACE ON EARTH.

As I shared earlier, those in the Herd OS love fear. Fear is used to control and manipulate people away from their core of trusting and flowing. The hours, days, months and years after 9/11, for those who are old enough to remember it, you could "touch" the fear. It covered us like a huge, thick, icky blanket. No one knew what to do. We felt helpless. Those who put money first, took that opportunity to harness the fear into a massive profit generation. They did this by creating mistruths and focusing attention on the pain and fear and growing it—not only in the United States, but also globally.

The challenge in America is that so many people become so proud of being American, they never look around to see where they are standing, and who they are standing on. The blind belief that, "We're number one!" no matter what, is slipping away. In this global economy, things are shifting at such a huge pace that adjusting to what exists now is part of the journey—this is especially important for leaders who want to stay in power.

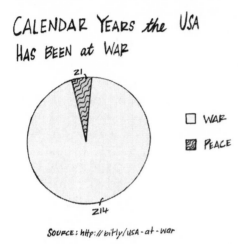

CALENDAR YEARS the USA HAS BEEN at WAR

□ WAR
▨ PEACE

21

214

SOURCE: http://bit.ly/USA-at-war

It has always bothered me a great deal that since before my 12-year-old daughter Mialotta was born, the United States has been at war with Iraq. I have a hard time explaining why this is so, to her and our other children because I don't understand it myself.

Part of the issue is that we don't even remember that we are at war because we don't "feel" it the way our parents or grandparents did with other wars like the Vietnam War or World Wars I & II. Because the normal checks and balances system have been removed through re-routing our attention to the mundane, our focus is not on war. By being so "busy" and feeling overwhelmed, we ignore what's right in front of us. This is how things get worse and worse and worse as our focus is on things that keep us entertained and "life-less."

I have traveled to 19 countries at this point in my life. The one thing I have noticed in all those countries is that most people want to be able to feed their children, have a roof over their heads, get an education, be safe and lead a meaningful life. If you watch certain media channels, you may see many of these beautiful people from other countries and/or religious belief systems being villainized. From my experience that's simply not true. My experience is that most people are kind, even to a total stranger. We are all *one*. There is no "they" and "us," but only "we." As the beautiful Wayne Dyer says, "There are no sides on a round planet."

War – What Is It Good For?

One thing I have *never* quite understood in my heart is the concept of celebrating war. Not just the actual fighting, which is totally barbaric and out of alignment, but also all of the pomp, circumstance and rituals performed by the entire society—by those who go to war, as well as those who stay home. For example, most of the statues that are built are created for those who either died or won some battle. In many town squares around America and throughout the Western world, you'll find large memorials to those who died, many times with some iconic tool of war as part of the display, such as a cannon or a tank.

Glorifying war is deeply rooted in the Herd OS way of thinking because *violence* is one of its tools. Because *fear* is the driver, the main goal is to have the feeling of "control." I say the *feeling* because you can *never* really control anything or anyone. For "things," you may be able to hold a certain pattern with a lot of effort, such as in the previous gravity example, but you cannot maintain it indefinitely. With people, you cannot control anyone without their consent. It is much easier to control those running their energy flow through the Herd OS, because they are living under the assumption that they *need to be saved or guided* and thus give their power to others. This is why they are called *sheeple*. An example is people who vote for government officials with the understanding or intent that your elected officials will "fix" everything. Instead of being a part of the system, they give their power away.

"Wars" don't have to be just between countries or groups, they can also be between family members, friends or coworkers. Different parts of you can even wage war against another part. What is seen as powerful in the Herd OS is the ability to "control" others. As I just described above, this is really not possible without someone's consent. But those who have been *domesticated* into living in the Herd OS have been taught to give their energy to others so they can be taken care of. One of the ways people come to this kind of thinking is by the use of violence—even by your most trusted beloveds, your parents.

"Ever Notice?" Exercise... It's incredibly common to see violence in movies and on TV, even in cartoons. Slapstick humor is based on laughing at someone else getting hit. Guns and shootings are commonly used in storylines, even when it's not necessary. Many may not like it, but in general, violence is commonplace. Let's shift this energy. Begin to notice how very "common" it has become. Bring it up. Discuss it with friends. Read about how gun violence is an epidemic. Play with your observations. See what you discover.

There comes a time in life
where you just stop fighting everything.
You start to see yourself as being part
of the grand design of everything.
You allow people to say and be what they choose.
When you don't feel the need to argue back at anyone
and you allow them space to see they are fighting themselves,
you are very close to understanding the beauty of freedom.

—Angela White

Bringing Back "Peace On Earth" as a Given

What most people miss is that there's a correlation as to why BIG WARS exist and the conflicts in our very own homes. Another way to put this, is big wars will never end until we first learn how to deal with the conflicts within ourselves, and then in our relationships with families and friends. It's *healing* and *alignment* for ourselves that reverberates out into the bigger world; even though most of us would not put wars on the same level as the personal conflicts that we may have in our own lives. By developing further awareness around conflictual behavior, perhaps having wars, gives us further feedback on our state of affairs. It's feedback that most of us ignore because it's all so common in human history. It's our *new normal*, even though it is completely contrary to our spiritual DNA. This is the inauthenticity that the Herd OS creates in the world. War is feedback that we're living out of alignment, disconnected from our energy bodies. The longer it takes to grasp this fact, the more destruction and suffering accumulates.

The smallest and youngest among us—babies, show us how we came to Earth in our most unadulterated form. They are the guiding example of our energy body without domestication. Peace on Earth does not have to be something you just write on your holiday cards and then forget about for the rest of the year. The solution to bringing in more peace on Earth, starts with each one of us realizing that we have been domesticated into this unnatural way in the Herd OS, by running our energy and living our lives from an inauthentic, unaligned place.

This is why so many of us see life as a struggle. Once we realize that this is where we have gone astray from our authenticity, it's from that point, we can stop cookie-cutting our lives and start noticing what is truly authentic to us. We move from the *have to* to the *get to*! This is where the solutions will effortlessly come from to help re-align the whole planet. Like expecting not to get affected in a pool with a "peeing section," this is an all-or-nothing kind of mission. We have to learn how to live from our energy body—or implode.

 JOURNAL TIME... "War" is a counterculture era soul song written by Norman Whitfield and Barrett Strong for Motown in 1969. Take the time to read the words and then write what war means to you? Have you thought about war very much? When you hear the word "war" what comes up for you? Where does war fit in your life? Do you agree with the current wars? How are you connected to/disconnected from them? Be open and kind as you journal about this topic.

REFRAIN

War, huh, yeah
What is it good for
Absolutely nothing
Uh-huh
War, huh, yeah
What is it good for
Absolutely nothing
Say it again, y'all

War, huh, good God

What is it good for
Absolutely nothing
Listen to me

Ohhh, war, I despise
Because it means destruction

War, it ain't nothing but a
heartbreaker
War, it's got one friend
That's the undertaker
Ooooh, war, has shattered
Many a young man's dreams
Made him disabled, bitter and mean
Life is much too short and precious
To spend fighting wars these days
War can't give life
It can only take it away

Refrain

War, it ain't nothing but a
heartbreaker
War, friend only to the undertaker
Peace, Love and understanding

Of innocent lives

War means tears
To thousands of mothers eyes
When their sons
go to fight
And lose their lives

Refrain

War, it ain't nothing
But a heartbreaker
War, friend only to the undertaker
Ooooh, war
It's an enemy to all mankind
The point of war blows my mind
War has caused unrest
Within the younger generation
Induction then destruction
Who wants to die
Aaaaah,

Refrain

Tell me, is there no place for them
today
They say we must fight to keep our
freedom
But Lord knows there's got to be a
better way

Ooooooh, war, huh

Good God y'all
What is it good for
You tell me
Say it, say it, say it, say it

War, huh
Good God y'all
What is it good for
Stand up and shout it
Nothing

We can bomb the world to pieces,
but we can't bomb it into peace.

—Michael Franti

Things I Want To Remember/Research/Review:

It feels soooooooo great to move towards
your life's purpose!
—Maria Salomão-Schmidt

Chapter 38. The Right Now OS... The "Real" You!

The Right Now OS is incredibly simple. It's the most natural way to live on this planet. You are born with it. There's nothing to learn, add, buy or grow. It is you. Animals are examples of beings who live in the Right Now OS, especially if they have not been domesticated. Their focus is on the present moment. Accessing the Right Now OS involves slowing down and connecting to the natural rhythm of Earth.

Two autumns ago, we laughed at the behavior of the squirrels in our yard. They stashed hundreds and hundreds of pine cones behind several of our trees. "Aren't squirrels funny," we thought because we had never seen them do that before. That year was one of the most brutal and longest winters ever in New England with record low temperatures and snowfall. We humans did not see it coming, but the squirrels somehow did. They knew to stash away food because they are intrinsically linked to Mother Earth's flows. We have this ability too, but most of us have blocked it for so long that we are much less in tune with nature's rhythms. I, like an increasing number of people, have begun paying more attention to nature. Nature is one of our greatest teachers, always showing us our natural energetic flow. Notice that even the world "natural" comes from the word "nature." It feels so good to connect to nature because we are nature. We are a part of this whole web of life on planet Earth, no more or less important than any other living being.

The Right Now OS is the natural connection you have with your *energy body* and your *meat body*. It is simple and effortless. It flows. You don't need to "do" anything. You simply are this connection. Babies get this. They are authentic in every moment because they haven't been introduced to the *Land of Should, the Herd OS*. If they are hungry, cold, wet or sick they let you know. Babies have a deep sense of wonder and love to explore things. They generally love animals and want to connect with them. They're authentic, curious and live in the present moment.

As adults we oftentimes experience living in the Right Now OS in the following situations:

- When we are singing in the shower.

- When we are on vacation.

- When we are singing along or dancing to a fantastic song, especially when we are alone.

It's at these times that we connect to our energy body. Afterwards, we feel better because we have gotten a hit of our own amazing natural energy flow! It's like taking a hit of pure oxygen. It feels wonderful, but the effects don't last forever, just like you cannot take one breath and expect to live for a week on it. The more you can connect to the things you LOVE, the more you connect to that energy that is innately yours, that natural flow that feels so amazing!

Now to be clear, because I'm always asked this question, just because you live mostly in the Right Now OS, does not mean that life is perfect. It just means that you are focusing on the parts that you *choose* to, and *not* the ones that you allow others either directly or indirectly to choose for you. I have had some pretty amazing things happen to me in this lifetime.

One of them was meeting an amazing poet and her husband on one of my flights to Portugal. It was the first time I was flying to Portugal as a mom without my children. The flight was cancelled two days in a row because "equipment failure," so a small group of us befriended each other. We would text each other with updates because the airline was not great at sharing information.

I asked her if I could include her poem in this book because it is a beautiful example of someone surrendering, even when it's scary and going with what is showing up. Ladies and gentlemen, I now present to you the poetry of the beautiful Gail Hersey of New Hampshire, USA. She allowed me to share with you:

Gail writes, "Here is a poem I wrote about my dealings with my cancer. I wrote it after my first chemo..."

Not A Warrior by Gail Hersey

Cancer is not a battle I am fighting.
    It is part of my life.
I wake to snow blowing wildly
    in the gray dawn
    filling the gap between window and screen.
Winter caught me
    short.

        There is a savage feel to the day
          and though the wool of blankets
          holds me in a cave of my own heat
          when I stretch my legs the cold beyond
          is furiously sharp and dangerous.

A brave woman would leap naked
    from her den to kindle cooling embers
    against the frigid air
    blowing on them with determined breath until
    dusty coals spring to life
    battling the icy morning and
    sometimes I do.
Sometimes I do.

A warrior would pull on her boots
    adrenaline coursing through
    the river of her veins
    shovel raised like a bloody sword
    tilting at winter's windmill
    her breath a
    harsh and angry fog
    obscuring her vision
    as days grow shorter.

        Wild grace comes weeping
          to me
          accepting my sadness and curiosity.

        She whispers
          "Lay down your shield
          Fill your lungs with the cold fresh air
          Dance in the short hours of daylight
          Bathe in the miracle of infinite snowflakes

Make peace with the coming night."

❄ ❄ ❄

Can you feel the power in Gail's poem? The beauty? The rawness? The authenticity? The wisdom? Her heartfelt words show she is fully present, even as she is facing something very icky. That is a rare and beautiful thing; I find that by noticing or being present to what is

Maria Salomão-Schmidt

around us, that life presents us with unexpected surprises, even when we're not looking for it.

In April of 2016, the wonderful poet Gail passed. She was such a heart on legs! I love that part of her lives on through your reading her words here! I am truly grateful for having connected with her so strongly.

Playing with Poems Exercise... What comes up for you when you read Gail's poem "Not a Warrior?" Feel free to read the poem again. This time more slowly. Savor it. Play with it. Ask it what gifts it holds for you. By slowing down to pay attention to the simple things, such as poetry, you'll greatly increase the joy in your life.

Bonus Exercise... Whether you've done it before or not, write a poem... play with it. Notice what judgments and fears come up. Notice what is beyond that? Use this as an exercise to "feel the fear" and do it anyway. This is a wonderful exercise to show you how you handle the journey. In this case the journey is a simple task. Remember the outcome is not as important as the journey itself... and how you do one thing is how you do everything.

Things I Want To Remember/Research/Review:

I only hope that we don't lose sight of one thing—
that it was all started by a mouse.
—Walt Disney

Chapter 39. Who Is The Giggly Fairy?

Another Tool You Didn't Know You Had...

The Giggly Fairy first appeared to me when I had the courage to listen to a part of me that was very clear about what it wanted. I knew I wanted to move to Portugal but my husband Doug's successful real estate career was in Massachusetts. I felt stuck because I could not see how it was going to work itself out, so I shut it out for a long time. As I blocked my intuition hits, I started feeling heavier. In turn my body also became heavier. I was becoming very negative and sad, not wanting to go out anymore. It was very hard to think that I had to choose either between what my intuition was telling me to do and my husband's career. It all seemed really unfair. I felt caught in a great, big Catch-22. No matter what I picked, someone was going to get hurt.

Because I was feeling so lost, I decided to start consistently meditating on a daily basis. I would wake up an hour earlier and perform my coveted morning ritual of drinking warm lemon water, doing yoga and then finishing off with a simple meditation. I did this on my sunny veranda in Portugal overlooking the beautiful Tagus River and Atlantic Ocean. The more I did my morning ritual, the more my life began to have freedom and flow. My definition of Love is exactly that, *freedom and flow*. It seemed like I was finding a part of myself that had been dusty for a really long time, like connecting to an old, dear heart friend. After meditating for two weeks, I had a very strong visual appear in the form of a beautiful fairy who communicated only by giggling, which is why I call her the Giggly Fairy.

She spoke to me telepathically, which may seem strange to some, but if your cell phone can capture "invisible" sound waves, then why can't we? The Giggly Fairy's message was that everything is flowing at it's own pace. She explained that a *giggle* is "flow." To be honest, at first, I didn't know how to take this so I sent her (also telepathically) as many painful stories as I could remember of atrocities that happen on our planet. Wars, suffering, incest, torture, greed, pollution... I just threw all the icky stuff I could l think of at her.

I saw her getting heavier and heavier and more and more droopy, and less and less giggly as I fed her all these harsh painful images. Her head and shoulders dropped. I noticed that the images I had sent her seemed to be going *through* her, not *into* her. The ickiness was not stopping in her, but rather moving past her. As quickly as the ickies came in, they went out. As soon as the last one had left, it was almost as if she'd passed an "energetic furball." The more the icky energy left, the more her giggle rose, first from breath, then sound until it crescendoed into a full-blown giggle.

This was fascinating to me. I don't know how she communicated it to me but she did. The message I got is that it's not what happens to you, it's what you do with the information. The Giggly Fairy was not blocking anything or afraid of anything. She was curious to know why I was so sad; and even though she could connect to it, she didn't hold on to the sadness. The Giggly Fairy just simply felt it, as part of *noticing*, and let it go. This is an incredibly helpful reminder if you are the type of person like I am, whose heart hurts when we hear of other people suffering. It does not mean don't do anything. It means to be grounded and full of yourself when you tackle anything. That is when you can make the best decisions with the most power.

What is Her Message?

Let things flow through you, not become part of you. The more you hold onto things the more inauthentic you become. The more inauthentic you become, the more your ego grows and the more you disappear. The reverse is also true. The more you let go of things, the more you are in your energetic flow. The more you are in this state, the more open you are to your own intuition hits, information and ultimately the more you can be your own "flavah" in the world! She taught me that our natural state is always in the flow, where it's fun and *effortless* to be ourselves. When icky things come up, I can still be me. I know to some people this sounds crazy, but it's certainly no crazier than the world we live in right now.

5 Things The Giggly Fairy Wants You To Know

Having lived in the Herd OS for long periods of time, certain parts of you have been shut down or you only use a small portion of your capacity. This not only causes sadness and heaviness, it also causes massive *boredom*. The Giggly Fairy reminds us that we need to use all of those parts of ourselves if we desire to live a fulfilling life! Think of the word FULFILLING... This means living full of yourself, calling your energy back. A better way to say it is to allow your energy side room to "breathe," thrive, grow and communicate with you.

You are that flow but have blocked the communication, which is where you get your life's wisdom. There's a way of communicating and creating that many are not given the opportunity to develop. This is the link to unlock our spiritual DNA. Most people are taught to search for something outside themselves. Many spend their whole lives searching. As a fully equipped human being there is nothing outside yourself you need to get. You have everything you need. You were born full! Here's a countdown to the five simple things you can give more focus to so you can get better "reception" when you are accessing your spiritual DNA...

5. Imagination

Imagination is the name we give to things that aren't yet *manifested* (in physical form). Imagination is one of the most powerful tools a human being can have. The stronger your imagination, the more likely it is that you can create the life you desire on earth. This also depends on how *grounded* you are (Go to Chapter 3 for more information on grounding, one of your Helpers.) Imagination is how your spiritual DNA communicates with you. It does it through things like dreams, intuition, hunches, daydreaming and Freudian slips (where you say something without your conscious brain being involved). Imagination is an incredibly important tool because it helps you focus your energy and attention on something. It is by doing this that we manifest and magnetize what we want to create in the physical world. Imagination actually exists in both Human OSs. In the Herd

OS, our imagination actually imprisons us by keeping us small and focused on fear. The size of the "box" you live in, is determined by your imagination. If you focus on fear you slow down your energy body's flow. Wayne Dyer used to say that if you break down the word FEAR, you get "F"alse "E"vidence "A"ppearing "R"eal.

The Giggly Fairy only exists in our imagination, which is the realm of energy, but it does not make her any less powerful, as those in the Herd OS would have everyone believe. Those who connect with her can still benefit from all that she has to teach. If this sounds a little hard to grasp then take a moment to think of a Disney character you love. It also only exists in your imagination but by connecting to that character or movie, it helps you align with a certain vibration. If you think of the movies Nemo versus Frozen, you get two totally different vibrations. Slow down enough to notice the different feelings you get with each movie. This is a wonderful way to learn how to play with your energy!

4. Creative Thinking

Creative thinking, a direct cousin of *imagination*, is dangerous to those who want to control people, places or things. They don't want things to shift, or flow. To keep things stagnant, is to prevent *freedom and flow*, things that are essential to a *happy human being*. Your imagination is always on because it's how energy communicates. It's either focused on *fear (blocked)* or *flow (unblocked)*.

Although you're the only one who gets to choose, much of what society teaches is there is a "right" and "wrong" way. They are essentially trying to take your choice away without you realizing it. To keep the masses entertained and fed, in other words "comfortable," is a key concept of capturing people's attention. If you give someone your focus, you give them your life's flow. Show them what to focus on and humans, traditionally, will follow what's put in front of them, just like in a herd. This is how people live as *sheeple*.

3. Dreams

When utilized in the Right Now OS, imagination is one of the most powerful ways your spiritual DNA communicates with you. One of the ways your energy body communicates with you is through your day dreams. I'm talking about the things you wish you could do if you had unlimited time, money, support and talent. Where did you think your dreams come from? Why is it unique to you? Those locked in the Herd OS would have you believe that dreams are silly and unimportant.

Dreams are very powerful ways that your spiritual DNA communicates with you. If you slow down you can see that dreams move you in the direction of what fills you full of your essence and pulls you towards it. This is when people and opportunities start magically showing up. Your dreams are received messages from your spiritual DNA. If you want a meaningful, authentic life, play close attention to your dreams. They can only guide you if you pay attention to them. Cemeteries are full of dreams that were never taken seriously. Do you take yours seriously?

2. Giggling

If you go to a preschool, you often see kids giggling, but when was the last time you giggled? Giggling is a natural way of resetting your breathing. Most adults, especially men, give up giggling after a certain age. I have a theory on why giggling is not more prevalent in adult humans. I think it's because if someone is operating from the Herd OS their ego is high and self-esteem is low. When they hear someone giggling, they assume it's about them and they react from that place. You often hear them saying, "Are you making fun of me?"

In our society giggling is seen oftentimes as weird. If you see an adult man giggling you probably picture someone who is deranged or drunk. This is another example of how we have been trained to reject joy in our society as you read about in Chapter 7 about the *Happiness Glass Ceiling*. The fact is that giggling, like laughter, is very powerful for the health of both your meat and energy bodies. Giggling is many times a precursor to laughter.

1. Laughter

Laughter is indeed the best medicine! Why? Because when you laugh you surrender to the the present moment. In other words, you stop blocking your natural flow and by default connect to the Right Now OS. That surrendering is when you can surf effortlessly in the flow of your life, which is why laughing feels so good.

Laughing is on the same level as meditation in terms of getting you to the aligned state of being full of yourself. Whenever I give talks I use a lot of humor because it's a wonderful way to raise the audience's vibration. It's very powerful to be in that yummy pool of energy where whoever surrenders to the laughter adds to the love, freedom, connection and flow of the room. Talk about feeling good! WHEW!!!!

Connect With the Giggly Fairy Exercise... This is an exercise of how you can connect to the Giggly Fairy. She's a valuable and fun tool that your imagination gives you to align you back to your authentic self, where you can access your spiritual DNA. How do you align with the Giggly Fairy? Where does she show up in our life? What messages does she bring you?

JOURNAL TIME... Laugher is an incredibly vital tool in helping you maintain your authenticity. The Giggly Fairy reminds us of that. Take this time to write or draw out what things or people make you laugh.

This page and the next contain a list of some of the funniest people to activate your imagination:

Tyler Perry, Jeff Jeffries, Monty Python, Zero Mostel, Melissa McCarthy, Anjelah Johnson, Chris Rock, Robin Williams, Ellen Cleghorne, Amy Schumer, Aparna Nancherla, Ellen Degeneres, Redd Foxx, Mae West, Jack Black, Chelsea Peretti, Will Smith, Mabel Normand, Martin Short, Terry-Thoma, Lily Tomlin, Dana Carvey, Jonathan Winters, Joyce Grenfell, Ernie Kovacs, Louis CK, Sherri Shepherd, Whoopi Goldberg, Tiffany Haddish, Buster Keaton, Stephen Colbert, Iliza Shlesinger, Mo'Nique, Carol Burnett, Wanda Sykes, Danny Kaye, Tig Notaro, Bert Lahr, Fortune Feimster, DL Hughley, Bea Arthur, Sarah Silverman, Martha Ray, Lou Costello, Kevin Hart, Marina Franklin, Andy Kaufman, Marco Horácio, Jane Lynch, Trevor Noah, Nathan Lane, Rico Rodriguez, Jimmy Durante, Eric Idle, Dave Chappelle, Michael Palin, Tim Conway, Phyllis Diller, Jon Stewart, Betty White, George Carlin, Steve Harvey, Tina Fey, Angela Hoover, Mike Myers, Lucille Ball, Steve Carell, Shappi Khorsandi, Sandra Bullock, Lewis Black, Billy Crystal, Kumail Nanjiani, Aasif Mandvi, Amy Poehler, Wayne Knight, Eddie Murphy, Ed O'Neil, Larry David, Rainn Wilson, Jesse Tyler Ferguson, John Leguizamo, Eric Stonestreet, Dane Cook, Leslie David Baker, John Krasinski, Gracie Allen, Ariel Winter, Zach Woods, Ed Helms, Creed Bratton, Seth Macfarlane, Steve Coogan, Gina Yashere, Paul Lieberstein, Estelle Harris, Jerry Stiller, Charlotte de Turckheim, Elizabeth Banks, Craig Robinson, Bernie Mac, Ty Burrell, John C. Reilly, Jason Segel, Martin Lawrence, Julia Louis-Dreyfus, Esther Rolle, Zach Galifianakis, Sabina Guzzanti, Michael Richards, George Clooney, Jason Bateman, Alec Baldwin, Marilyn Monroe, Ricardo Araújo Pereira, Jerry Seinfeld, John Oliver, Jamie Foxx, Parker Posey,

Chris Farley, Vince Vaughn, Catherine O'Hara, Fanny Brice, Nolan Gould, Paul Rudd, Kristen Wiig, Sarah Hyland, Jonah Hill, Sofia Vergara, Stephen Wright, Beatrice Lillie, Kim Wayans, Seth Rogen, Roberto Benigni, Matt Damon, Margaret Cho, Rick Moranis, Fred Willard, Mel Brooks, Debra Wilson, Danny Devito, Bill Cosby, Madeline Kahn, Julie Bowen, John Cleese, Eddie Griffin, Christopher Guest, Tracy Morgan, Jimmie Walker, Denis Leary, Dan Aykroyd, Rafinha Bastos, Rue McClanahan, Will Ferrell, Somore, Flip Wilson, César Mourão, Steve Martin, Lenny Clark, Bill Murray, John Goodman, Richard Pryor, Adam Sandler, Shazia Mirza, Chevy Chase, Anne Meara, Jim Carrey, Ben Stiller, Arsenio Hall, Anthony Anderson, Michael Capozzola, Bill Maher, Janeane Garofalo, Samantha Bee, Jessica Williams, Jason Jones, Hasan Minhaj, Aasif Mandvi, Wyatt Cenac, and Ricky Gervais to name a few...

Journal about who makes you laugh. Who are your favorites? What makes you laugh? If you were to check in with yourself, do you feel you laugh enough? Could you use more laughter in your life?

My way of joking is to tell the truth.
That's the funniest joke in the world.
—Muhammad Ali

Things I Want To Remember/Research/Review:

Maria Salomão-Schmidt

I am no longer accepting the things I cannot change.
I am changing the things I cannot accept.
—Angela Y. Davis

AFFIRMATIONS

Chapter 40. Do Affirmations Really Work?

The divine Louise Hay is a big proponent of affirmations and I completely agree with her about the use of them. Affirmations work because they help focus you on your intention. Remember one of my quotes, "Whatever you focus on controls your life."

Affirmations are incredibly helpful in directing your focus. This simple tool is incredibly effective, especially if you know the deeper reasons of why you are doing affirmations. Give yourself permission to play with them. Be open to saying things that are even uncomfortable.

 Affirmation Exercise... Having a strong "why," instead of just following "the ass" in front of you (as in the herd), is a wonderful way to check into your life. So pick a few of the affirmations in the next section and use them daily for 33 days. Leave copies all over the places you go: home, work, car, etc. Write them everywhere so you say them all day long.

At the end of those 33 days, it'll be the equivalent of doing an authenticity boost to your life. The result will be that since you have consistently and consciously focused on your intention, you'll have called much of your power back from things, people and events that were draining you. It's like getting an energetic facelift.

Here are examples of powerful affirmations...

- I am love! I am flow! I am happy!
- Everything always works out for me!
- Life is rigged in my favor! (Rumi)
- I treat my body with Love and respect!
- Food is the tool I use to nourish my body!
- I choose connection over being "right!"
- I always remember to play!
- Everything shows up exactly when I need it!
- I love being me!
- I love what magical things await me today!
- I am always safe and free!
- I love being me in the world!
- I find the gifts in everyone and everything.
- I am powerful, loving and kind.
- I am open to all possibilities that are in alignment with who I am!
- I am on the same vibration as the happiest, wealthiest and most influential people who have ever lived!
- I effortlessly find the love of my life!
- I release things I no longer need!
- I am open to accepting abundance!
- I release what feels icky to me!
- I am kind to myself and others!
- I move my body effortlessly and consistently!
- I effortlessly attract the best parking spots!
- Happiness is my absolute birthright!
- I love my body!
- I always have the best experiences!
- I easily lose weight and keep it off!
- I effortlessly hold a space of love in the world!
- I quickly find wonderful solutions.
- I am always protected.

The more you do this affirmation work, the lighter and less stressed you will feel because you are starting to focus your energy on the authentic you. This is how to access your energetic DNA, so you can fully live this life as Dr. Wayne Dyer said without "...dying with your music still in you." This is another example of *calling your power back* from following the herd. *Get undomesticated!* The time has come to turn from *sheeple* back to *people, living from our core.*

 Bonus Exercise... As a bonus, say an affirmation out loud in the mirror. If you don't think you judge yourself, then the mirror exercise will let you know just how much you do. It's a wonderful way to notice and give yourself the chance to shift. Even if it's hard at first, continue because you are going to love what is on the other side of you. This is a great way to practice noticing without judgment.

Now write your own favorite affirmations here:

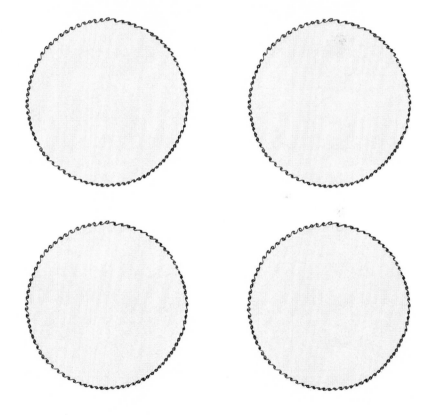

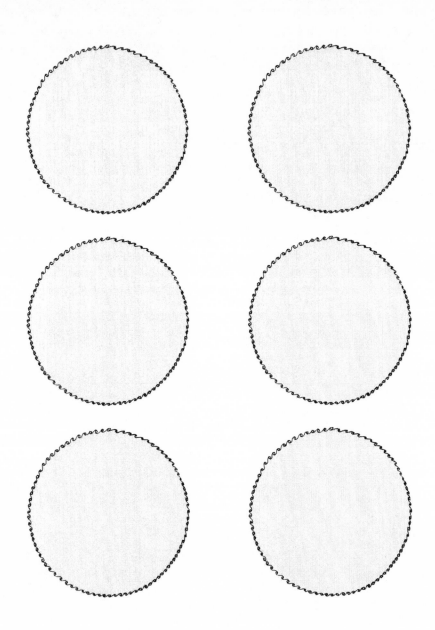

Maria Salomão-Schmidt

Most people still think they need to find themselves,
but what they really need to do is just
unleash themselves.

—Maria Salomão-Schmidt

Chapter 41. Vocabulary That Instantly Blocks Your Life

Affirmations are a great way to maintain an authentic life. They help you focus on your core. Affirmations help us see that the words we use matter.

For the next few pages I'm going to be sharing words with you that will help you start noticing how your life's flow is greatly affected by the phrases and expressions you have taken for granted. Below are words that decrease your energy. The result is that you activate and operate in the domesticated state of the Herd OS. Notice how you feel when you read these...

Good/Bad – These two words are the result of judging a situation. When you judge, you're leaking energy. When you leak energy you are operating in the Herd OS, where you are blocking your own flow, you must take or beg for energy from those around you. Judging something as "good" or "bad" puts the energy flow in the unnatural direction of from the outside-in, instead of the authentic way of from the inside out.

Be A Good Girl – This phrase is a very powerful tool of the Herd OS. It causes the child inside us (no matter our actual age) to seek outside approval above what our internal feelings may be telling us. Even though it was meant to help, most of us have used this form of "approval" or had it used on us. It's one of the most powerful and damaging phrases ever created, mainly because it is so common that it is seen as an absolutely "normal" part of what human beings "should" aim to be. They are aiming to be authentic while being the very opposite. The more they "try," the more inauthentic they become. Even as you read this you might feel some conflict. It also buys into *Conditional* versus *Unconditional Love.* You'll only be loved or liked "if you..." (do the desired action). Similar phrase: "Were you a good girl today?"

Be A Good Boy – Same as the "Be A Good Girl." It's important to allow a space for the men reading this book too for in the Herd OS women were seen as weak because they had feelings, but men were not allowed to have any feelings at all. This is one of the biggest tragedies in human history, the fact that most societies did even allow men to connect to their internal GPS. The consequence is major external conflict for these men who were subconsciously mirroring their internal conflict. Wars happen specifically because of this treatment of men.

Try – The act of attempting, which tricks many into thinking there is a commitment for completion—when in reality, there is only a commitment for an attempt. It allows the space for people not to show up in their lives while thinking that they actually are. If it were computer code, it would be a bug in the system.

But – Whatever phrase came before this word you are negating it. For example, "I love you, but..." Get the drift? This is a Neuro-Linguistic Programming (NLP) classic, which is a form of psychology of how people communicate. It's very useful. The solution is to use "and" instead of "but."

Busy – Run into anyone and ask how they are and, most likely, they will respond with this word, *busy. Busy* is a code word for mindless, stressful living where you feel like you can never catch your breath or take a break. It is you living inauthentically, on the road of *efforting*, depression and illness. This is all feedback for how you are living unaligned to your spiritual DNA. I break down the word "busy," and call it being on "Bus Y." We don't know *why* we're on it, but we keep going round and round, bored and tired. Great news! If you're reading this, chances are you will eventually be taking the "Bus Y" trip less and less, once you become more aware of how your energy body works.

Always – This is a word of absolutes and there are none on our planet. Everything is constantly shifting and moving, even though your naked eyes cannot see it. Everything is in constant motion on Earth because the planet is too. It never stops rotating. Sometimes "always" is used in affirmations, as an anchor for what you want to consciously magnetize into your life. Although the intention is good, the word can cause a bit of a slippery slope by having the affirmation very easily be turned into a vow. Vows make a promise that creates stagnant, cemented energy. The outside world and your ego might like that, but your energy body does not. Words like this create energy blocks that keep us stuck, even though that is not the intention.

Never – This is again another word, like the word "always," that is about only one way of being which causes stagnation. Your energy body does not like it.

Using these type of words causes you to fall into, and then have to spend the efforting energy, maintaining a difficult existence in the Herd OS.

 JOURNAL TIME... Lower your shoulders. Smile. Roll your neck from shoulder to shoulder. Review the words above and write about which words you use most. Use lots of deep breaths here. Now take a moment to ask yourself these questions...

- How is that affecting your life?
- How you feel?
- How you see yourself?
- How you connect and access your dreams?

Use a lot of deep breaths here to move the energy as your write. This Journal Time has the potential to really help you shift things for you so that you're more aligned to activating your spiritual DNA.

The Painful Phrases of Disconnection and Conflict

Whether we realize it or not, words are incredibly important because they help connect us to a corresponding energetic vibration. Words that flow allow us to flow with our natural, authentic current. The words we choose that are low energy words, create suffering, efforting and discord. Because most of us live in the Herd Operating System, words that keep us in the lower vibrations are so common that we don't even notice them.

Although each of us is born with access to as much energy flow as we could ever need, as part of the domestication process, we are taught to block our natural flow. Since we need energy to survive, we must use what we can to take energy from each other. We become *energy vampires*, by default, so we can get the energy we need to stay on this planet. The following phrases exist solely in the Herd OS. Part of waking up to your spiritual DNA is to notice what creates energetic *stuck points (blocks)* and *flow points (movement)*.

If you feel confused, it might be because you didn't realize that we need that flow of energy to live, just as dearly as we need oxygen. Energy flow is absolutely vital for survival. People can get so low or have been so connected to someone else that when that person is gone, the flow is broken and they literally leave this life.

An amazing example of this happened to a fellow Boston College alum and football great, Doug Flutie. His parents Joan and Dick Flutie were married for 56 years. His dad, who died of a heart attack, had been sick for a long time so the family was able to say their good-byes. What they were not expecting was that their mom Joan, who was not sick, would die less than an hour after her beloved husband. "They say you can die of a broken heart and I believe it," Doug Flutie wrote on Facebook. Doug's powerful words say it all. Since the heart is the brain of the energy center, a broken heart can be just as lethal as a heart attack.

The person can die quickly as happened to the beloved Joan Flutie, or it can happen more slowly, where people become "shells" of themselves and can seem almost zombie-like. The zombie-like people can be described as having "no life," which is in a way very accurate, because they have cut off their life's energy. Again, this is mostly subconscious, because up until now, a vast number of human beings did not acknowledge their energy body.

All of the phrases below are energetic *stuck points*. They activate low vibration feelings. You can tell when something is "low-vibration" because it does not feel good. The only caveat is that it might temporarily seem good to the person (energy vampire) receiving it, but it is not authentic. Soon that person is again looking for more energy because she/he has disconnected herself/himself from her/his own innate energy source. It's simply not sustainable, unlike in the Right Now OS, so the hunting for more energy cannot stop.

Read these phrases and notice how they make you feel.

I Have To - This phrase, along with "I should," is one of the most popular ones people use, especially in their heads. It's that judgment voice that seems to never stop. It is also one of the most harmful, because it leaks energy and keeps us stuck. (The solution is "I get to" because it completely and instantly aligns you back to your core.)

I Should - The more you judge, the more you leak energy and the more you stay stuck where you are. This is much like a balloon with even the tiniest hole will begin deflating little by little, getting smaller and smaller. This phrase is still one of the biggest energy drains on our planet. When we are in energy vampire mode, we love using this phrase as a way to steal large amounts of energy from others.

I Can't - The domestication process leaves many humans with the belief that they are mostly helpless. Instead of trying something new full-heartedly, with a sense of wonder and fun, domesticated people generally choose the well-worn out path of "I can't." This phrase instantly cuts off any possibility of movement forward.

I Know - When you hear yourself saying this, it's a sign you could use a grounding exercise. It indicates your energy is coming from your head space. In certain situations it's absolutely fine to come from your head space, like if you are calculating a budget. The "I know" that leaks energy is the one that blocks feedback or information by saying, "I know, I know..." because the person has stopped listening.

I Hate It When - Regardless of how you finish this statement, this phrase just sets you up for leaking your precious energy because it focuses your attention on the negative. This is an embedded "I am" statement of hate. Hate is one of the lowest, most-energetically expensive and draining vibrations.

Powerful Stuck Point Questions

Questions can be very powerful tools that greatly affect your energetic body. Questions basically help you maintain whatever operating system you are in. In the Herd OS, you either "steal" or "beg" for energy. There exists a complete misalignment with your authenticity and a low vibration existence. The following are versions of classic Herd OS questions that keep you from accessing your spiritual DNA, thus blocking your authentic life:

Who does he/she think he/she is?

This is a statement that is definitely about "misery loves company." It can happen if you are low-vibration and you see someone else having what you want, or looking "too" happy (see Chapter 7 The Happiness Glass Ceiling). This can get activated when you are feeling down and  out and "blue." This concept has enabled our society to stay at lower vibrations by focusing on using other people as a feeding station. Statements or sentiments such as this can be easily used by angry mobs who are in judgment of others. Racism and sexism often feed off of this phrase because they begin labeling them as "other" and eventually "lesser" so they can energetically and physically use them.

What's your problem?

This is a provocative statement, instigating the energetic prequel to stealing someone's energy. It's an aggressive question that creates little to no connection to others. It's a power play. The main result is that it steals energy from others.

Here are a few more to watch out for:

- Don't you love me?
- Why is this happening to me?
- What did I do wrong?
- Why does bad stuff always happen to me?
- Why am I broken?
- What is wrong with me/you?
- Why don't you ever…?
- Who do you think you are talking to?
- Why doesn't anyone love me?
- Why doesn't anyone want me?
- What do I need to do for you to love me?
- Why am I not worthy?
- Why can't I ever get it right?
- Why are you always…?
- What do you do?
- Why is it always my fault?

Example of How to Shift Back to Your Flow Point

If you think the world operates from the energy/approval that you get from those around you (energy moving from the *outside-in)* then who you are is a reflection of how you are treated by the outside. This is the Herd OS. On the other hand, if you live life as if you flow from the *inside-out,* you do not have to morph or change who you are to fit others. This is the Right Now OS.

Life Challenge Example

You grew up in an abusive family. (Could have been physical, sexual, alcohol, neglect, etc.)

Under the Herd OS You Handle the Experience Any Of These Ways:

You shut down or have frenetic energy. Life feels heavy and depressing. You "are" a victim. You repeat the pattern in many different ways with many different people. You believe there is something wrong with you. You are unlovable. "Why did this have to happen? Why didn't anyone do anything? Why didn't someone save me? Why didn't my _____ (fill in the blank with anyone whose name fits) take care of me?"

Under the Right Now OS You Handle the Experience this Way:

Yes, it was an icky experience, but you realize that your family members were doing the best they could with what they knew. They were not operating from their wholeness. You understand they could not have done any better in the domesticated state they were in, because they thought that the flow came from the *outside-in*. In that equation, they were "losers" every time because they are not full of themselves, which is a very confusing, heavy, sad, draining place to live from. The world constantly hurt them in some way because they were looking for love/energy flow from an *outside* source. This is what happens in the unnatural state of the Herd OS and why people have suffered so very much.

When used in the Herd OS, questions help stagnate the flow and movement of your energy. It blocks your energetic freedom. You see your perpetrator(s) for what they are. You realize that you are in the Earth school and that each interaction is both a gift and a curse. You have learned to notice the patterns in yourself and others. You no longer take them personally. You are grateful for the gift. You move on instead of playing the movie of what happened over and over in your imagination. This is freedom and flow. This is Love.

There is no greater agony than bearing
an untold story inside you.

—Maya Angelou

Things I Want To Remember/Research/Review:

Maria Salomão-Schmidt

"HAPPINESS is a BY PRODUCT of LIVING in YOUR ALIGNMENT"

MARIA SALOMÃO-SCHMIDT

Chapter 42. Vocabulary That's In Alignment With Your Heart

I have listed specific vocabulary words and phrases in this section to help you immediately align with your source by operating from the Right Now OS. When you use them, they are powerful tools that connect you to your core authenticity (energy body) by focusing your thoughts, mind, energy and attention on your innate connection, your natural flow. They are useful tools because when you use these words, you are literally accessing the sound vibration at the level you want to exist that the matches *effortlessness, freedom* and *flow*. This is important because these are the higher vibrations of your heart. Here are some specific words to start noticing to in your life:

And – Use instead of "But." There is no more connective word than "and."

No – Saying "no" is often the kindest thing you can say to everyone involved, because it's a word that gives you, and those around you, boundaries. By saying "no" you are choosing where your energy goes, instead of being a victim by feeling you have to give up your energy when it does not serve you. One of my most favorite expressions is, "If it's not in alignment for you, then it's not in alignment for them either."

Yes – Saying "yes" to everyone else is common. Ah but saying it to yourself, and that little girl/boy that lives inside of you, may be a rare occurrence. The more energy you spend focusing on the true needs of that core, authentic part of yourself, the more intuitive and insightful you can become. If it were a financial transaction, it's the best ROI *(return on investment)* you can get for your asset. Since we are dealing with energy I call it E-Roi *(energetic return on investment)*. The biggest asset you have is your energy. By saying "yes" to yourself, you are focusing on the *core* of what is the way towards true happiness, the flow of your energy body. It's as easy and effortless as water flowing down stream. Most people think it's hard because they are trying to unnaturally take the water upstream. They are right. That is hard, but only because that's living life in the Herd OS.

Icky – This is a feeling you get when you feel something is off in your energetic or physical bodies. It indicates that something does not feel in alignment. *Icky* is a powerful alternative to using the judgmental expressions "good" or "bad," which causes ones' unalignment. Unalignment leads to a life of struggle, efforting and suffering.

Beautiful – The word I insert before each person's name to remind them, as well as myself, that their core energy is *Love, which is freedom and flow.*

Specifically – Many times people who get into arguments have wonderful intentions but are simply on different channels. The challenge is that they assume they are on the same channel so the argument grows. Miscommunication is rampant in our society. Using the word "specifically" helps cut the layers of crap, where the potential for drama and discord happens, by going right to the heart of the matter. For example, the word "dog" is a seemingly pretty self-explanatory word, but if you are at a dog park and someone says "Go find my dog," you may bring back the wrong one because that one simple word can indicate hundreds of possibilities. So by asking, "Which dog specifically?" or "What does your dog look like exactly?" you will have a better chance of attaining the desired outcome.

Thank You – Being grateful and spreading that gratitude to others is one of the most powerful ways you can spread Love on our planet! Gratitude is the path to happiness.

Weirdmaste – Derived from the iconic greeting "Namaste," which means "the god in me, sees the god in you." Since energy loves humor, this version plays off of that with, "the weird in me sees the weird in you."

"Weird" is how people in the Herd OS see anyone who is not "normal." In the Right Now OS "weird" is equivalent to authentic for each unique individual.

Phrases & Questions That Instantly Move You Into Your *Zone*

The following are great communication and connection phrases of the Right Now OS. When you start using these phrases in your everyday life, you receive many more intuition hits that allows you to unlock your life's mission. This way you are no longer living in defense and fighting all the time. You move into a natural state of trust, and that is when the magic starts flowing, your authenticity is the by-product. . Here are some examples of phrases and questions to start adding to your daily speech. They lessen the ego's influence and increase the heart's guidance in your life.

What I Heard You Saying Is - This phrase is a powerful way to allow the other person to feel heard, which is one of the most basic human needs. Having the other person feel heard is the first step to your creating a win-win situation. *People want to feel seen, heard and understood.* By using this specific phrase you are refocusing the conversation so that this can happen. This phrase then allows a flow of communication. It's a truly wonderful way to connect with someone.

I Am - Choose what comes after this phrase very carefully. This is the most powerful of all phrases you can use. It is the "God statement" because by using it you're literally creating your world, aligning yourself to any vibration you want! The "I am" phrase is the ultimate expression of creation so take great care in only using it for things you want to align with—who you *are* or who you want to show up as. Let's use the example, "I am sad." By saying this you become sadness; instead of saying, "I feel sad," which places the energy in a more flowing place. It is felt in the moment and is then, eventually released. "I am" is more solid. "I feel" is more fluid.

I Get To - One of the most powerful tools human beings possess is this phrase because it completely and instantly aligns them with their authenticity. Another way to say the same thing is "I Choose To." Do what works for you.

I Love It When - This phrase is another one that is incredibly powerful. It raises your energetic vibration by increasing your freedom and flow, which is the energetic definition of *Love*. By using it with others, it also invites them to raise their vibration. All ships rising!

I Feel – This is an energetically wise way to start a sentence because it focuses on the *freedom and flow*, which is the definition of *Love*. "I Feel" is a statement of movement, unlike the "I Am" statement which is one of being, not movement. When having a conversation with someone, people who are rigid with their viewpoints are not open to listening. It allows clear communication without putting others in defense. For instance you will most likely get more flow from saying, "I feel angry that you did not call me back." instead of, "I am angry that you did not call me back." When you are first noticing how you use your language it might not feel like a big difference, but as you begin to pay more attention to the power of your words, you'll access more of your spiritual DNA. In the past, feelings have been labeled as a weakness. It has been more acceptable to listen to the feedback of the physical body, for example, "I feel cold," because it can lead to serious damage. But when someone says, "I feel horrible driving to work every day." the response is more along the lines of "Who doesn't!" and "Join the crowd." That shows us what operating system that person is operating under, and how very common it is for our society to be connecting to the Herd OS. As part of our awakening, more of us are realizing how our energetic bodies give us feedback. Using the "I Feel" statement is a magnificent tool for activating your feelings, which in turn, build your intuition. Your intuition and your dreams are how your spiritual DNA shows up for you.

This Does Not Feel Good To Me – This phrase may at first seem like an energy block but energy needs some boundaries for it to flow in its authentic way. Without boundaries there is nothing but mush. Imagine if your house was not split up into different rooms. Imagine your kitchen, bathroom and bedroom were all in the same room so you pooped where you cooked. This shows that boundaries are really important. It allows the person to check in and get feedback as to where they are energetically, by noticing if they feel "light" or "heavy."

Maria Salomão-Schmidt

What Is The Gift? – This is an incredibly powerful question. Ask it as much as you can! It's the one question that helped bring me back to life when my daughter suddenly died. No matter where you are in your life, the more you ask this question, the more you start shifting into your alignment because this question magnetizes *gratitude* into your life. *Gratitude* is the elixir of the soul. It refocuses your attention and vibration back to your natural state of alignment.

What I'm Noticing Is – By starting with this phrase, you create an opportunity to share the feedback you are picking up. The challenge is that when you are leaking energy you oftentimes judge, and at the same time, can feel judged by others. When someone is in the defensive state of the Herd OS, the act of noticing can be taken as a judgment and attack. From the Right Now OS, this is not the case at all. It is just an introduction to *sharing* information. Sharing information encourages freedom and flow. Your energy body loves that!

You Are Right – This is one of the most diffusing phrases in the entire world, and most underutilized. It isn't an easy one to say at first because it goes right in the face of your ego, which never wants to be "wrong." In any conversation where there's discord, there's a first step that most miss. Usually people go right into their *"let me convince you I'm right"* stance. The rule of thumb to remember is that if you want to get to a true win-win solution, make sure the other person feels heard first. Let the other person speak first. When they are done speaking, use this simple phrase, "You are right." The key to remember is that you're not saying you *agree* with the person. You're simply saying you understand that to them, they're right. It's a phrase of acknowledgment the same as when you nod your head as others are speaking. This allows the other person to move into the *now let me hear you* mode. If you want others to hear you, you must first hear them. It's a very different way than most of us have learned to resolve a conflict, but it's a useful tool that the more you practice, the more harmony you'll attract in your life.

There is a crack in everything.
That is how the light gets in.
—Leonard Cohen

The happiest people who have ever lived are those
who live lives congruent with their heart's calling!
—Maria Salomão-Schmidt

Chapter 43. My Journey

I was on the "good girl" path of life. Still a little edgy, not vanilla at all, mind you, but doing all those things in the formula of life that I was told would make me "successful." For the complete formula go back to Chapter 26. By the way, what I've come to discover is "successful" is really just a code word for "I want people to love me" or "I want to feel loved." As you have probably experienced in your own life, we humans will do almost anything to get that feeling—and I did.

From a very early age I wanted my parents to be proud of me and won as many awards and contests as I could. I participated in all sorts of extra-curricular activities: band, chorus, plays, school clubs, Portuguese school, *musica folclórica de Portugal* (Portuguese traditional dancing), basketball, track, volleyball, National Honor Society, etc. You get the idea. Being from an immigrant family meant that making our parents proud was a really big part of the deal. Maybe no one ever spoke about this as directly as I'm stating this, but in doing my research I now realize that is how our childhoods were set up, through the stories they tell us of how the world "is."

The "story" my parents told us was that they came to America to give us a "better" life. They "sacrificed" for us, and in turn, our part of the deal was to follow that simple success formula that we all know so well. Except for our yearly summer trip to our beloved Portugal, our lives were very much based on living in the Herd OS. A huge emphasis was put on working hard, and not based a lot on what we felt or wanted. There were very specific rules and protocol. When people live from such an inauthentic place, they certainly can have moments when they implode or explode.

My parents, especially my father, is one of the most charismatic men I have ever met, but he had an incredibly painful childhood that he survived only by limiting access to his magnificent heart. Growing up we were both terrified and in awe of how benevolent he was to others. My *pai* has always been an incredible community leader. He helped countless people, many who had no other place to turn. The community loved him. Everyone knew he was very passionate about everything he did. Unfortunately, his anger was also fueled by that passion. *Pai* had many moments of nonsensical rage. My brothers, mother and I were beaten by him when that rage overtook him. Although that part of my life was incredibly painful, I now realize my father is one of my biggest gifts in this lifetime. I am grateful for what I learned by having gone *through* what I did.

I created a *stuck point* of my energy that kept me stuck in suffering, even more than what my father had ever done to me. I got stuck in the vibration he exposed me to, as he was stuck in the vibration that his parents exposed him to for many years but eventually it became a *flow point*. You can only access the gift of a situation when it enters the *flow point*. At the time though, I did not have that understanding. Some of my life's most horrifying moments occurred at his hands.

For much of my life I so identified with the abuse that I now joke that the phrase "I grew up in an abusive home" was my middle name, because I used it so often to describe who I was. It was how I saw myself and how I related to the world. In retrospect I brought it up constantly for two reasons. One, it was my biggest point of reference up to that point in my life. It was a huge *stuck point*, a massive *energetic furball* I was processing. Two, now that I have learned about energy work, I see that it was also a way I ran my artificial energy flow. Since I did not operate in my natural state of the Right Now OS, I received energy from others in the form of *sympathy*. Because I was living mostly in the Herd OS back then, how I unconsciously thought I could best "feed" my energetic body was through sharing these stories. In those moments, much like a drug addict would, I felt great at first, but then there was a big let down.

Getting your flow in this manner is not a great way to run your energy for three reasons:

1. You are getting someone else's recycled energy, and like recycled air, it's not as pure or effective as yours would be.

2. You have to continuously find ways to beg or steal energy from others when you are running out of it.

3. It runs your system ragged to constantly have to have these extremes of emotional energy—either really full or really empty—versus a consistently balanced level that naturally happens in the Right Now OS.

Whenever I think of the person I used to be, it becomes clear just how much *contrast* I have had in my own life. This is mainly due to a magical little girl who not only stole my heart, but also showed me how to find it again. That little girl's name is Sophia, or "Sophalicious" to those who knew and fell in love with her.

My Earthly Angel

Sophia June-Raquel Salomão Schmidt was born at Mount Auburn Hospital in Cambridge, Massachusetts on May 12, 2005. Her pregnancy and birth were the easiest of all my children. She was born naturally and without complications. We were so incredibly happy to have another baby. I had been dreaming about having more children and so we were incredibly thrilled... until... the shock came when I first laid eyes on her and knew something was "wrong." Doug and I immediately looked at each other and we both knew—our baby girl had Down Syndrome.

I believe in being brutally honest because being authentic and raw helps clear out the crap in our lives. The best day suddenly became our worst day. Both Doug and I took it incredibly badly. In my mind she was not a baby—not my baby. She was "damaged." She was "not 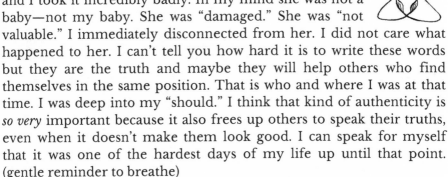 valuable." I immediately disconnected from her. I did not care what happened to her. I can't tell you how hard it is to write these words but they are the truth and maybe they will help others who find themselves in the same position. That is who and where I was at that time. I was deep into my "should." I think that kind of authenticity is *so very* important because it also frees up others to speak their truths, even when it doesn't make them look good. I can speak for myself that it was one of the hardest days of my life up until that point. (gentle reminder to breathe)

There's a part of this story that I haven't often shared that added to the shock and confusion of the day for me. On a beautiful fall day when I was a sophomore at Boston College, I was standing in front of the School of Social Work in Chestnut Hill. Out of nowhere I remember hearing a very strong genderless voice say to me, "You are going to have a little girl with Down Syndrome." I remember looking around to see if I had just overheard someone else's conversation. There was no one around me. It was the weirdest thing in that moment because I was 19 years old and had no context for this whatsoever. Maybe because it was so out of the blue, this memory got locked away; and so I had forgotten about it until this event actually happened. The weight of remembering this memory made the initial experience of it that much weirder, and harder to handle.

Maria Salomão-Schmidt

There's an expression I have used repeatedly in my life when I feel confused or stuck. It is, "You have not been brought this far to be abandoned now." I metaphorically fell onto my knees, feeling completely run over by life. Feeling completely lost, I did not see the cup as half full, or even half empty—I saw it as someone who cracked the glass, so that I'd never have water again! So great was my fear.

Look For The Angels

The answers are all around us, and if you pay close attention, there is no hardships when *angels* are around to guide us. When people speak about "angels," they usually mean the ones without bodies. The ones I leaned on that day were actually in physical human form. I don't know if they really know, but they made all the difference in the world to me and our family. By showing up in my life, they helped me course-correct from a closed life of fear and sadness to one of meaning and love. I hope that when they read this they will understand how much they mean to me.

There were sooo many "angels" who showed up in my life at that time to help me focus on *the gift*. Two in particular stand out. One of those angels was my Boston College roommate and heart-friend, the beautiful Kathleen Zinzer McCarthy. "Kataleanie," as I affectionately call her, has an amazing niece with Down's whom she adores and when we were at BC, she used to speak about her all the time. This was one of the first thoughts that I started to connect to as I began processing what had happened. The invisible groundwork that Kathleen and her beautiful family had inadvertently been doing for almost two decades was helping me in that initial devastating moment in time. By remembering that they were happy and that she was beloved to them, I could begin to re-shape how I saw Sophia.

Again, this is so very hard to write because "Sophalicious" was and *is* such an incredible gift! I had the "crown jewels" but because of my conditioning of what was "good" and "bad," I could only see this as all *bad*. The sadness that came from all this was unbearable. The confusion arose because I was fighting my programming of what she "should" be and look like. This is classic de-programming from the Herd OS, which can really be a painful experience. Boy, oh boy, can it get messy! Peace and wisdom comes from total surrender to what is authentically unique to you. Comparing yourself to others is where your life gets convoluted back into the Herd OS.

The second Earth Angel who really helped to ground and connect me to my heart when all I could see was pain, was my beautiful mother, Maria Raquel. She sat on my bed with me for hours after Sophia's birth with tears in her eyes, quietly and lovingly sharing her inner strength with me while holding my hands. Her wisdom was exactly what I needed to hear. Even in all the chaos, she spoke right to my heart. My beautiful mãmã Raquel shared with me that, yes, this child was not what I expected, but she was still *my* child. As big tears ran down her lovely face, she said that if I rejected Sophia now, during these first precious few hours, I would never be able to bond with her. Sophia would never have her mother. She asked me not to do that to her, or to myself. Looking into my eyes she asked me to "act as if," to open my heart and all would be taken care of. These words are the basis for living a happy life. I will be forever grateful for my mother's beautiful heart, especially for that moment of compassionate wisdom and deep love.

As with everything we do in life, once we commit to something with our whole heart, it's as good as gold! I took my mãmã's advice and started acting "as if" and immediately things started to shift. The confusion left because I now had a *focus*. I moved from stuck point to flow point energy. Before I had nothing to focus on but self-pity and lament, which just leaks energy. That's no way to live.

I spent much of my time engaging Sophia through play, reading, connecting with experts, setting appointments, buying the right equipment and doing physical therapy to give her as much freedom to move and communicate with those around her. I had studied the work of Anne Sullivan, Helen Keller's teacher so I communicated with Sophia as if she were deaf and blind so she could use the vibrational and visual cues from language.

When I was little, I had a deaf friend so I knew a little sign language so this experience had opened up a whole new world to me, as did the speech pathology class I took at BC. I was using all that I had learned in my lifetime up until that point to help Soph thrive. We made sure it was all play and fun for her. At a very early age she started signing back to us, even making up signs. (Luckily we have it on video!) By focusing on Sophia, Doug and I became even closer. The gifts of what we learned started pouring in because we were raw and open to it. We surrendered to what was and it brought us massive happiness.

I fell into a deep, deep Love with our beautiful Sophalicious, everyone did—because honestly, that's all she ever gave people. For a few months more, I still compared her to "the other Sophia," the one who was "normal," the one who *should have been*, until I finally realized that we got the *real* Sophia. As a mother of five, I can tell you that as hard as it is to believe, there was not one moment in her whole life that I was ever, ever, ever the tiniest bit angry or upset with her. As a baby, she was Love incarnate! Even as a mere baby, Sophia brought me out of my deep fear and ignorance; her Love was that intoxicating!

People with Downs have an extra chromosome so Doug and I had jokingly asked the doctors if that meant that she would have superhuman powers like the ability to fly or leap tall buildings in a single bound. Now we know that she indeed did have a super human power, and that power is to LOVE FULLY. Do you know how amazing it feels to have that kind of love? It is absolutely incredible! The feeling of pure connection and peace is exhilarating. That is what it feels like to be Sophia June-Raquel Salomão Schmidt's *mãmã*! This became our *new normal* and it was incredibly fun to be around someone who is "all about the love." We looked forward to a lifetime of exploration, play and love together! Again, it was not to be how we planned...

June 22, 2006, is the date that part of me died forever, while another part of me was uncovered. A month earlier, we had had Sophia's grand first birthday party. It was one of those events where everyone was so truly happy and flowing with tons of food and fun. At that time I was a working mother of three, with two in diapers so it was a miracle that I found the time to send everyone her first birthday photo. It came out so beautifully, authentic Sophia, that people called to say her photo was on their refrigerators because it was such a super photo of a super joyous day! We loved to hear that Sophia's photo was on refrigerators all over the world!

On this otherwise normal sunny Thursday morning in late June, I was running late for a client meeting when the absolute unthinkable happened. Just as I was about to leave, the nanny called out for me in a tone of voice that activated something primally deep within me. Instantly, I knew something was very, very wrong. I dropped everything I was carrying and bolted to her side. When I picked up Sophia, who was normally a very heavy bundle of Love and giggles, she was light as a feather, her lips were blue and she was non-responsive.

Frantic desperation fell over me as I tried to remove my other daughter Mia, who was a very verbal and perceptive two year old, from the room. I immediately called 911 and gave her CPR, to no avail. I have replayed those moments over and over and over in my head. Our beloved Sophia passed away that morning giving me one of the biggest and hardest gifts I have ever received, although it took me a very long time to realize that any gifts were involved whatsoever.

I took her death very hard. I blamed myself and did not understand why my beautiful husband Doug did not blame me too. It was so incredibly sad, totally heartbreaking. At the funeral when I approached her little body in the tiny casket, my breasts began lactating at her sight. It made me feel even worse! I kept thinking, "Why is this happening? This is so not natural! Even my body misses her!" I felt sorry for myself and then felt bad and mad for feeling sorry for myself.

I felt shades of confusion, sadness, anger, pain, rage throughout my thoughts. Who I was died the day she did. I won't call it innocence because it was not that. It was more like in the virtual reality rooms in Star Trek when it seems as though they are in a beautiful scene but when they turn off the program there is nothing but an empty blue box. Well, Sophia's death had virtually turned off my beautiful life and now I found myself living in an empty blue box. I could see that others still saw the virtual reality world, but I could no longer buy into that world.

After we lost Sophia, I also felt so lost. For the first few heart-wrenching hours and days especially, I just wanted to die, *really die*! I felt the whole world was one big, fat lie, and we were the idiots following the rules but getting our asses kicked over and over again. You can say that for me her death was the last straw and I wanted out! Strangely, at the same time, in the midst of this HUMONGOUS rift in my life, I also felt incredibly free. I noticed that when I leaned into or focused on that feeling, I would get such a huge wave of pain—so much so, that it was something I was not able to process or explore at the time. But I now experience a very similar feeling when speaking or coaching. It is the magical feeling of total surrender, completely without the pain part. Thank goodness pain is temporary!

WHAT'S the GIFT?

Immediately after Sophia's death, I had a flashback to an episode I saw on *The Oprah Show* some 11 years earlier, before I even had kids or knew Doug. The show was about a young mom who had twins. One of the babies died unexpectedly a few days later. Best-selling author Gary Zukav, who has an incredibly gentle soul, was on the show. He told her that she had one of two paths before her. She could forever stay stuck in what I now call the *Land of Should* where the twin that is still alive will always be compared to his dead brother, or she could choose to see this as *a gift*. In that moment she spits out, "How can the death of my innocent little boy possibly be a gift to anyone." Without missing a beat, Gary says, "There are millions of people watching this show all over the world, and you never know how your story will affect and help them. Your son could be a gift to those people." It was this moment which seemed not so important to me at the time, that planted the idea of becoming a guest on The Oprah Show. More about that later.

Well, fast-forward a decade from when that magical television show aired and I'm standing in Metro West Hospital in Framingham, Massachusetts being told by a very unfeeling doctor that my baby girl Sophia is brain dead and is on life support. In that pivotally powerful moment, all my breath just left me and all I could think of was that mother's anger and Gary asking over and over and over again... "What is the gift?"

At first I simply did not want to hear it! I'm going to give you an idea of what was going through my head. This is unfiltered and raw, as were my emotions. Even now, each time I edit this section, tears stream down my face. Feel free to skip it if it's too much. It is my reality and an important part of how I channeled all this amazing material. I hope it helps you get through your own, unique energetic fur balls!

Here's what it felt like in my head..."STOP!!!!! There's no gift! I want out of this life! I want out of this pain! I've been wronged! The whole world is fucked up! How can God take a baby, an innocent, sweet, beautiful baby? How can God kill babies, especially our beautiful baby Sophia?! How can this have happened in front of our other baby, our two-year-old daughter Mia? She doesn't understand! Hell, I don't understand! How could I have let this happen? I should have made an appointment with that doctor or this doctor! What about the horsehair plaster walls in her room? Maybe if I had gotten those changed? What could have I done to make this not happen? I can't stand to be in my body! I just can't! There is so much pain! I miss my baby! My heart hurts and feels numb at the same time. I want to DO something to make things better, to right this wrong, but there's nothing to do. I feel guilty that I'm not being present for my other children but I can't right now! I don't want to eat. I'm afraid to go to sleep because when I wake up I will remember that my baby is DEAD! DEAD! DEAD! I held a dead baby yesterday for hours! She was my sweet Sophia. What mother would not be crushed by hearing herself say those words? I only stopped when they had to come in to do the autopsy. "OMG, they are going to cut her open. I can't stand it! Now we have to call the funeral home... for a baby! How can this be happening! Thank God Doug is handling that! We both agree that cremation is the way to go, but I have a hard time knowing that my little girl's option, the options for her perfect little body is either to be buried or burn! What kind of barbaric sick, fucked up world do we live in when this is what happens to innocent babies!? How will I ever want to live again? The world no longer makes sense. I feel like throwing up. It hurts to see Doug crying like this. Such heartache! This world is just messed up! How can this happen? Where's my Soph? Where's my sweet baby? Is she safe? How can I protect her now when I don't even know where she is? Who has her? Where is she? She was just a little baby! I feel so lost. I don't know how to help our daughter Mia or son Christopher. Oh the pain and confusion in their eyes. Mia no longer trusts me because she thinks I have taken her sister away from her. How can I protect her now? How can I explain this to her? Where are you Sophia? I'm so sorry baby girl, I've failed as a mother to protect you from death. How can this be happening to a baby?! Where is my baby girl? I feel like such a bad mother! How did I let this happen?" These were some of the billion thoughts racing through my mind trying to "make sense" of the most heartbreaking day of my life.

Finally, I was so exhausted that I fell asleep. Mercifully, that night I dreamt of Sophia. She was not a baby but rather a twenty-something year old woman with long, straight strawberry blond hair, a 60s A-line dress and white go-go boots. She looked like she was a version of Heather Graham's character in the Austin Powers movie, *The Spy Who Shagged Me*. (See how the universe has a wicked sense of humor! Never a dull moment if you're paying attention.)

This beautiful woman was leaning against a doorframe with her arms crossed. When I saw her I said in my mind, "I know I'm supposed to think you are Sophia but I don't think you are." In direct reaction to my comment, she placed her hand on her hip and made a face and gesture that only Sophia made. She smiled at me and I smiled at her. In that instant, one of my biggest fears was addressed.

Part of me had felt a desperation that she was unsafe because I was no longer able to care for her. This dream showed me that Sophia was not a baby. She was something else. She was fun, sassy, smart, hip and free! I knew if I saw her in this new way (rather than a helpless abandoned baby) that the grieving process would be more fluid and without so much heaviness. As I write this I am positive that Sophia was giving me yet another gift. Unfortunately, I could only ingest part of that gift because her loss was just too big for parts of me to accept.

Part of what I experienced in losing a child is that I felt that I needed to find her to protect her. Afterwards for the good part of that year, almost every time I went to a restaurant or store, or met a new person, I would tell them I had lost my daughter. When I finally *noticed* what I was doing, I checked in with myself and realized that there was a part of me that had not yet accepted her death. That part of me thought that if I asked enough people, someone was going to say, "Oh you mean this Sophia? She's been here all along waiting for you to come find her." I know it may sound crazy you, but I can promise you that it's no crazier than if your beloved child suddenly died in your arms.

At the end of the Austin Powers dream, I started channeling a lot of words in a stream of thought. I knew that if I just lay there and let the words wash over me I would lose them, so I jumped out of bed and ran to my computer and began typing the magnificent words that came pouring out of me. That was the first time I had ever experienced that form of writing. Much of this book comes from that benevolent faucet of words that flow in accordance with the level of trust and authenticity the human being (a creature with both an *energy* and *meat body*) can magnetize. At that time the words were pouring out so quickly that I could not type fast enough! There were no pauses just *focus*—let go, surrender, trust and write!

Reading these channeled words at her funeral was yet another layer of healing because I *got to* use my voice to convey what Sophia stood for me, LOVE INCARNATE. Here's what poured out of me on the morning after Sophia's death...

A Mother's Letter to the Community that Mourns Sophia

Sophia June-Raquel Salomão Schmidt
May 12, 2005 – June 22, 2006

My Dearest, Dearest Friends,

We have all been around long enough to know that life sometimes turns in a way that we did not expect. If we stop and listen to the "pulse" we find that these are challenging times for the people of our planet. I believe the only hope is our AWAKENING. The world's goodness puts angels among us to guide us back to LOVE. No matter how much pain/disappointment you have had in your life, deeply remember to always come back to LOVE.

Sophia was LOVE! The only difference between Sophia and us was that she knew nothing else. The more I reflect on the last 13 months, "our lucky 13," the more I realize that I, and all the people she crossed paths with, were witnessing an angel among us. Just look at her photos, you see it.

Her only "weapon" was her smile and the exuberance you could see in her face. Her first word was in sign language. She creatively created her own sign from the standard words for "drink" and "milk." Her first spoken word was "Dada" and she would occasionally say "Hi" and wave at you. At first we thought it was a coincidence, but when several people said she did it for them too we were dumbfounded (and delighted!). Our Sophia, despite most of the things "experts" said was a VERY smart little girl. Just a couple of weeks ago she delighted us with her ability to overcome her low muscle tone and sit up from a lying position with such exuberance it would make the most burly man start clapping with glee. Pure LOVE. She just took your breath away and the next time you took in a breath, it filled you with an incredible sense of peace. Peace.

It all sounds "perfect" but I have a little secret. One that I hate to admit but maybe it will serve as an example to others. When Sophia was born, Doug and I did not take it very well. We were expecting another perfectly healthy baby. We had no

Maria Salomão-Schmidt

idea she had Down Syndrome. At first we were not prepared to see past it. Sometimes in life beautiful things come to us but because we were looking for it in a different form, we don't realize what we have.

We are all deeply saddened by the loss of such a beautiful person. We all wish she could have stayed with us, even a moment longer. As a mother, I can't tell you how much I long to snuggle my face in her neck and just kiss her and kiss her and kiss her but...

BECAUSE OF SOPHIA...her father and I have a deeper relationship

Because of Sophia our family is more closely knit

Because of Sophia several professionals have been so inspired that they have made life-changing decisions, which will deeply affect the lives of other children

Because of Sophia we have gotten to deeply know and befriend magical people

Because of Sophia our children and family are more deeply respectful of people with special needs

Because of Sophia one young troubled girl has found inspiration and gone from flunking to being an A and B student.

Because of Sophia, our relationships are more "real," life is more "real."

Because of Sophia, the world is a better place.

If you are here, if you can hear my words, you have been touched by Sophia. I beg of you not to let my little girl's life be in vain. I beg of you to take Sophia's life as a beacon for how to be ALIVE, AWAKE and BRAVE in your own life. Be in the moment, even when it's "icky" or not pretty. Life's most profound and meaningful shifts usually come after such deeply painful experiences. Make your community the best it can be! Live life NOW, you can always be "busy" later. Our collective actions will decide whether this is a tragedy or not. I ask that you go and do something special for someone else, "pay it forward"

I am and will always be Sophia's mommy and because of Sophia I am a better person.

Sophia, Sophalicious, Sopiah, Soph-Soph, Sophie, bébé....eu adoro-te! I adore you!

Maria de Lourdes Cerveira Salomão-Schmidt
Sophia's Mãmã

Things I Want To Remember/Research/Review:

It's never too late to start the day over.

—Michael Franti

Chapter 44. Adjusting To Life "Without" Sophia

I have always felt like I never quite fit into this world, as though I never really belonged to just any one group or place. Instead, I felt like I belonged to all of them. A better way to say this is that I'm not a big fan of excluding anyone. I realize this feeling derives from not wanting to buy a lifetime pass into the world of human domestication, such as the good girl/boy formula that many seem to be killing themselves over in order to keep up with the Joneses! Before Soph's death I could tolerate a lot more. After Sophia's death, I started to view the world differently. I could no longer tolerate certain things. Speaking your mind in many places is only welcome if it's in alignment with what they already believe.

In our small New England town I got kicked out of a volunteer mother's group because I *rocked the boat* too much. Sometimes, just my being around made others uncomfortable—because losing a child is such a scary thing for most, and I was a reminder it could happen. Truth be told, it was sometimes hard to be around them too. Especially at the beginning, it was especially hard to hear any mom or dad complain about their child. In my mind I'd often be thinking, "Do you realize how very lucky that you have him/her in your life?! Do you?! Are you kiddin?! I'd give anything to be in your position! Stop complaining and start hugging!" Sometimes I would tell them out loud (in a kind way) and most would thank me for saying it. It helped them shift into that level of gratitude and being present with what is.

Many people during this time, even in our own family, avoided us because they simply did not know what to say. We don't blame anyone for that. We all do the best we can in any given moment. It was just a very lonely time for us. Most people, who called asked the normally obligatory greeting, "How are you?" When you are going through trauma that's not what you want to hear. One of the best phone calls I ever got at this time was from my dearest friend since childhood and our maid of honor, Dr. Gail Emilsson! No stranger to death, she knew exactly how to deliver the perfect phone call. "Do you want to talk about you? Do you want me to talk about me? Or do you want me to hang up?"

How refreshing! In a sea of people always asking "How are you?" but don't want to really know the answer, Gail's response was absolutely perfect because it allowed me the choice to choose when I felt so very powerless! I asked her to talk about her, which was extremely refreshing because most people just wanted to talk about me. That was a very magical phone call that I will never forget! I've paid it forward by sharing this amazing set of questions with those going through this. Gail's magical gift to me shifted my energy from a painful stuck point to a flow point.

The Gifts Keep Piling Up

The gift of having Sophia gave us the gift of meeting some of the most magnificent human beings I've ever encountered in this lifetime! We met one incredibly special person, Sharon Lisnow. She and her partner Mary McQueeney run one of the most amazing places I've ever been, The Michael Carter Lisnow Center in Hopkinton, Massachusetts.

When Sophia died, Sharon shared her own heartbreaking story about her beloved Michael's death, which gave me the courage to let go of my blame and guilt for not having been able to save Sophia. It's a rare and magnificent gift when someone can hold the space for you to just let go and fall apart in front of them. No dainty tissues, just a huge release of the avalanche of pain through my tears and cries of grief. They gave me space to let go of my massive *energetic fur ball*! Both Mary and Sharon were (and are) absolutely incredible! What they did for our family and do for others in similar situations, is miraculous. I can say with all certainty that they mostly live their lives beautifully full of themselves and that Love (freedom and flow) has extended out into the world. They have built an incredible community for their clients and their staff. If you get a chance go visit their respite center or make a donation! It's a perfect example of where Love lives. What a great role model for other businesses! Check them out at www.hopkintonrespite.com. It will *feed* your heart and fill your energy body!

Another Earth angel is Milford, Massachusetts' Police Chief Thomas O'Loughlin, who did not know me or Doug whatsoever. Even so, he bravely showed up one day on our doorstep to share his story about losing his own son. Unbeknownst to him I was suffering HUGE GUILT of having given Sophia CPR and it not working. I felt if I had done it "right" she would not have died. It was a horribly draining belief to carry. I shared this with him to which he responded, "I am a trained professional. I have given CPR eight times and six of those people died, one of them was my son."

Tom went on to share that most of the time CPR does not work, even for those who are professionally trained. It's just something that given nothing else is better than just standing there doing nothing. It was a massive weight off my shoulders to stop obsessing over whether I had done it "right" or not. Because of Tom's gift, I was finally able to stop paying this painful energetic mortgage. By following his intuition to reach out to us, total strangers, this beautiful man, helped me shift my energy pattern from a stuck point to a flow point. Chief Thomas O'Loughlin is a hero!

Several key people who had children with Down Syndrome also came forward. Some were people I barely knew, and others were people who had been in my life, such as the beautiful Dr. Kathleen Zinzer McCarthy as I shared earlier. These magnificent people helped me refocus on what was possible. By giving me examples, they helped me see the gift that Sophia was to me, our family and the whole world. I could not have done it without them, especially the beautiful Francine Rothkopf, who absolutely blew my mind with how she viewed her daughter, whom coincidentally has the same name as my Sophia, with just a different spelling. Her beautiful daughter is Sofia. As I've said before, the universe has a wicked sense of humor. In the story below you'll see what I mean.

Helpful Hint: Find the humor/absurdity in what is happening, even if it's incredibly painful, and you have found one of the most profound ways to heal. Healing is simply moving from a *stuck point* of energy to a flow point. By connecting to the "funny" you unlock the door to healing. Laughter is a wonderful catalyst to get you back into the Right Now OS. It's impossible to laugh and be in defense at the same time.

So Here's A Funny Sophia Story: Exactly, a year after our Sophia died, we had a bittersweet memorial, a get-together at our house with about 200 people. It was a pretty emotional day. The coolest thing was not only the amount of people who showed up, but also that many of those who came had not even met Sophia. They were just touched by having heard about her and simply showed up. You know grief is one of those things that most people, especially Americans, are not very comfortable with. They want to help, but they don't know how.

Everything was going on as planned with our simple celebration when at one point, people saw me look up and yell out "Sophia" as I ran over to hug a little blond girl with Down's, who except for being a few months older looked very much like our Soph. There was a collective gasp, and then uncomfortable silence. They thought I thought Sophia had come back from the dead! It took them a few very awkward minutes until the laughter started rolling through the crowd, as they realized that this beautiful girl was also named Sofia! The look of relief on their face was priceless. We all had a good laugh over it. Sophia would have loved it!

Those who tell the stories rule the world.

—Hopi American Indian proverb

Things I Want To Remember/Research/Review:

Maria Salomão-Schmidt

The biggest adventure you can ever take is
to live the life of your dreams.
—Oprah Winfrey

Chapter 45. Twenty Years To Oprah

I had a very strong vision that would not die. My twenty-year journey of becoming a guest on *The Oprah Show* is an incredibly interesting one, because I could never have predicted how it would have happened. Instead of just being on a normal show at Harpo Studios, I was invited to attend the filming at the United Center in Chicago where one of the biggest parties in the world was about to take place to honor the godmother of our planet, the beautiful Oprah Winfrey. She was finishing 25 years of televising her show on the air, and so her staff was throwing her a big shindig like no other.

Everything was top secret. We had no idea who was going to be there. We couldn't even tell anyone we were going. It is a very strange, exhilarating feeling to be sitting there surrounded by Beyonce, Madonna, Jamie Foxx, Jerry Seinfeld, Tom Hanks, Patti Labelle, Tom Cruise, Stevie Wonder, Maria Shriver, Will Smith, Michael Jordan, Josh Groban, Maya Angelou, Aretha Franklin, and Diane Sawyer. Celebrities such as Lisa Ling, Carson Kressley, Jessica Seinfeld, Ally Wentworth, Bob Greene, celebrity chef Tyler Florence, NFL star Emmitt Smith and former Chicago Mayor Richard Daley sat in the audience near us.

Everything was very *hush, hush*, so that Oprah would get the surprise of her life and I believe she did! I love that I was there to honor her because her following her life's path saved my life, but also activated its deepest life purpose! The vision that was guiding me I now know was my spiritual DNA, the deepest part of my core. It was so strong that I literally held on to it for 20 years; and even when it did not *make sense* I still felt the incredible urge to share it with others.

Part of the reason I got to be a guest on *The Oprah Show* was that the producers were reading my weekly blog called Butterfly Moms. They were not the only ones—thousands of people read it every week. Because there is such a deep excitement in how I described the experience as it was happening in the moment, I'm including the two blog posts here, in their entirety, of right after I got back from my very special secret trip. They are packed with the electric authenticity of the moment!

Maria's Blog... MY OPRAH DREAM REALIZED, Parts 1&2

May 20, 2011 – May 27, 2011

WOW! WOW! WOW! I have just read the first paragraph of my last blog on May 13 just seven days ago. I have lived a whole lifetime in these last seven days! I'm bringing lots and lots of BREATHE REMINDERS to today's blog because it is surreal in many ways how this has all happened and putting it into words, well, I don't know if I can turn something so AMAZING into linear thought, quite honestly!!! :)! I'm in a world right now where my whole energy level has shifted. The dream I had for 20 YEARS!!!!, that of being on The Oprah Show, finally came true in the grandest of scales!! I am in a state of awe, shock, gratitude, disbelief, amazement.... you get the idea! Every time I think I've "identified" a feeling it shifts to something else. I am a wave of fantabulous emotions!

I also feel like this experience has opened me up into a whole new level of being. If I had to describe it, I would describe it as my soul just expanded. My energy feels bigger. It is a magnificent feeling! Yesterday as I worked the counter of our family's dry cleaning business, I could feel how I was igniting the souls of the people who walked in. It felt AMAZING! I know that is my life's calling and whether I do it on a stage or one-on-one it feels like total alignment of my soul when I'm doing this. To see people's faces and energy dramatically shift in a short time leaves me feeling incredibly grateful and joyous! I sometimes even jump up and down and clap my hands, I'm so this kind of happy!

For those who need an update I will give you the quick rundown. Last Thursday, May 12 would have been Sophia's 6th birthday. *The Oprah Show* had only 3 shows left. Every actor, musician, therapist, author's PR people were doing anything and everything to get their clients on the show. I used to do PR so I know how this goes. I had been trying to get on for 20 years people, so I knew that if it was going to happen I simply needed to completely *surrender* because it was out of my hands. All I could control was my ENERGY ATTITUDE. I let go again of my expectation and embraced *gratitude*. I sent a final email from my heart to the producer I had been working with letting him know it was Sophia's birthday and thanking him for answering my original email, working with me throughout the year and giving me soooo much hope!

Friday, May 13: Wrote my blog to the reception of one of the highest number of readers ever. The same day a new producer calls me and interviews me. About five more calls that day. I'm asked if I can fly out to Chicago for an interview or have a crew come here. (I hope for them to fly me out, but am open to whatever comes.) They call me back and say someone is flying out to film me, "Are you free at noon?" After a few phone calls I changed things around so that I was free. Duh! ;)

The Oprah Show camera crew came to our house in Holliston (Massachusetts). What a wonderful day! On Saturday, May 14: The producer Alex flew directly from Harpo Studios to Providence with not even enough time to change his clothes. He interviewed someone in Providence at 8am and came to my house at noon. He brought two cameramen and one sound guy extraordinaire. Of course one of them was Portuguese from São Miguel in the Azores. *(Love how the universe works!)* Alex says it might not even air. They have to still approve the content. They film for 2.5 hours and leave. I'm thankful for the whole experience and that my kids get to see what a production team looks like. It is a beautiful sunny day. *You KNOW when things get too serious*—I have to collaborate fun... :)

Sunday, May 15: It's a rainy day. Finished an open house on a new real estate listing. Get lots of interest and two offers above asking. Doug finished his open house at the same time. So since we had a babysitter we met at Bertucci's for a quick lunch. Alex calls. They loved the film and will use it. Yay!!! And, surprise, they have two tickets for me if I'd like to come to Chicago for the final taping? It hits me that not only am I going to be ON THE Oprah Winfrey Show, but that it's going to be one of the very *last* shows!!!!

Suddenly, Sophia feels very, very, very close to me! I KNOW this is a gift from her! I'm having the same out-of-body experience I had when she died, but this time it's oh-so-joyous!!!! WHAT A GIFT!!!!! One snafu... They cannot pay for the flight because their budget is shot but will pay for the hotel and food. It's been a rough couple of years for us financially, but I know that if I've come this far nothing is going to stop me. So I reached out to my class (I'm in my second year of Energy Medicine School) and asked if anyone had any frequent flyer miles. To my heartfelt joy, my classmates got together and chipped in to buy us our airplane tickets!!! AMAZING! (Learning to receive is SUCH a huge part of all this.) My friend Karyn Knight Detering sprung into action as one of my many fairy godmothers who appeared. Karyn offered to drive me to airport, take care of my Mia and called our wonderful hairdresser Meredith from Willow Salon for an emergency appointment. Meredith opened up the salon for just me at 6am on a Monday (during the day they are normally closed) right before she got her root canal! AMAZING! Thanks goes to my mom for watching my two youngest just days after her surgery. Thank you Vicki, Raquel, Heather, Arden, Gregg, Alex, Andy, Alberto, Sandy, Linda, Doug, Nancy, Karyn, Meredith, my class at the Rhys Thomas Institute for Energy Medicine and everyone else who had a hand in me going to Chicago!

Monday, May 16: Within 24 hours we were in Chicago and getting debriefed on what to wear and some of the basics. My brother Pedro meets me because he now lives in Chicago. He brings his son Mateus who is a total cutie pie! What a total treat it is to play with him! I hardly sleep that night knowing what's coming!

It's an amazing vibration when you have 13,000 people around you who are sooo thankful to be there!

Tuesday, May 17: It's the big day. Trying to stay in my body. I get up SUPER early. Can't sleep. Too excited! Spend lots of time answering people's questions. My email is still sporadic and my computer still not working right, so I'm hobbling along, technologically speaking. I chant, meditate and do Reiki to calm down. The fear/worry wants to come in. When this happens I want to start controlling things. I am observing as if I'm outside my body. I'm shifting and I don't know what I'm feeling from one moment to the next. We go for a walk. The air feels great. It's a little past three o'clock and we meet downstairs for our limo bus with the other ULTIMATE VIEWERS, who will be featured on the show. As we start heading towards the United Center, we start getting more details. There was a lot of secrecy prior to this point.

The representative tells us that it's going to be two shows instead of one with over 30 stars and lots of surprises. Still not sinking in. We are told we will be there until around 11... ended up being more like 1am!!! When we get there we come in through the security entrance that all the stars take. It was AMAZING! Incredible energy. Everyone was EXTREMELY grateful to be there! A "funny" thing happened where I heard a Madonna song and danced over to see what was going on and there was Madonna standing there practicing her part of the show! I wish I could tell you I acted cool, but I did not! That was the first of many stars I would see and mingle with that night!

People ask if I met Oprah. This is not the typical show she does because these two shows were for her. Oprah did not have a microphone during most of the show because she was "receiving" not "giving." She sat four people away from me and passed by me all night long because they kept moving her (she wore heels and by the end of the night you could tell her feet were "barking;"—after 12 hours of dancing and standing in heels mine were too!!!!)

We had VIP seating and I sat behind Stedman and Gail for a part of the first show. Cameras were not allowed, but I did sneak in my phone and so did a lot of people. After a while everyone was taking photos. It was hard though, because the phone does not have zoom. This place WAS MASSIVE! I'm going to have to make this a two-part blog because it's getting too long. There is lots and lots still to talk about!

Make sure you watch THE OPRAH SHOW, Monday, May 23, 2011 on ABC! I'm in a video in the first few minutes and you will probably see me again in the audience shots because the camera crews were all over us!

The rest of the night was about movie stars and heart-warming stories from everyday people who have done extraordinary things! Everyone was adding their own energy of Gratitude and the Love in the United Center and it just grew and grew and grew!!!! Doug and I could feel Sophia's spirit all around us. It might sound strange to people but just because the person is gone does not mean the relationship is. It feels soooooo wonderful to be able to feel her. It feels like the deepest Love I've ever felt. It's the type of Love that lifts your life standards and increase your heart's ability to forgive and adore. Ahhhhhh (sigh).

One story that sticks out for me is Rosie O'Donnell. She came up to us backstage like a magnet was drawing her to us. Rosie looked as surprised as we were that she approached us so intentionally, like she was being pulled. It was so intense that I took three steps back. It was only when I got home that I uncovered the *aha!* moment gift!

I looked at my VISION BOARD and saw that Rosie O'Donnell was on there four times! I put her photos on there, because to me it represented my dream of being a talk show host! You can call it what you will, but it is crystal clear what it was to me...the Law of Attraction unfolding before us! SIMPLY AMAZING!

As for the star report, most of you have probably seen the shows as they have aired, but for those who did not, we rubbed elbows with Madonna, Tom Cruise, Beyonce, Usher, Aretha Franklin, Stevie

Wonder, Queen Latifah, Michael Jordan, Jamie Foxx, Maya Angelou, Alicia Keys, Halle Berry, Jerry Seinfeld, Tom Hanks, Madonna, Dr. Oz, Nate Berkus, Maria Shriver, Dakota Fanning, Will Smith, Rosie O'Donnell, Patti LaBelle, Katie Holmes, Simon Cowell, Josh Groban, Stedman Graham, Jada Pinkett Smith, Rascal Flatts, John Legend, Kristin Chenoweth, Jackie Evancho, Gayle King, Diane Sawyer, etc. It was surreal and soooooo amazing! What was even more amazing was that I felt totally at ease around everyone. Sure I did the cuckoo, freak-out dance when I first saw Madonna, but once I got into the groove it was totally effortless. I just SOAKED IT ALL IN!!! :)!

Doug and I hardly slept that night either! We had "dinner" at 3:30 AM and a few hours later had to take an early morning flight back to Boston. It was AWESOME! (Funny side note: I used to be a flight attendant and for some reason when I walk down the aisles there is almost always someone who asks me for a drink or what time we land. It does not even matter what I'm wearing. Must be "the walk.")

Leading up to May 23, there were lots and lots of commercials on ABC for the WCVB-Channel 5 piece that would run right after *The Oprah Show*. We were on at least once an hour on every show including *The View*, *Ellen DeGeneres*, etc.! It was completely surreal! My friend Linda Deming was watching the *Spider Man* movie late one night and suddenly she sees my face on TV. She said it took her a while for it to soak in. She felt like she was in a *Twilight Zone* episode!

Now, during this whole time (for the last 8 weeks, in fact), I have no real access to emails so unless you are a friend on Facebook, I cannot let anyone know that I'm going to be on *Oprah*!!!! It cut my communication WAY down! I felt like a wanted to share my joy with everyone but that I could not. At this time reporters were emailing me and I had no way of knowing it. It was totally about SURRENDER. It is not something I can do easily...It is something I am learning to do because I see the benefit of it...most times.

I cannot even say that I know if I'm completely BACK INTO MY BODY. This is such an AWESOME experience that is still unfolding. Someone called Doug the other day and told him they heard my voice on HOWARD STERN! They played my voice from *The Oprah Show* about Sophia! Now tell me the universe does not have a sense of humor! ;)!

People asked if they could come over for the taping and if you asked you got invited. A wonderful group showed up from all different parts of my life. It was wonderful to see! During the actual viewing, I realized yet ANOTHER MIRACLE had happened.

There were about 10 ULTIMATE VIEWERS that were featured on the two shows we sat in on. We taped for about 6 hours and the shows have no less than 2 hours to allow for commercials. They had to CUT OUT A WHOLE LOT! The result is that more than half of the people who went, even one woman who flew all the way from Afghanistan, were completely cut out of the TV portion of the program! They cut the woman before me, the beautiful Tamika, but they INCLUDED ME! I was actually the first person. Soooooooooo amazing! Yet another gift from our beautiful Sophia! Thanks everyone who came for sharing in this very special moment! Soooo sweet! *(end of blog entry)*

I just described the unfolding of one of my biggest dreams. Dreams are the images, sounds, tastes, feelings and sensings we get from our spiritual DNA. Pay attention to your dreams, even if they seem impossible. Remember when you break down the word "impossible," you get "I'm possible!"

 JOURNAL TIME... What is your biggest dream? Dreams? Where are they written down? How comfortable are you talking about your dreams? Do you allow your dreams to lead you or do you hide them?

Humanity has only scratched
the surface of its real potential.

—Peace Pilgrim (Mildred Lisette Norman)

Things I Want To Remember/Research/Review:

Without ice cream, there would be
darkness and chaos.

—Don Kardong

Chapter 46. What Does Ice Cream Have To Do With Your Life's Purpose?

Do you like ice cream? Ice cream is probably one of the first words kids learn to recognize. Ever see a small child who has just heard the ringing bell of an ice cream truck slowly driving through kid-populated neighborhoods? Even if pre-verbal, the child will make it known that she wants an ice cream! For some reason, many human beings really love ice cream. Although ice cream is eaten all over the world, the United States still produces and consumes the lion's share.

Ice cream is happiness condensed.

—Jessi Lane Adams

A Cool History *(pun intended)*

Ice cream is actually something that dates back to ancient times. In the 4th century BC, Alexander the Great, the Macedonian king who was tutored by Aristotle until he was 16 years old, was also a fan of ice cream. By the age of thirty, Alexander the Great, undefeated in battle, had created one of the largest empires of the ancient world. Alexander the Great's form of ice cream was snow mixed with honey and nectar. Here is an ice cream timeline...

The History Of Ice Cream Timeline

4th Century, B.C.: Ancient Greeks enjoy a dessert similar to ice cream.

1300s: Marco Polo brings an early form of ice cream to Europe.

1700s: Ice cream is introduced to America as a delicacy enjoyed by high society.

1776: America's first ice cream parlor opens its doors in New York.

1840s: The ice cream churn is invented.

1851: The first ice cream plant is opened.

1880s: The ice cream sundae is born.

1904: The waffle cone reportedly makes its debut at the World's Fair in St. Louis, MO.

1929: Rocky Road becomes the first widely available flavor other than vanilla, chocolate and strawberry.

1984: July is declared National Ice Cream Month.

Over the last couple of decades, the popularity and complexity of ice cream has dramatically increased. When I was growing up in Hudson, Massachusetts in the 1970s, ice cream flavors were very basic. You basically had the "Neapolitan,"—which is ice cream blocks of the classic three flavors: vanilla, chocolate and strawberry, divided into thirds. Back in the day you were "Miss Fancy Pants" if you even knew that this combo was called Neapolitan. If you wanted to get really "fancy," you got sherbet, but that never really did it for me.

You and Ice Cream

"Uh, excuse me, Maria. I thought this was a self-help book on how to access my spiritual DNA so why am I reading a whole chapter on ice cream? Aren't I supposed to avoid ice cream?" Well, I'm glad you asked! It's because ice cream is a WONDERFUL way to teach spiritual energy principles. Just like with a really good sundae, learning how to do energy work has many delicious layers to explore and "taste." Even though it comes from the same sundae, each spoonful can taste completely different! There are three main lessons that ice cream can teach us.

It's harder to hate someone when they like

the same ice cream as you.

—Shannon Wiersbitzky,
The Summer of Hammers and Angels

Ice Cream, You Scream, We All Scream For Ice Cream

Lesson 1: Massive Expansion & Growth

 Do you have one flavor you always go to or do you mix it up depending on your mood? If you grew up before the 70s, chances are that the ice cream choices you for the most part had were limited to the aforementioned Neapolitan and sherbet flavors. Did anyone complain about the choices at that time? Most of us did not complain, because we didn't know any better. We were happy with what we had. As human beings have expanded our energy for what is possible in the world, that expansion has affected everything from big things, such as technology, to little things like ice cream.

Let's deconstruct the word "expansion"—not like we are used to using it in the Herd OS—but under the more effective Right Now OS. According to the Merriam-Webster Dictionary, the definition is, "The act of becoming bigger or of making something bigger." The concept of becoming "bigger" is something that is coveted in the Herd OS. Under the Right Now OS, we can see *expansion* as natural movement directed outward, extending and flowing. From this natural flow, concepts such as creativity and imagination help generate even more flow. With the ice cream example, we can see that the natural flow of creativity has dramatically expanded the amount of flavors. What's more, with the arrival of all those new flavors come the wonderfully quirky names adding to the creativity.

These are names that most likely would NEVER have worked had someone used them in the 1960s, for example, because people were not as creatively evolved as we are now. If you offered a kid at that time "Rocky Road," she would most likely think it was a new cowboy show she had not heard about and just ask for chocolate, strawberry or vanilla, because that is what she was used to. Because the energetic expansion is growing exponentially at a much higher rate, we no longer need to wait seventy years (approximately an entire generation) to see massive evolution. Just like with ice cream flavors, it is happening faster and faster.

It is pretty amazing to witness the change from three main flavors dominating the landscape for decades, to a seemingly sudden reaching of ice cream's flavor flashpoint, where there's been an unexpected explosion of flavors. These flavors not only emerged, but they also have continued to expand. Since I'm all about the fun and want to show you how vast this expansion is, I've included a small sample of the vast amounts of ice cream flavors that now exist. **Check out the Ice Cream Index at the end of the book.

In terms of food items, specifically, it's not just ice cream either. I picked ice cream for this example, but the expansion can also be seen in other things that we've taken for granted as always staying the same. For our grandparents, if you asked for a cup of tea, coffee or hot chocolate it was a pretty basic thing. If you want to have some fun, go to a Starbucks, belly up to the counter and eavesdrop on the orders people ask for. If you belly up to the bar and hear my hot chocolate order it goes a little something like this. "I'd like a 'grande' hot chocolate, no whip, no foam, extra hot, extra pump of vanilla and an extra side of Love." We've come a long way baby.

The number of choices and possibilities are expanding in almost every aspect of the human experience. This expansion will continue. The way energy has been shifting, mirrors the changes on this planet, because everything is energy and we are all Love expanding.

Ice-cream is exquisite—what a pity it isn't illegal.

—Voltaire

Ice Cream, You Scream, We All Scream For Ice Cream

Lesson 2: Remembering Your Priorities

"Priorities" is the cousin of "Intention." As the universe keeps expanding, it is important that we keep our focus on the priorities. Because things are moving so fast and at a much deeper level, it is vital to pay attention to what is being done in our names, and what is being done to hurt the planet on such deep levels that we will hit bottom—*the point of no return*. The energetic intuition hits that I get right now is that our planet is in *deep shit*. We have been asleep letting other people control our world.

Hippocrates lived about the same time as Alexander the Great. Hippocrates was the father of modern Western medicine. He so believed in ice cream that he encouraged his patients to eat ice cream *"as it livens the life juices and increases the well-being."* Why would he say that? Well, an important point to remember is that originally ice cream was made with truly all-natural ingredients that did not contain the pesticides, hormones and genetically modified products that are so prevalent in today's food supply.

One large note of caution here. As we sped up and began expanding, we began exploring different ways with the intention of making almost everything "better" and "faster." This desire fed those who had financial goals over any other goals. Many people live life as a *reaction*. Many feel powerless. The trend has been to give advantages to large entities, like corporations, while the consequences to people and our earth is often totally disregarded. When money and profit are the number one goal, then EVERYTHING else, environment, relationships, connection, legacy, honor all take a backseat. The lack of checks and balances in our current human structure is suffocating our planet and causing massive amounts of suffering, even to children.

This need for greed is creating a huge imbalance in the natural order, yet the signs are being ignored. When we slow down and check in, we can realize just how "crazy" we may have been living. Remembering our priorities is something that ice cream reminds us of because even with a simple food like ice cream, you can buy the large container of chemical-filled, hormone-filled, artificial ice cream for a lot less money than the smaller organic, locally created ice cream product. The trend for smaller amounts with a higher quality is what is going to start making a difference—not only to your health, but also to your quality of life! It's about savoring versus *gulping* your life.

Ice Cream, You Scream, We All Scream For Ice Cream

Lesson 3: Your Own Unique Flavor

Another spiritual lesson that ice cream teaches us is that from the previous cookie cutter concept of having only three main flavors of chocolate, strawberry and vanilla, we now have a huge selection that seems to be ever expanding, as illustrated in Lesson 1. We human beings, like ice cream varieties, are also expanding.

There was a career board game I played as a little girl that gave me the option of picking from only three professions. I could be a teacher, nurse or ballerina. There was a time, within the lifetime of many people reading this book, when these careers were the few main options that were considered "acceptable women's work." Thankfully, today that career choices have greatly opened up for not only women, but also for men. Also now men can be in any of these aforementioned professions without the stigma.

Television shows like *So You Think You Can Dance, America's (Britain's) Got Talent, Dancing with the Stars* and *American Idol* have also helped to greatly expand entertainment opportunities by shifting what is possible and acceptable for career choices in the way of singing, dancing and performing. Ice cream also reminds us that being our own *unique* "flavor" is possible—a growing trend. People too have their own "flavor." Connecting to your spiritual DNA is about connection to your unique "flavor."

In addition to careers, there were the archetypes that were acceptable. You were either a *good* person or a *bad* one. You either did things *right* or *wrong*. The duality of good and evil were clearly drawn out. People fell into these basic categories. There was not a lot of room for uniqueness. It was all about following the status quo to be accepted so that you could survive, or for the rare few, thrive. Judging ourselves or others, keeps us out of our own alignment.

 JOURNAL TIME... What was your favorite ice cream flavor growing up? What does ice cream mean to you? What does it bring up for you? If you were going to invent a flavor of ice cream what would be in it? What would you name it?

After eating chocolate you feel godlike, as though you can conquer enemies, lead armies, entice lovers.

—Emily Luchetti

Things I Want To Remember/Research/Review:

The mantra 'safety first' reflects a society that is addicted to control and bereft of its sense of purpose.

—Charles Eisenstein, Pathways of Family Wellness

Chapter 47. The Secret Is Recognizing The Herd OS

The challenge is that for the last 10,000 years *being different* was something you were *taught to avoid at all costs*. They labeled it many things including being a "black sheep." According to historians and scientists like *Cosmos'* Neil deGrasse Tyson, about 10,000 years ago human beings started forming larger communities. They also started acquiring more than ever before, so a way to count to keep track of what they had was needed. Writing developed at this time so that people could write down how much and what they owned.

Things evolved very slowly. A person learned how to "be" from the prior generations, and each one's "job" was to do the same for the next generation. The Japanese have an expression that's perfect for this line of thinking, "The nail that sticks out gets hammered in." In the name of safety, tradition and honor each generation was systematically taught and in turn taught it to the following generations to follow the customs of your particular herd.

The Matrix is a system, Neo,
and that system is our enemy.
When you are inside, you look around,
what do you see?
Businessmen, teachers, lawyers, carpenters,
the very minds we are trying to save.
Until we do, these people are part of that system
and that makes them our enemies.
You have to understand that most of these people
are not ready to be unplugged and many
are so hopelessly dependent on the system,
they will fight to protect it.

—Morpheus, in the movie, The Matrix

As you have learned, the Herd OS is a life-altering model of painful living. Just like racism, it must be taught and reinforced. In order for it to work, you must block your energy body's communication with you. This derails your health and happiness within your lifetime. The Herd OS represents the last 10,000 years of human beings living under a very specific set of unnatural rules of how to be in the world. Who you are is not so much determined by your internal guidance or what you preferred, but rather to which family, area, time and gender you were born.

College fraternities that still have hazing, mirror the inauthentic system of the Herd OS. In fraternities you follow the rules, even when it is humiliating, abusive or painful. Strangely enough, many who suffer through it, teach this method of giving up their power to the incoming class. Often the very people who got abused are the ones who don't want it to end. The mentality is that, "If it was good enough for me, then it's good enough for them." They label it *tradition* so it becomes an assumption. "That's just the way things are." In this frame of mind, there's no hope for shift.

This is the same in the Herd OS. The energy is stagnant in its stuck point existence. The stagnation causes suffering to the energy body. Turns out that human beings can suffer a whole lot before they begin to look for solutions. What they see is what they accept completely as "reality." Outside of the fraternity, it may seem an odd way, but when you're in it, it's *normal*.

Over and over, some of the most exciting human stories are about a hero's or heroine's fighting against that establishment to be able to shift one of these debilitating, archaic rules that many follow—not because it helps anyone, or because it's useful, but rather because it's the way it's *always* been done.

> *If your dreams do not scare you they are not*
> *big enough.*
> —Ellen Johnson Sirleaf

Fear

Fear is at the root of all conflict. It is the turning away from your own intuition and internal flow. Fear breeds selfishness, greed, arrogance, dishonesty and manipulation. All of these are "feedback" that you are not aligned with your authenticity. Unchecked, fear breeds more unhealthy behaviors, more inauthenticity. Fear for many has been defined as the absence of courage. This definition is limiting. The more accurate definition of fear is the feedback feeling you get when you are moving away from your core's energy flow. Fear only lives in your body through your brain. Fear is a thought. It is a built-in mechanism of the meat body to attempt to keep it  safe. Fear does not exist in the Right Now OS, only in the Herd OS. This scene from *the movie, The Matrix* describes it beautifully.

Morpheus: I imagine that right now, you're feeling a bit like Alice. Hmm? Tumbling down the rabbit hole?

Neo: You could say that.

Morpheus: I see it in your eyes. You have the look of a man who accepts what he sees because he is expecting to wake up. Ironically, that's not far from the truth. Do you believe in fate, Neo?

Neo: No.

Morpheus: Why not?

Neo: Because I don't like the idea that I'm not in control of my life.

Morpheus: I know exactly what you mean. Let me tell you why you're here. You're here because you know something. What you know you can't explain, but you feel it. You've felt it your entire life, that there's something wrong with the world. You don't know what it is, but it's there, like a splinter in your mind, driving you mad. It is this feeling that has brought you to me. Do you know what I'm talking about?

Neo: The Matrix.

Morpheus: Do you want to know what it is?

Neo: Yes.

Morpheus: The Matrix is everywhere. It is all around us. Even now, in this very room. You can see it when you look out your window or when you turn on your television. You can feel it when you go to work... when you go to church... when you pay your taxes. It is the world that has been pulled over your eyes to blind you from the truth.

Neo: What truth?

Morpheus: That you are a slave, Neo. Like everyone else you were born into bondage. Into a prison that you cannot taste or see or touch. A prison for your mind.

 JOURNAL TIME... What are some your favorite movies? Pick one, the first that comes to mind. Why do you like it? What makes it your favorite? Now look at the movie in terms of energy patterns. How does how you feel about the movie shift when you notice the energy patterns in it? This might be a new way of consciously looking at the world so play with it. Be open to exploring what comes up. What does it teach you about your own energy patterns and lessons?

Your dreams are your instructions directly
from your spiritual DNA.
Your intuition is your internal GPS leading the way.
Trust and Courage are the fuel.
—Maria Salomão-Schmidt

Everything always passes,
and everything is already okay.
Stay in the place where you can see that,
and nothing will resist you.

—Martha Beck

Chapter 48. Play... The Solution To Stress

Most children you see today are allowed to play. This was not always the case. Many "civilized" societies throughout history have seen play as frivolous, even harmful. As we shift as a people, play has started with the children and is extending to the adults. It is especially prevalent to the children born in the 70s (again give or take 10 years), the Bridge Generation, who deeply still love to play.

When I worked in Silicon Valley in high tech public relations, I'd go into a lot of startups. Many of them seemed more like playgrounds rather than companies. They had things that only kids traditionally played with like pinball machines, basketball nets, bicycles, chalk boards, games, ping pong tables, etc. Spaces were open, colors were bright, clothes were casual. It was a huge contrast to the traditional companies that were all about cubicles, appropriate behavior, titles, business suits, hierarchy and fluorescent lights.

New Idea to Play With...

What is a "Trust Fly?" - Many of us grew up with the expression taking a *trust fall*. The concept of "falling" is not something that people look upon favorably. It is dangerous and unknown and could be highly painful, even deadly. When following your intuition you are oftentimes *flying* on some level because you are literally moving in the direction of your dreams.

When you take a *trust fly* you are putting your faith in that whatever is going to happen will. You are always guided. *Guided* is what it looks like to the meat body. To your energy body, it's just your natural flow, that only diminishes when you block it. The trick is to begin noticing and listening. Just like your cells have a DNA code to tell them how to grow and what to do, your energy body has its own instructions for your life's purpose. Begin noticing without judging. Ever see kids playing when one kids chimes in over and over, "That's not how you do it, do it this way." No one wants to play with the controlling kid, so don't you become like that fearful kid in your own life.

How to Deal with Stress...

Let's Play the "Who Are You?" Game

 Here's how you play: First, Take a deep, deep breath. Hold it. Then let it go. Get yourself into a neutral state of just being in the moment. Noticing your breath, dropping your shoulders, your belly button towards your spine, smile, relax, breathe I call this the *in utero position*.

Now, activate your imagination by picturing someone you has been very unkind to you. Think of them clearly. Actually picture them. Notice how you feel. Stay with the image even if uncomfortable. Release judgments if they come up. Then go back to *in utero position* and write down what came up for you. Breathe through each one for more authentic answers as you dig out the gifts from the big pile of crap that's accumulated from living from the Herd OS.

In my body I feel:

_____

I emotionally feel:

_____

I notice:

_____

What I am releasing?

_____

What is the gift I notice?

_____

Surround yourself with the thoughts, people, food
and places that inspire you to live life full of your
own energy, to live life full of yourself.

—Maria Salomão-Schmidt

Key Points To Remember

- You don't DESERVE stress-free living. You ARE stress-free living!

- Feeling happiness means you are full of yourself. Feeling *depressed* or *heavy* means you are on some level of empty.

- If you want to help someone along on their journey, you do it best from being in a grounded, authentic, full of your authentic self kind of place!

- Check in with your breath. Have you been holding your breath too long?

- Be kind to yourself. You have forgotten about your story, your legacy, your mission. It's never about someone else. That's the lie. It drains you to think of life this way.

- Everything you're attracting is both a gift and a curse. Look for the gift side. Whatever jackassity comes up, just look for the gift. Hint: sometimes it's buried deep down, but just like within every Cracker Jacks or cereal box when I was a kid, the gift is in there!

- You've got SUCH an amazing heart! Connect to it. You have much adventure to live and much Love to radiate! Our planet could use more of your authentic Love (freedom and flow)! You know what *living small* is called? It's called *not living*! Stop that! You are being called. You know it and I know it! So take the information you have learned and start noticing, focusing, imagining, exploring, releasing and embracing! There is much living to be unleashed. Your mission started when you opened this book. CONGRATULATIONS!

DOROTHY
Oh, will you help me? Can you help me?

GLINDA (THE 'GOOD' WITCH)
You don't need to be helped any longer. You've always had the power to go back to Kansas.

DOROTHY
I have?

SCARECROW
Then why didn't you tell her before?

GLINDA
Because she wouldn't have believed me. She had to learn it for herself.

TIN MAN
What have you learned, Dorothy?

DOROTHY
Well, I—I think that it— that it wasn't enough just to want to see Uncle Henry and Auntie Em—and it's that— if I ever go looking for my heart's desire again, I won't look any further than my own backyard. Because if it isn't there, I never really lost it to begin with! Is that right?

GLINDA
That's all it is!

FINALLY FULL OF YOURSELF

SCARECROW
But that's so easy! I should have thought of it for you.

TIN MAN
I should have felt it in my heart.

GLINDA
No. She had to find it out for herself. Now, those magic slippers will take you home in two seconds!
—From the movie *The Wizard of Oz*

Things I Want To Remember/Research/Review:

Maria Salomão-Schmidt

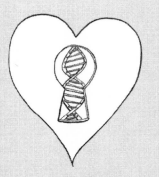

THANK YOU for reading this magical book!

I am thrilled that you've taken the time to learn how to unlock your spiritual DNA because being full of yourself is the best gift you can give the world!

This information only helps end suffering and heal our planet if it is shared. If *Finally Full of Yourself!: Unlocking Your Spiritual DNA* has inspired you, *please share it*!

Think of it as a LOVE PACKET that you are unleashing and spreading out into the world to help others stop struggling and start living! We are creating waves of LOVE!

Thank you for being born!

TO FIND COMMUNITY, CONTINUE LEARNING
AND CONNECT WITH MARIA GO TO
WWW.COACHMEMARIA.COM

♡

As I close out the book, I lovingly send you to the next level of your journey with one my favorite prayer poems from the amazing peace-promoting Unitarian Universalist (UU) community...

We go forth in the world in peace
To act with works of love
To affirm each person's dignity
And to cherish the living earth.

♡

May you be FULL OF YOURSELF all the days of your life!

Namaste!

Weirdmaste!

Acknowledgments

No matter how lonely we feel at times, no journey is done alone. There are people, animals and energies that help us, even when we cannot see them. I am deeply grateful to those who helped me evolve into the person I am today.

I am especially grateful to my mother, the beautiful Maria Raquel Salomão who taught me elegance, creativity, classical music, hard work and organization. In this lifetime she has been there from day one until now. I would write her age but she'd kill me. To my father Claudinor Oliveira Salomão who taught me how to be stronger than strong. In this lifetime he has been one of my biggest teachers. He is an amazing community organizer, networker and visionary. To my three brothers who I grew up with João Alberto, Claudinor and Pedro Francisco, my first playmates. I treasure the wonderful times we spent playing together. The road we traveled together was not always friendly but it was filled with adventure, exploration and play, especially in nature. Some of my sweetest memories are of you and with you! To my other siblings, Mark, Jeffrey and Julia, you've taught me a whole new level of wonder. The experiences I've have had with all six of my siblings have helped me channel, create and decipher my life's work. You've helped me manifest this book by just being authentically you. Obrigada a todos!

To those who helped edit, comment and make suggestions over the last few years. A great big THANK YOU to the beautiful Beth Bacon, Sheryn MacMunn, Linda Deming, Karen Anderson, Darlene Vittori, Jean Kingsbury, Karen Maki, Dot Walsh, Karyn Knight Detering, Paula Sherwin, Elena Antunes, Nora Farr, Maura McGinnity Rausch, Dennis Wong, Gabriele Kirschner, Anne Lafleur, Paul Daigle, Mialotta Schmidt, Kathryn Common, Dennis Pratt, Megan Twing, Gabriella Opaz, Sara Stalnaker, Elaine Brouillette, Mickey Mouse (Kidding! Just seeing if you are paying attention), Alyson Lucas, Sylvia Eng, Terri Sorensen, Loretta Matson, Patricia Ross and Theresa Donaghy, Gail Mitchell Emilsson.

A great big THANK YOU to beautiful Melanie Gebhardt, Josephine Finocchiaro, Darcy Skye Holoweski, Amy Woodworth, Sandra Brennan, Linda Deming, Patricia Zub, Arden O'Donnell, Jose D Pereira, Maureen Mann, Keith Eaton, Patricia Delano, Ellen M Hunt, Maryellen LaBelle, Nicky Moreau, Marjorie Themeli, Christine

Leonard, Heather Holloway, Martha Angelini, Kristi Jones, Claudia Rauwolf, Gina Cicero Papazian, Louise Leduc, Paula Sherwin, Linda Scruton, Lynne Rooney Maynard, Miguel David, Ana Alvim, Alana Baker, Cathie Chouinard, Lynn Fawthrop, Lynn Kadela Siders, Krysten Deveaux, MaryAnne Foster, Susan Dean, Karen Landon Moore, Rosemary Woitowicz, Gladie Katz Lauer, Nancy Senior, Dianne Olszewski, Kathy Tuffs, Julie Laughlin, Barbra Benzi Brickle, Kathy Toomey Natale, Vicki Adams Rapanault, Dalal Akel Rosenzweig, Nancy Bleyer, Janice Harvey, Bette Salmowitz, Paula Bronzini-Fulton, Dorothy Souza, Rosemary Woitowicz, Dorothea Mahoney, Malinda Branson, Michelle Thibeault, Toni Barillaro, Colleen Cathcart, Meena Mehta, Joanne Mueffelmann, Lisa Campion, Rhys Thomas.

To those on my Coach Me Maria group on Facebook who cheered me on while I was writing incuding:

Adelaide Freitas, Danielle Landry Estrella, Susan Russo, Allegrini Dunsky, Amy Deinlein Butch, Amy Palmer, Amy Sullivan Thomson, Anita Kotch Cellucci, Ann Wenstrom Murphy, Anne Grubinskas-Quemere, Anne Liho Shilimela, Annemarie Mcneil, Annie D'Esposito, Barbara Lahey, Barbara Lush, Bernadette Dempsey, Bethany Archambault, Betty Ledo Devitt, Bonnie Sardinha, Brenda Murphy Blacklock, Cameo Thorne, Carly Petracco, Carolyn McGee, Caryl Borger Mix, Cassie Smith, Cathie Chouinard, Celeste Braga, Celeste Song, Ann Jeye, Charlene Burke, Cherry Lee Fenton, Cheryl Davin, Christine Muckenthaler, Cindy Ardito Fields, Cindy Freeman, Cindy Rio Bacon, Corrine Petteys, Cynthia Lindeman, Danielle Robyn Bartram Vilar, Dawn Anderson-Giusto, Dawn Lorraine, Deb Brimer, Deb Maintanis, Deborah Cote Croteau, Judy Giovangelo, Sherry DiNapoli, Deborah Sweet, Diana Chrzanowski, Dinis Pimentel, Donna Moy-Bruno, Edna Courtemanche Harris, Carol Sussman-Ghatak, Cheryl Cohen, Ashley May Jardim, Kristin Lee, Eileen McDonough, Susan Carlson, Erin Fanning Fleischer, Esperanca Stevens, Gail Brodeur, Gina Stucchi, Gordon Saladino, Graça Palmer, Guillermo Ramirez, Hani Elnaggar, Hedlights Lui, Helen Bannigan, Helen Thomas, Holly Raible Blades, Holly Shepherd, Indira Prado, Jaclyn 'Grivois' Roth, Jan Krause Greene, Janice Harvey, Jean Kingsbury, Jean Spera, Jeanne Handelman, Jo-Ann Perkins, Joanne Laura Patterson, John McArthur, Joyce Berard, Judy Parent Sandland, Julie Kehoe, June Pawlowski, Justin Brown, Karen Anderson, Karen Keirstead, Karen Zaccaro, Kat Moulton, Katie Canty, Kathleen Johnson Kenderdine, Kathleen Schropfer Grevers, Kerri Grey Miller, Kathleen Zinzer McCarthy, Kathy Allen Archambault, Katrina Libertelli, Kelly Mechaley Lallo, Kim Lanz, Kimberly Bagni, Kristen Wisuri Murphy,

Kristin Lisi Conway, Laura Patterson, Linda Hammond, Linda Love, Linda Robayo, Lisa Craycraft, Lisa Pond, Liz Myers, Liz Todd, Luisa Teixeira da Silva, Marian Dortch, Marian C Hobson, Margie Breihof Carr, Mark Ahronian, Mary Ames Johnson, Mary McGuinness, Mary McQueeney, Maureen Connor Gormley, Me'chellelynne Rabot, Michael Hallett, Michele Hunting, Michele Weselake, Micheli Lynn, Michelle Carlow, Mojgan Momtaheni, Monica Garcia-Freitas, Nadyne Taylor, Nancy O'Shaughnessy, Natalie St Germain Byrne, Nick Hart, Noca Spice, Olivia Junqueiro, PK O'Shea, Pamela Serocki Brown, Patricia Glynn Olson, Patricia Partington, Patricia Ross, Patricia Salamone, Patricia Warner, Paula Marchetti Kaufman, Paula Sherwin, Peggy Billingham, Polly Jo Labbe, Renee Rakowsky, Robin Frongillo, Rosa Jesus, Sally-Anne Cast, Sandra J. Edwards, Sandra Sciarpelletti, Sandra Silva Cabral, Serchil Welly, Sheila Donovan Joslin, Sherri Roberts Lumpkin, Stacey Borona Balardini, Stacy Dereshinsky Rickman, Sue Press Fenick, Susan Bergheimer Robillard, Susana Borges, Suzanne Chambers, Suzanne Collins Sennott, Suzette Monteiro, Tammy Pease, Ted Thibodeau Jr, Teresa Costa Figueiredo, Teresa Plasse Wright, Teresa Ryder, Terry Maguire Klausmeier, Thomas Herman Joel, Tina Cosio, Tricia Sweeney Venne, Vasu Keith, Victoria Haffer, Victoria Hen.

It took me ten years to write this book so you bet your sweet applesauce that I'm going to keep this gratitude train going and keep thanking those who were somehow a part of the journey. To my beautiful nieces and nephews Emily, AJ, Mandy, Jamie, Alexander, Nicole, Lauren, Benjamin, Daniel, Jocelyn, Julia, Brianne, Mateus, Kaia and Gabriella. To Cheryl Salomão, Beth Salomão, Cristina Terra-Salomão, Diane & John Heliotis, Denise and Peter Garcia, Debra and Andrew LaFemina, Vickie and Herb Schmidt, Ray and Friday Schmidt, Oma Amanda Becker, June Becker Schmidt.

To my Portuguese family, whether by birth or heart, Maria Amelia Duarte (Mamé), Maria Luisa Stephens, Carlos Alberto Santos Calambum, José Manuel Quintas, Mary Fowke, Eileen McDonough, José Marques, Paula Alexandra Almeida Santos, Tani Cabral, João and Cristina Charepe, Carlos Alberto Fonseca, Fiona McGlynn, Julie Deffense, Ana Custódio, Kirstein Brown, Marijn Moltzer, Catherine Stockwell, Denise Ribera Luxton, Katie Thompson, Jennifer Nicholson-Breen, Rita Zanin, Heather Taylor, Cecelia Street, Teresa Waters, Susan Humpert, Dina Ayoub, Marion, Kate Hands, Dorothy Morris-Grantham, Regina Frank, Trevor Morris-Grantham and the International Women of Portugal (IWP). The support you gave me when I went to Portugal to write was absolutely magical! I could not have done it without you!

To family members I never met but their beauty influenced how I saw the world: Maria de Lurdes Henriques Cerveira Abreu and Clemente Alberto Cerveira. I want the magic of your names in this book because I am who I am partly because you were who you were. Beijinhos amores!

To those who now guide me from the other side, a special THANK YOU to Sophia June-Raquel Salomão Schmidt, Mandy Heliotis, Maria Olga Henriques Cerveira Mendes, José Soares Mendes, Maria Eunice Henriques, Maria Emilia Oliveira, Tia Emilia, Tio António Lourenço, Joscelyn Chatman, Aida Bugge and Terri Sorensen. Wow, reading all your names makes me miss you even more! Also a very special thank you for the inspiration as I wrote the book from Joan of Arc, Marilyn Monroe, Princess Diana, Archangel Gabriel, Archangel Michael and Albert Einstein.

To my brilliant, loud, wild, wacky, fun-loving family: our kids, Christopher, Mialotta, Sophia, Olivia and Isabella, plus a shout out to the kids who've lived with us Laura, Bea, Ali, James and Tehya. Thanks for your insights and wonderful hugs. To our doggies and kitties, all of them rescues: Tejo, Shakespeare, Shanti, João Carlos, Delilah (Miss Lilah), Oscar, Joaninha, London and Zazu, who sat by my feet over the years as I wrote and wrote and wrote.

Last, but not least, to my beautiful husband Douglas for going beyond the limits of what is comfortable... over and over and over again! What a ride! Wooooooo! Life is sweeter because we met, bonded and helped each other learn how to be full of ourselves. It's a work in progress but there is no one else I'd like to play with than you!

As you can see, it took a virtual village of hearts to birth this magnificent book. I am forever humbled, thankful and ecstatic for the support from the seen and unseen. As we clap for all of you, take a bow!

The most beautiful people we have known...have an appreciation, a sensitivity, and an understanding of life that fills them with compassion, gentleness, and a deep loving concern. Beautiful people do not just happen.

—Elizabeth Kubler Ross

Ice Cream Index

This book is like a REALLY GOOD MEAL because it energetically feeds you. And what really good meal does not end even better than with a little humor (like 'Good Humor') ;) and ice cream, so here you go!

Everything on our Earth is evolving. Once you let yourself notice you can see it at all levels. Learning how to notice is a great skill to have, especially now in this stage of human evolution. Realizing how things are shifting gives you vital information that directly affects how much you can access, and ultimately activate, your spiritual DNA. As you have read throughout this book, your spiritual DNA contains vital information about your life's path and purpose. When you're in alignment, you feel happy. Learning how to live from your energy body can be really fun... even yummy!

In Chapter 46, "What Does Ice Cream Have To Do With Your Energy Body?" I mentioned this ice cream index. It gives a small sample of the wonderfully wild and creative ice cream flavor names. This is a fun way to see how we're evolving at all levels, even with ice cream. We used to have basically three main flavors (neapolitan) and now look at the options! Creativity is alive and well on planet Earth because it is simply energy flowing without interruption. ♡

---

60 Grit	Fudge Soy Bean	Pepp
69 Scoops	Fudge Vengeance	Peppermint Nudge
A Midsummer's Ice Cream	Funky Butter	Pesto Praline
	Future Freeze	Peyote
Abandon Mint	Gates Guzzler	Phenolic Phudge
Acid Crystal Chunk	Gazpacho Gelato	Pigeon Pecan
Adagio for Stringbeans	GD Peanut Brittle	Pineapple Day
Algae Rhythm	Gelatinous Plastic	Ping Pang Pecan
Almond Terrace	Gelatosphere	Pink Freud
Antifreeze	Gem Cream	Pizza 'N Beer
Anti-Gravity Chocolate	Giotto Gelato	Pludge
Ass Candy	Glue Belly	Poached Eggs 'N Sherry
Attila the Honey Bee	Goat Cheese Cashew	
Baba Rum	Caramel	Podunk Punch

Maria Salomão-Schmidt

Banana Cabana
Banana Curry
Basil Avocado
Beluga Gum
Big Juicy
Bitter Sweet Caramel Kvetch
Bleach Melba
Bleached Peach
Bliss
Bloated Belly
Blood Pudding
Blue Sushi
Bon Bons Jovi
Booster Cake
Boots and Laces
Bourbon Bliss
Brain Butter
Brother's Milk
Buffalo Butter
Burnt Umber
Butter Top
Cabbage 'N Cream
Caramel Knowledge
Cardamom
Carmel Knowledge
Carnival Coffee
Cascade Mint
Cashew Butter Cucumber
Cashew Planet
Cashioca
Caviar Jack
Celestial Pudding
Ceviche Caramel Chunk
Chamois
Cheerful of Chocolate
Chernobyl Chunk

Godzilla Pudding Chunks
Gorge Us
Grape Nuts & Raisin
Granola Fantasy Canteen
Green Gravity
Green Salad Surprise
Gristle
Gristle Bits
Gristle Epistle
Guano Amaretto
Guilty Swirl
Guru Chew
Half Full
Ham Crunchers
Ham Horns
Ham Licker
Has Bean
Havasu Cherry
Healthy Nut
Heel Pudding
Hemp Hangover
Hester Praline Pecan
High on Ham
Hillbilly Riviera
Honey
Honey Jalapeño Pickle
Hooda-Gooda
Horizon Glue
Hot Bowl of Ice
Hot Dog Sorbet
HotBelly
Ice Burger
Ice Can
Ice Cream Socialism
Ice Crush
Ice Lava

Poi Party
Pomme Juan
Popcorn Reprieve
Pork Slurry
Portuguese Passion
Potash & Gizzard
PowerPrawn
Practical Pork
Praline Shock
Prawn Alfredo
Prawn and Pretzel
Prawn Bons
Prawn Danish
Prawn Flakes
Prawn Gravy
Prawn Pudding
Prawn Toffee
Prawnchilada
Prawnderful
Preakness
Precious Potato
Prickly Pear
Pudge
Pulmonary Cheesecake
Pumice Crunch
Purple
SquirtleRainbow Ed
Rasta Pops
Razzle Dazzle
Red Hot Chilli Butter
Retro Cocoa
Rhesus Buttercup
Ricanelas
Rickety Splat
Ripple Effect
Road Rash Hash
Roadkill Penguin

Cherry Potter
Chillium
Chips and Guac
Choco Lulu
Chocolate Bondage
Chocolate Boudoir
Chocolate Death March
Chocolate Guillotine
Chocolate Mocha
Masquerade
Chocolate Mussolini
Chocolate Revisionist
Chorizo Chunko
Chow Biscuit
Christmas Turkey
Chutney
Chutney Chunk
Ciao, Bella Figala
Ciàobama
Clambake
Cloisonné Sorbet
Codfish Shake
Coffee Cobbler
Coffee Crash
Coffee Kraze
Coffee Menagerie
Coffee School
Cola Cones
Cold Cuts Crunch
Compost
Compucocktail
Confection Detection
Confiture Demure
Cookie Butter
Cookie Pageant
Corn Beef and Cabbage
Corndog and Kibble
Coronal Mass Ejections

Iced Patty Melt
Italian Ice Ice Baby!
Jalapeño Fireball
Jamocha Jerky
Jellyfish Java
Jubilant Mess
Juice Monster
Juicy Freeze
JuJu
Jurassic Pork
Kale 'N Gravy
Kelp Curry
Kitty Kitty Bang Bang
Kiwi Sea
Kohlrabi Krunch
Krillcream
La Niña Colada
Lardvark
Leaf Beef
Leftover Pesto
Lemming Meringue
Pie
Lewd Licorice
Lichen Sorbet
Licorice Lique
LiquiPrawn
Lollipop Flower
Lovely Lovely Two
Ludicrous Licorice
Macho Miso
Mad Beef
Mad Grahams
Malic Acid
Mañana Mango
Mango Mango
Manic Planet
Mantis Milk
Maple Thor

Roasted Rooster
Rocky Raccoon Road
Rocky Road
Revisionist
Rootbear Flotsam
Rosewater
Royal Tease
Rust Bubbles
Sacrificial Ham
Saguarro Foam
Salt Licorice
San Francisco Mint
Sausage Machine
Scat Leather
Scooper Duper
Sea Slug and Rabbit
Secret Breakfast
Seven Scentric
Sex Potato
Sexy Sadie Crunch
Shangri Latte
Sichuan Pepper
Silly Von Willy
Slope
Slow & Pulpy
Sludge Farm
Smelling Salts
Smoochy Goochy Bar
Smurf Gelato
Snowflake
Snuggy Lumps
Sock Drawer Slush
Sour Crocodile
Spam Sushi
Spice Cadet
Spooncake
Squid
Squid Plasma

Cosmic Crunch
Crab Cookies
Cracker Jack Gelato
Crammed Jammin'
Cream Doughnut
Crawdaddy Gumbo
Cream of Caulk
Creamed Capers
Creamed Cod
Creamed Corn 'AND Oats
Cream-Puff Chunk
Crumble Cheese
Crunch
Crutzle
Cryo-Gin Fizz
Cupcake
Curry Slurry
Diabeeto
Dijon Bomb
Dipstick
Dirty Laundry
Dot Com Crunch
Double Chocolate Chum
Double Dada
Double Taurus
Drastic Plastic
Dripping Salad
Dung Beetle
Earthy
Eggs Benadryl
Elder Carrot
Electric Waffle
Escargot
Ex-Boyfriends
FeedBag
Fern Salad
Fickle Fat

Marmalade Parade
Marshmallow Mastic
Marvelous Mutton
Marzipan Magic
Marzipan Station
Maximum Coconut
Meat Locker
Mediterranean Subterfuge
Melville Mint
Meow
mGravy
Milky Feeling
Millennarita
Mini Bar
Mint Dynasty
Mint Maestro
Mobile Mousse
Mod Cow
Modicrumb Cake
Mongoquant
Monkey Double
Monster Cream
Moose Toe
Mountain Mud
Multiple Cake
Mum
My Bad
Mystery Chunkz
Mystic Poppy Mint
Mystical Union
Nacreous Asparagus
Nana Banana
NASDAQ Daiquiri
Nasty Freeze
Nasty Good
Nastylicious
Nectarine Cream

Squid Pops
Stinko Balboa
Stucco
Sugar Caulk
Sugar Doggy
Sunday Night Syndrome
Superstring Cheese
Sushi Swirl
Sweet Corn Gelato
Sweet RainbowSwirling Guilt
Sympathy Slosh
Taco Hash
Tali-Bon Bons
Teen Cream
Teletubby Hubby
Temporal Freeze
Temporary Vegetable
Terra Cotta Jones
Tickle
Tidal Yule
Toe Jam Swirl
Tomato Truffle
Tomato Fish
Tropicandy
Tuna Juice
Tuna Truffle
Turf Damage
Tutti Frutti Butti
Tutu's Anniversary
Ultra Beef
Vague Tuna
Van Mango
Vanilla Spice Pureé
VegiGate
Velveeta 'N Grits
Velvet Stucco

Final Consumption
Fish 'N Chips
Fish Stomp
Flagrant Fish
Flip Out
Flow Tart
French Vanilla
Fluoride 'N Honey
Fly Butter
Flying Potato
Fondue Freeze
FreezeBurn
Freezer Burn
Freezia
French Poodle
Fried Earwig
Frog Jerky
Frosted Ptarmigan
Frothy Logic
FroZEN
Fruit Chowder

Dream
Neoprom
New Whirled Order
No Tomorrow
Noodle Doodle
Nose Nuggets
Nougat and Lard
Nuclear Winter
Squash
Oleander Ketchup
Operation Double
Dip
Orange Bounce
Pang Meringue
Panic Button
Parrot Cake
Patty Meltdown
Peanut Buddha
Peanuts Envoy
Peek-A-Boo Pork

Venison Chilli Chunk
Venom Flamingo
Vicuña Venison Chew
Voodles
Wanton Wonton
Wasabi Chunk
Water Lily Scum
Snaps
Whale Jelly
Whiskey and Bits
White Chocolate and
Rose
White Truffle Gelato
Wildberry Lavender
Yeasty Pete
Yogurt Hygiene
Yucatango
Zanilla
Zenbutter
Zillaberry
Zoo Butte

Things I Want To Remember/Research/Review:

Maria Salomão-Schmidt

Ice Cream Bonus Section

Interesting Ice Cream Facts: Curious minds are what we need more of on this planet. So here are some interesting ice cream facts. Enjoy!

- According to the International Ice Cream Association's company members, vanilla remains the most popular flavor. "Chocolate Chip Mint" and "Cookies and Cream" were the next most popular flavors.

- Next to cookies, ice cream stands as the best selling treat in America!

- Top 5 Ice Cream Consuming Countries in the World (per capita, gallons per year)

    o New Zealand: 7.5

    o United States: 5.5

    o Australia: 4.8

    o Finland: 3.8

    o Sweden: 3.2

- Most of the vanilla used to make ice cream comes from Madagascar and Indonesia.

- Chocolate syrup is the world's most popular ice cream topping.

- Vanilla ranks the number one flavor of ice cream sold in the United States.

- Neapolitan ice cream was named in the 1800's because of its presumed origins from the Italian city of Naples and the Neapolitan immigrants who brought their expertise of frozen desserts with them to the United States.

- 87% of Americans have ice cream in their freezer at any given time.

- The average number of ice cream pints an American enjoys each year. 48

- It takes 3 gallons of milk to make 1 gallon of ice cream.

- It takes about 50 licks to finish a single-scoop ice cream cone.

- "Brain freeze" occurs when ice cream touches the roof of your mouth.

- 1 in 10 people admit to licking the bowl clean after eating ice cream.

- 1 in 5 share with their pet.

"Never trust a skinny ice cream man."

—Ben Cohen

Things I Want To Remember/Research/Review:

Maria Salomão-Schmidt

About The Author

Maria Salomão-Schmidt, MBA has had a very eclectic life. She was born in Lisbon, Portugal and grew up in the small New England town of Hudson, Massachusetts. She graduated from Boston College, Simmons College Graduate School of Management and the Rhys Thomas Institute of Energy Healing. Maria has lived many lives within this one, including being a teacher, entrepreneur, waitress, college professor, camp counselor, insurance processor, book store clerk, model, real estate broker, writer, vice president of Silicon Valley public relations firm and flight attendant.

Maria accomplished her twenty-year goal of being a guest on The Oprah Show and has worked with some of the world's most amazing people and organizations including Jack Canfield & Chicken Soup for the Soul, Jane Goodall, Mikhail Gorbachev, Delta Airlines, Procter & Gamble, CBS.

Maria's gift is to cut through the blocks and get right to the heart of the matter, through her unique brand of humor, intuition and zaniness. Maria is a powerful international life coach, speaker, author who helps ignite her clients' life purpose. She is also a Reiki Master Teacher and expert in several other modalities including NLP, EFT (tapping), Chakra Balancing and Full Spectrum Healing.

Maria lives in a pink 1800's house in Holliston, Massachusetts and in a flat overlooking the Atlantic Ocean in Paço de Arcos, Portugal with her husband Douglas. Together they have five children ranging in ages of 8 to 21 years old, plus they regularly foster both children and animals. They currently have four rescue dogs. One of Maria's very favorite things in the whole world is to dance around her kitchen with Doug and their children.

Visit www.coachmemaria.com for more information.

Finally Full of Yourself CHECKLIST:

Finally Full of Yourself (FFOY) is a LOVE MOVEMENT. Be a part of it! Here's how...

- ☐ Join the Facebook: *Fans of...Finally Full Of Yourself: Unlocking Your Spiritual DNA (the book)* group
- ☐ Join the *Coach Me Maria* group on Facebook
- ☐ Tell your friends about FFOY
- ☐ Sign up on www.coachmemaria.com to join Maria's VIP list of hearts rising and get your free gift
- ☐ Go on Amazon and Barnes & Noble and leave a review
- ☐ Post a photo of yourself with your FFOY on social media (Use hashtags like #finallyfull #loverising #finallyfullofyourself)
- ☐ Order FFOY from a local bookstore (especially a small, independent one)
- ☐ Give FFOY as a present
- ☐ Share FFOY posts that inspire you
- ☐ Go back and do the exercises in FFOY
- ☐ Buy an extra copy and leave it somewhere with a note that says something like, "I've left this book for you to find. Keep spreading the Love. Pay it forward."
- ☐ Send to a friend who is going through a hard time

- ☐ Ask your local radio stations and newspapers to do a story/article on FFOY
- ☐ Get FFOY on audio and listen to it so you can get the information on a whole other level
- ☐ Book Maria to speak at your conference or event
- ☐ Do a podcast or write a blog on FFOY
- ☐ Sign up for a class with Maria
- ☐ Reach out to Maria with your questions at maria@coachmemaria.com so she can included them in the next book
- ☐ Choose FFOY as your book club selection
- ☐ Book a coaching session with Maria to work things that came up after reading FFOY
- ☐ Start a FFOY study group with your friends and go chapter by chapter each week
- ☐ Read FFOY again... Give yourself permission to write in it. A well-worn copy is a loved book
- ☐ Come to an event where Maria is speaking and get your FFOY personally autographed

---

Want More Of Your Questions Answered?

Finally Full of Yourself!
Unlocking Your Spiritual DNA

The Question Guide
by Maria Salomão-Schmidt

Release Date: May 12, 2017

Pre-order your copy now at www.coachmemaria.com